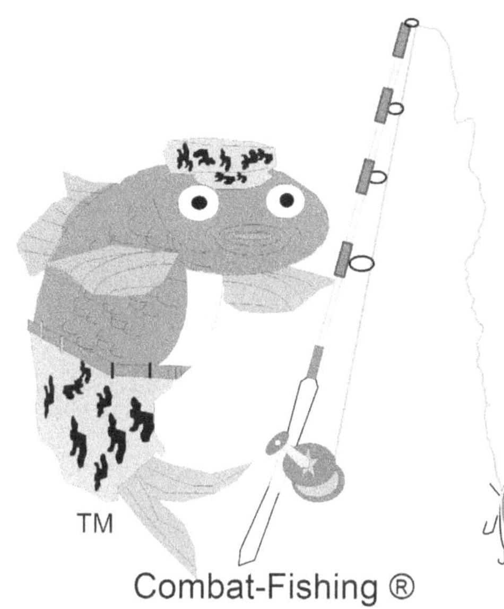

Of Oceans and Rivers, Fishes and Whales

A Coloring Book of Marine Life for Grown-ups and other Children

Do not be afraid to color outside the lines.

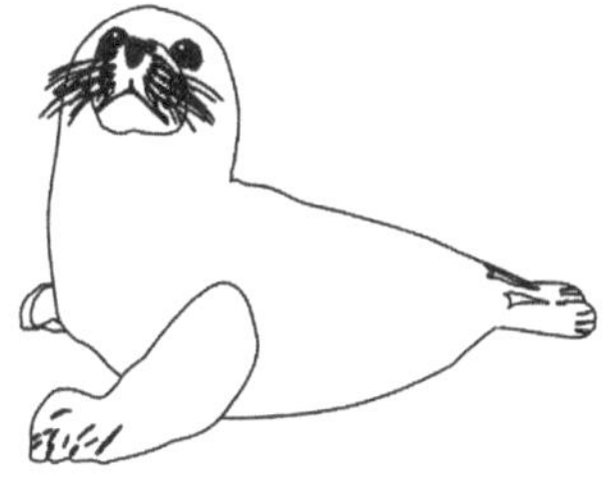

ISBN-13: 978-1523855735
ISBN-10: 1523855738
Library of Congress Control Number: 2016902619
CreateSpace Independent Publishing Platform, North Charleston, SC

Best attempts were made to depict species and ecologies as known to science or my observations, but simplifications were required for the intended audience .
When in doubt refer to a scientifically accurate detailed source.

How to use this book:

1) Each drawing page is printed on one side to avoid print showing into your artwork. Use a scissors or a paper knife to pull out your page if you want to frame or hang it.

2) Use coloring pencils if you leave the pages in the book! Markers may bleed through, and crayons are not fine enough for the details on these pages. Alternatively, cut out the page in question, then use paints or markers to your heart's content.

3) All the species in the images (scenes) are real species, in real ecosystems, though I took some license to reformat and rescale elements to make it easier to color in the items. I also simplified the fish, by removing the fin rays and other parts to have coloring space. Feel free to re-add details, or make up your own.

4) At the end, is a scene index, though there are only even page numbers (to allow framing). In the index is a guide where in nature to find the scene, and names of some of the species in the scene.

5) Hopefully the coloring experience not only provides fun and stress relief, but also a bit of knowledge about the watery world.

Enjoy,
Bryce

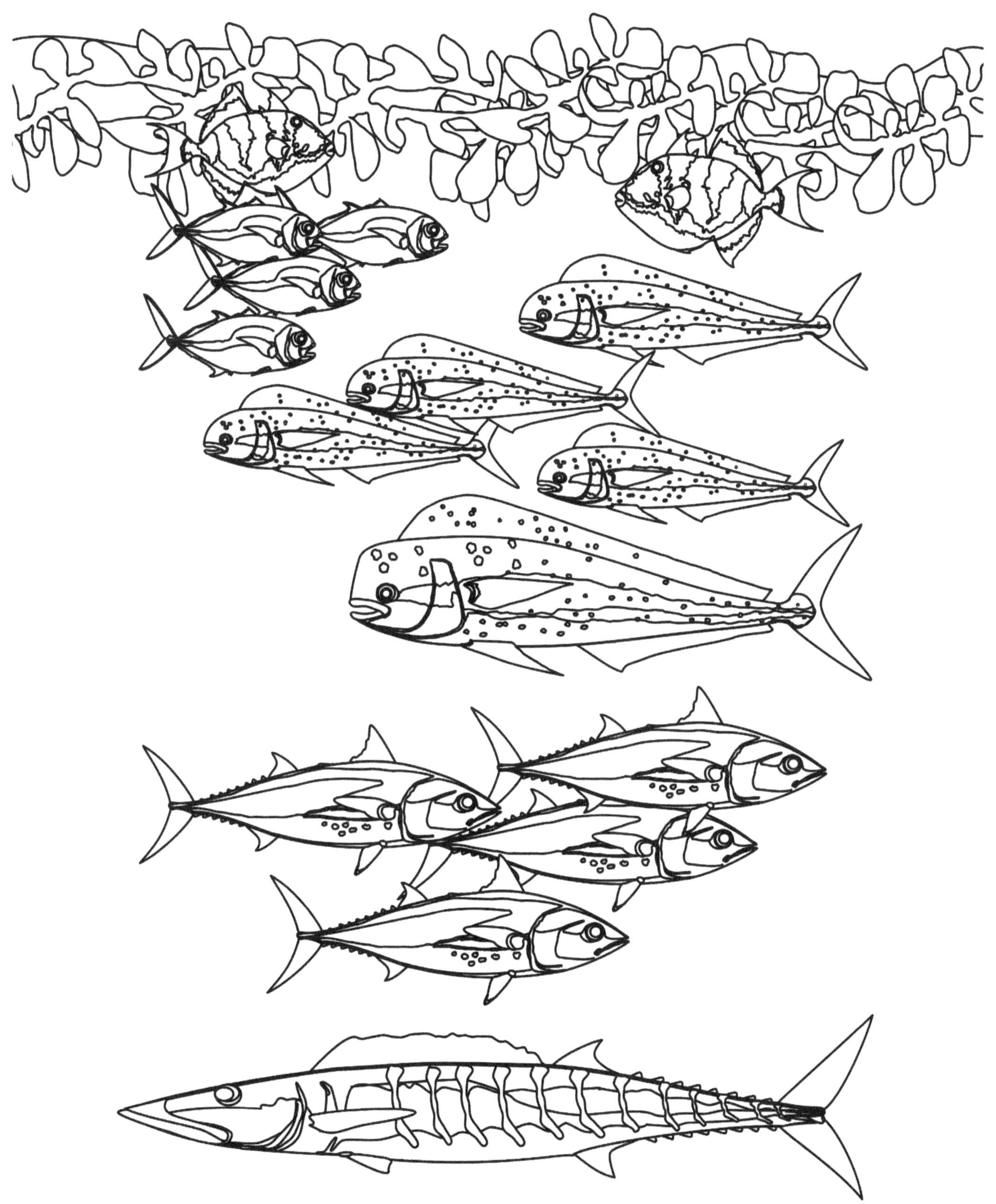

THIS PAGE LEFT INTENTIONALLY BLANK

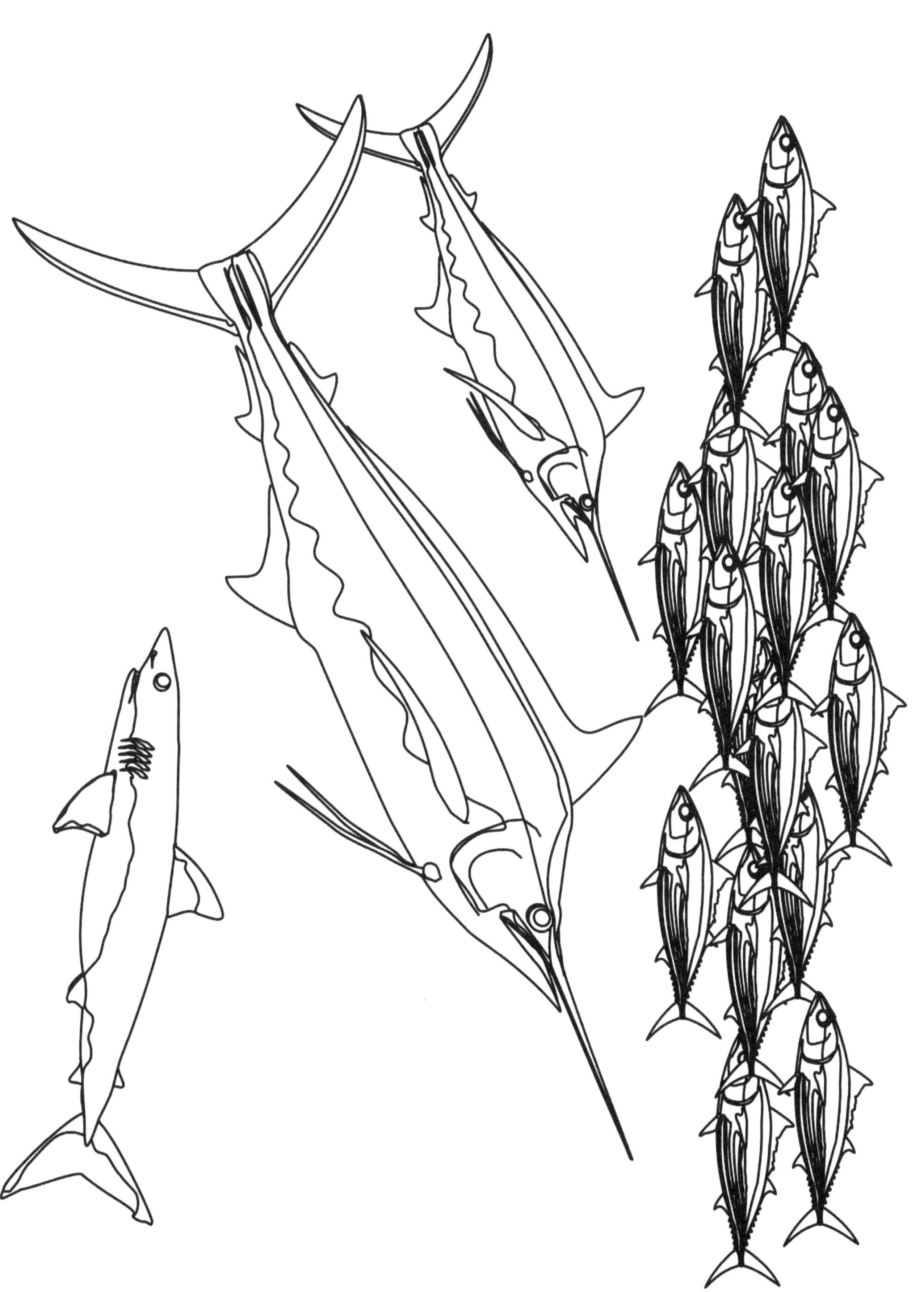

THIS PAGE LEFT INTENTIONALLY BLANK

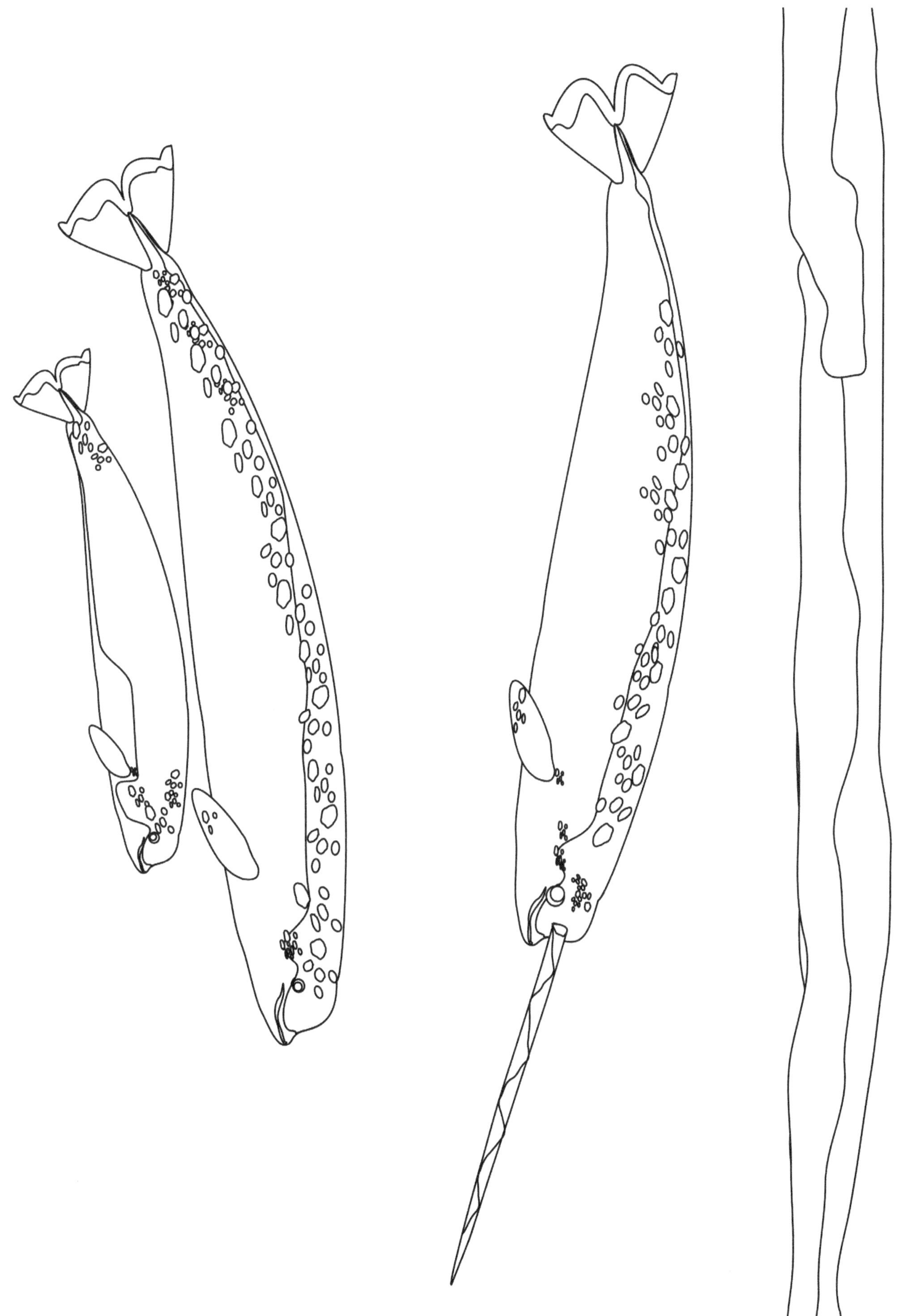

THIS PAGE LEFT INTENTIONALLY BLANK

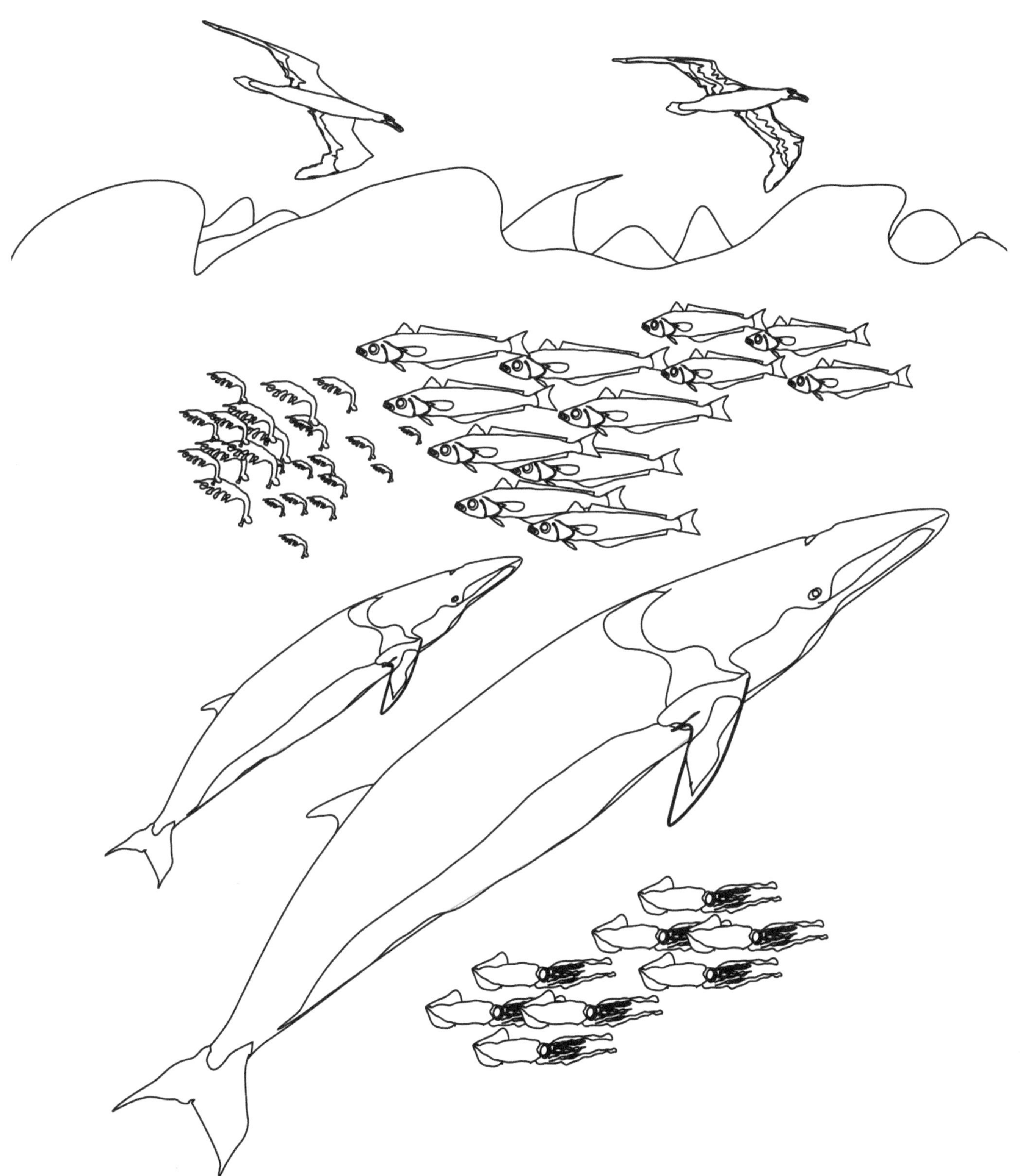

THIS PAGE LEFT INTENTIONALLY BLANK

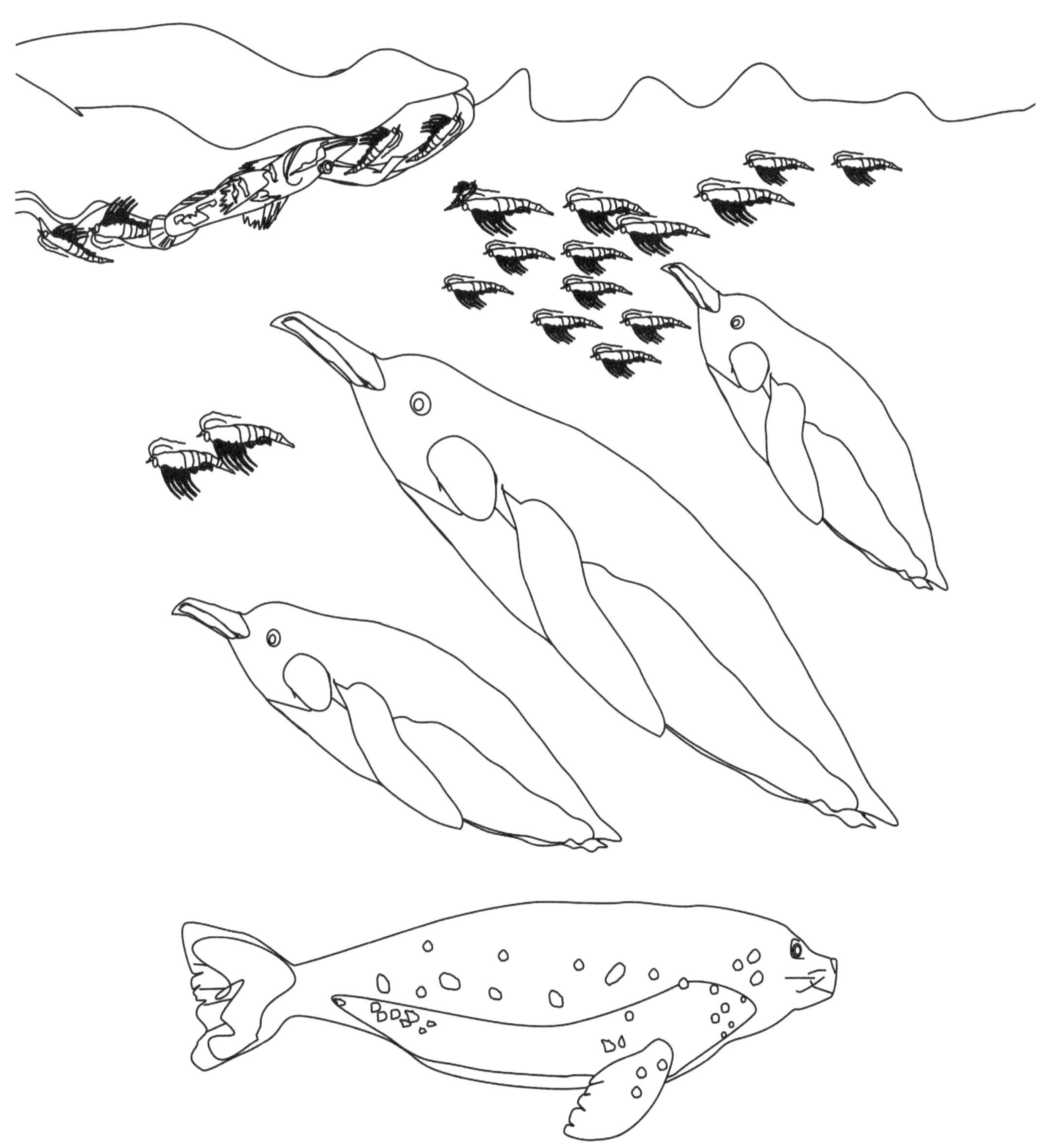

THIS PAGE LEFT INTENTIONALLY BLANK

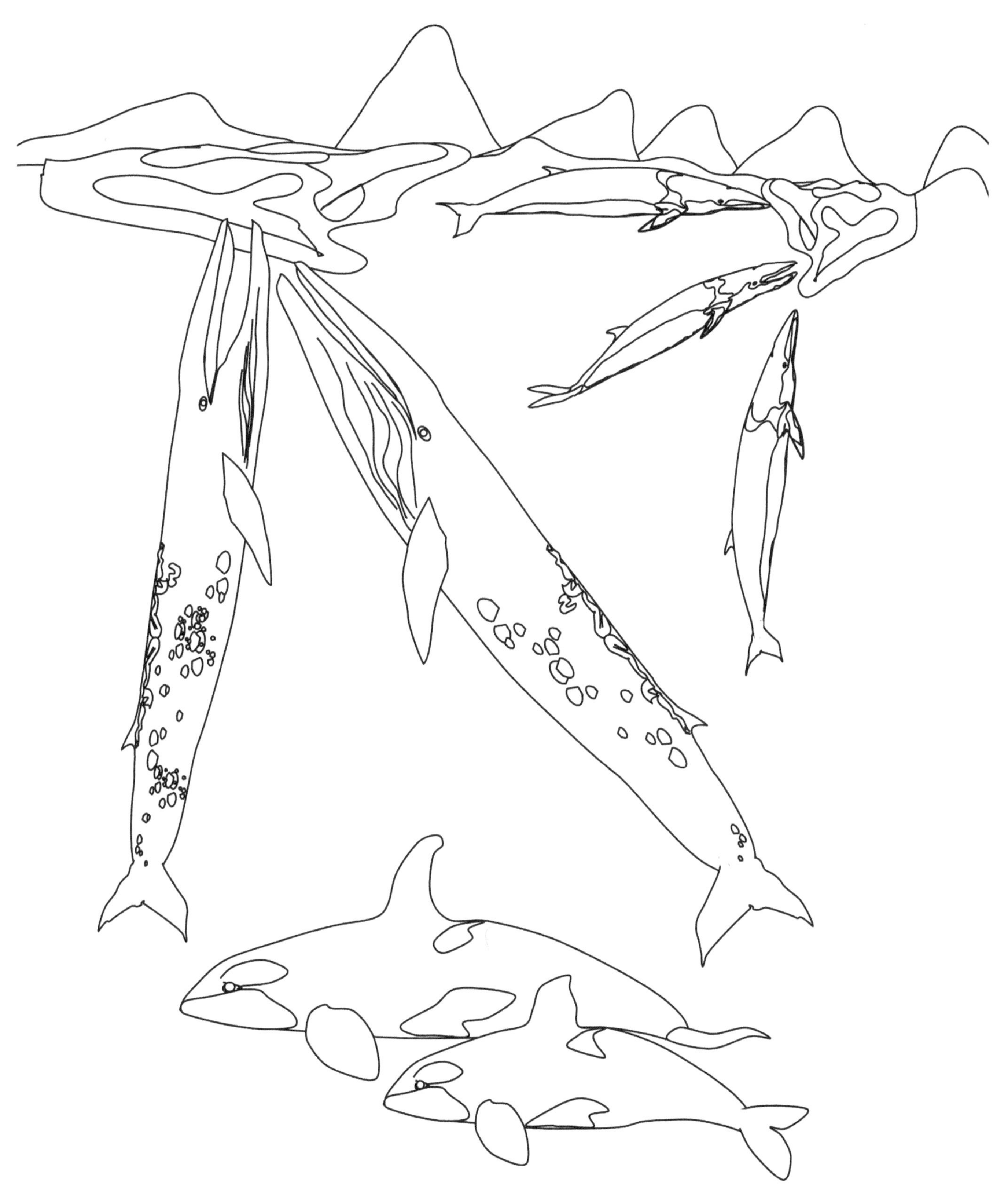

THIS PAGE LEFT INTENTIONALLY BLANK

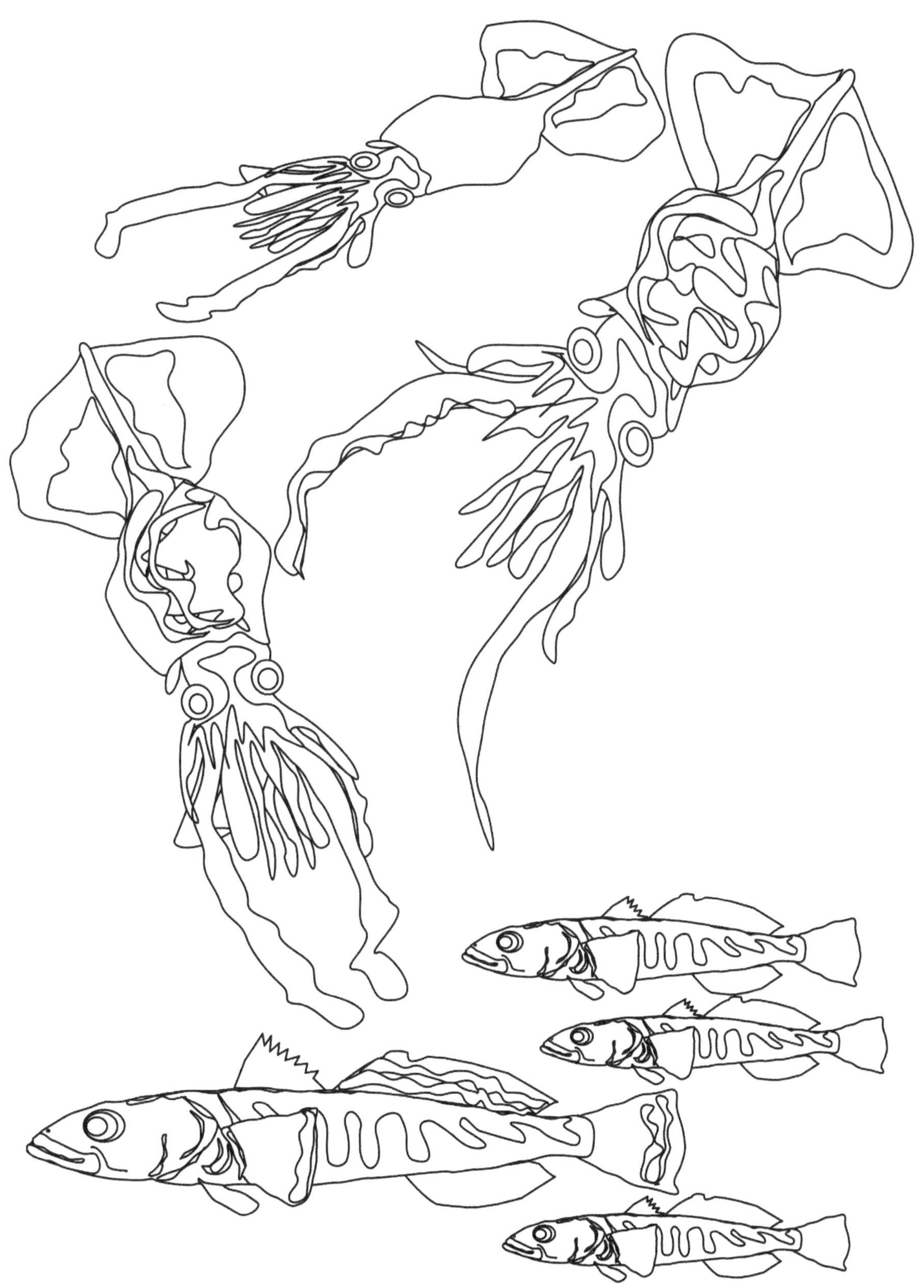

THIS PAGE LEFT INTENTIONALLY BLANK

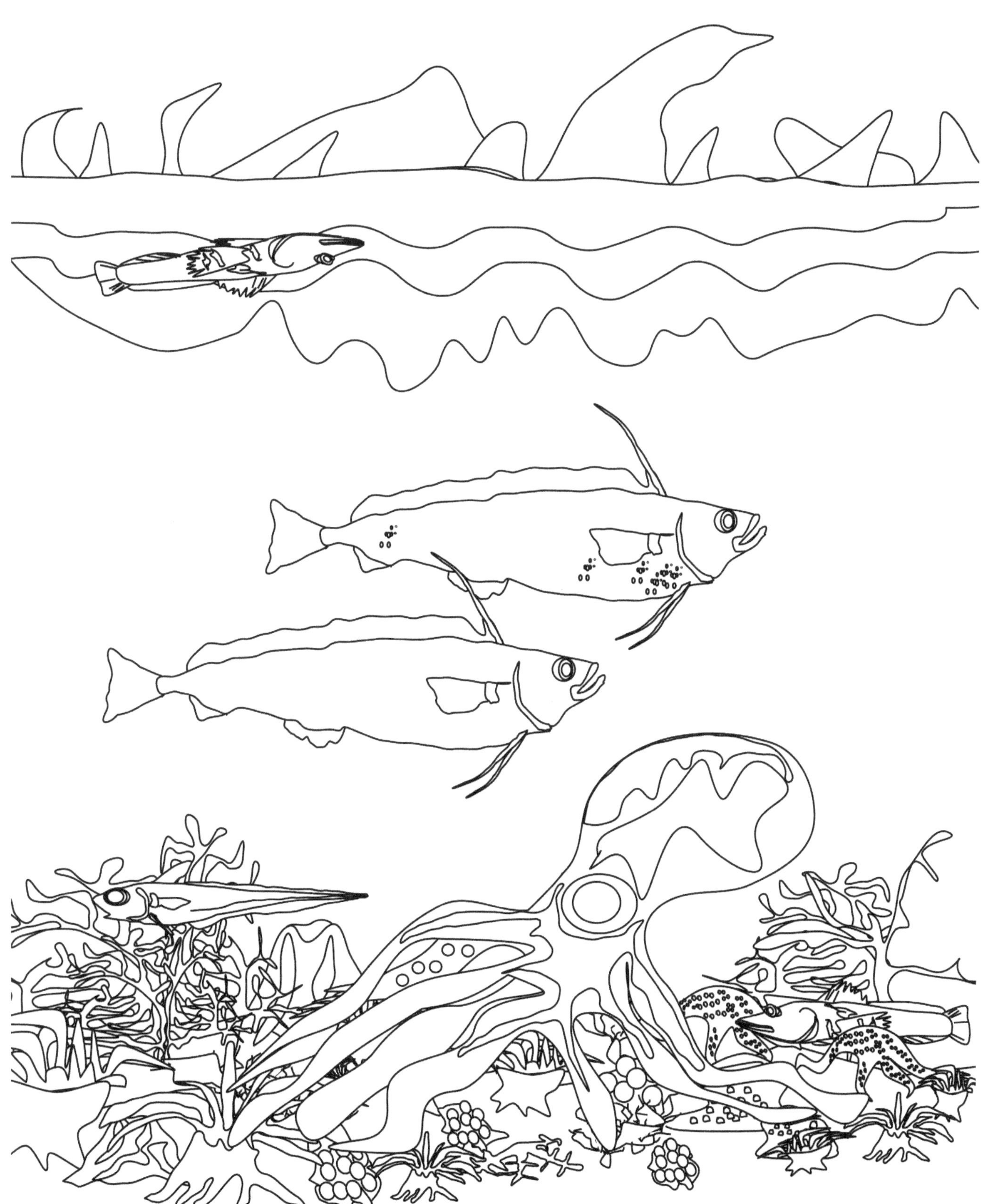

THIS PAGE LEFT INTENTIONALLY BLANK

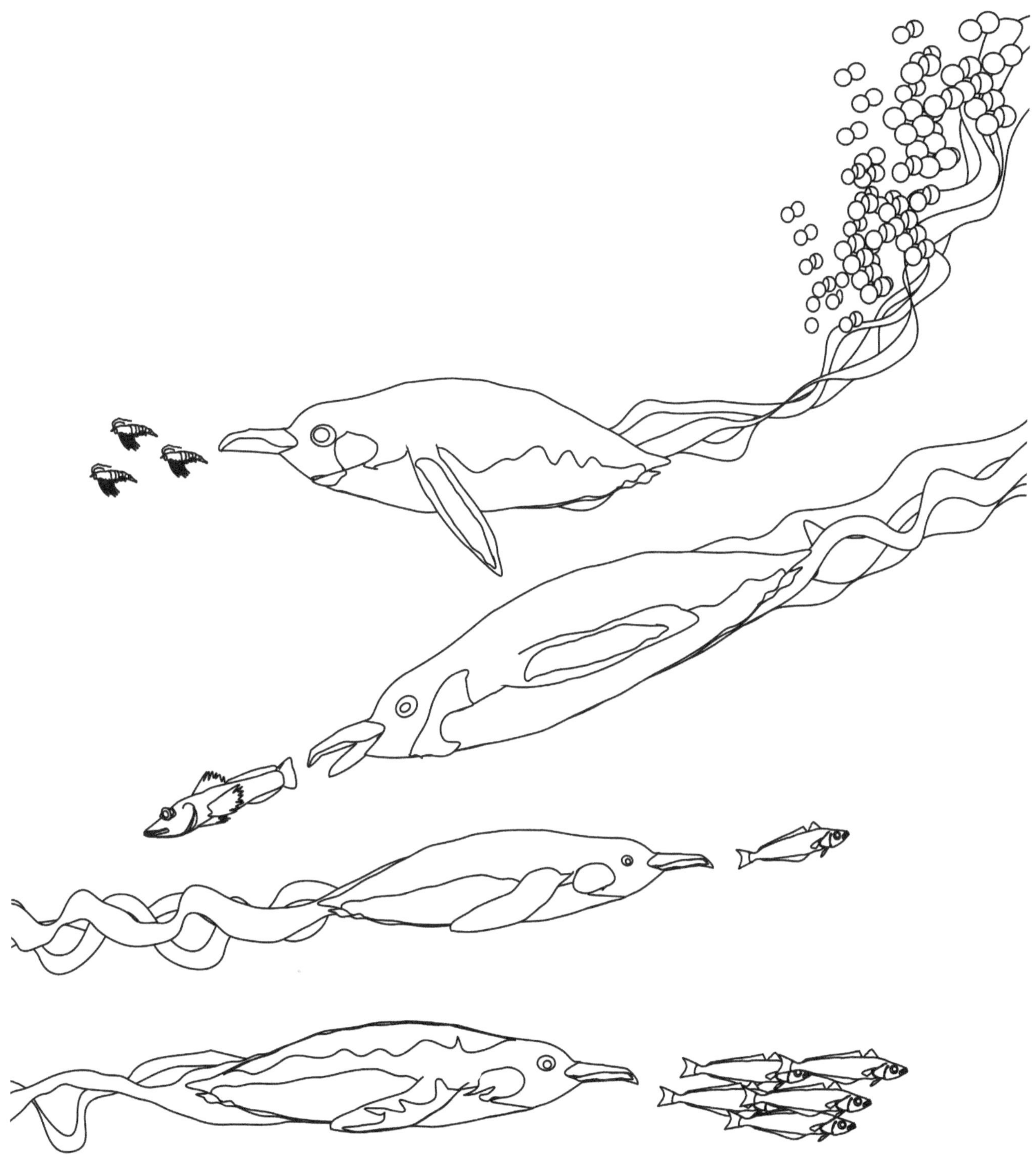

THIS PAGE LEFT INTENTIONALLY BLANK

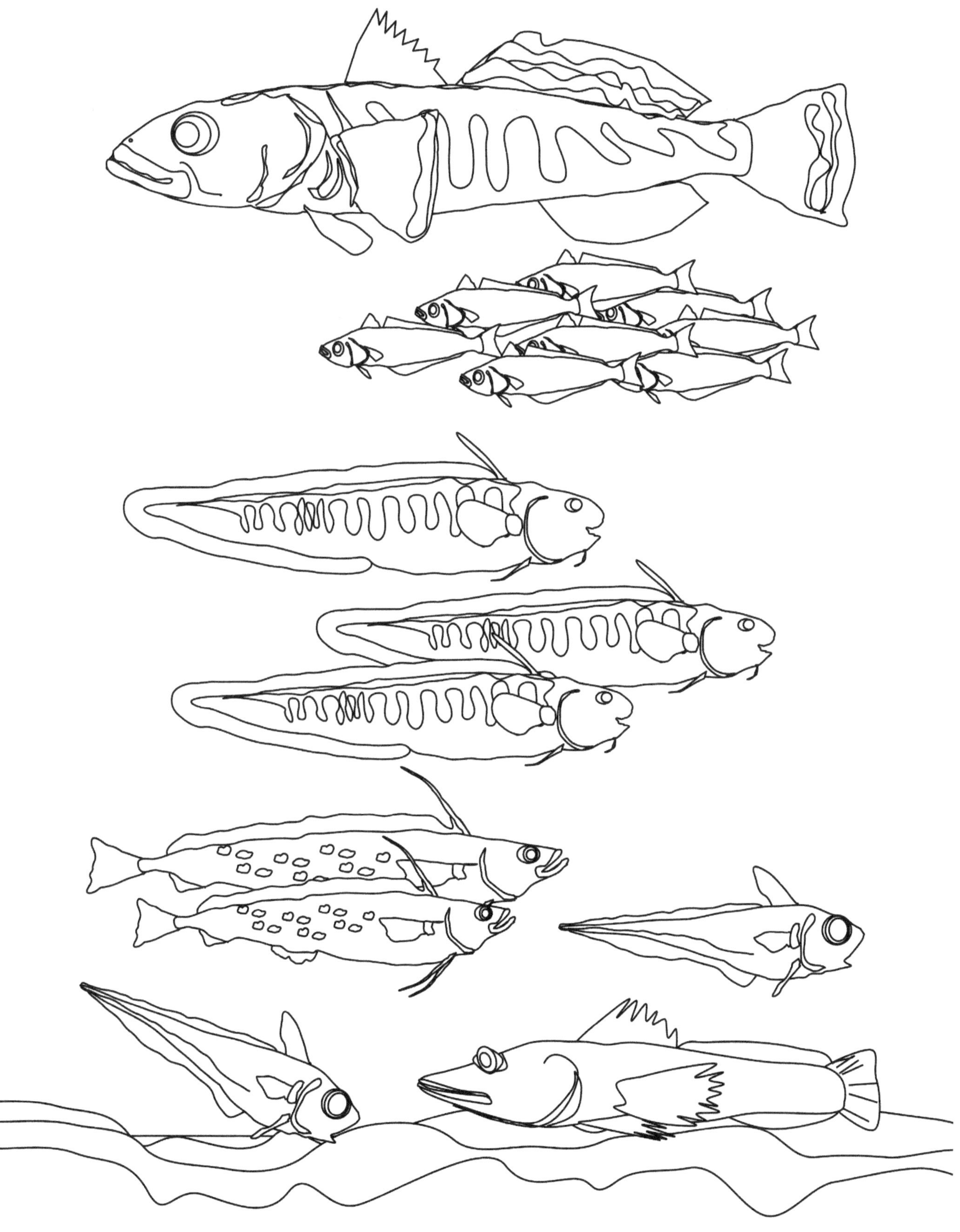

THIS PAGE LEFT INTENTIONALLY BLANK

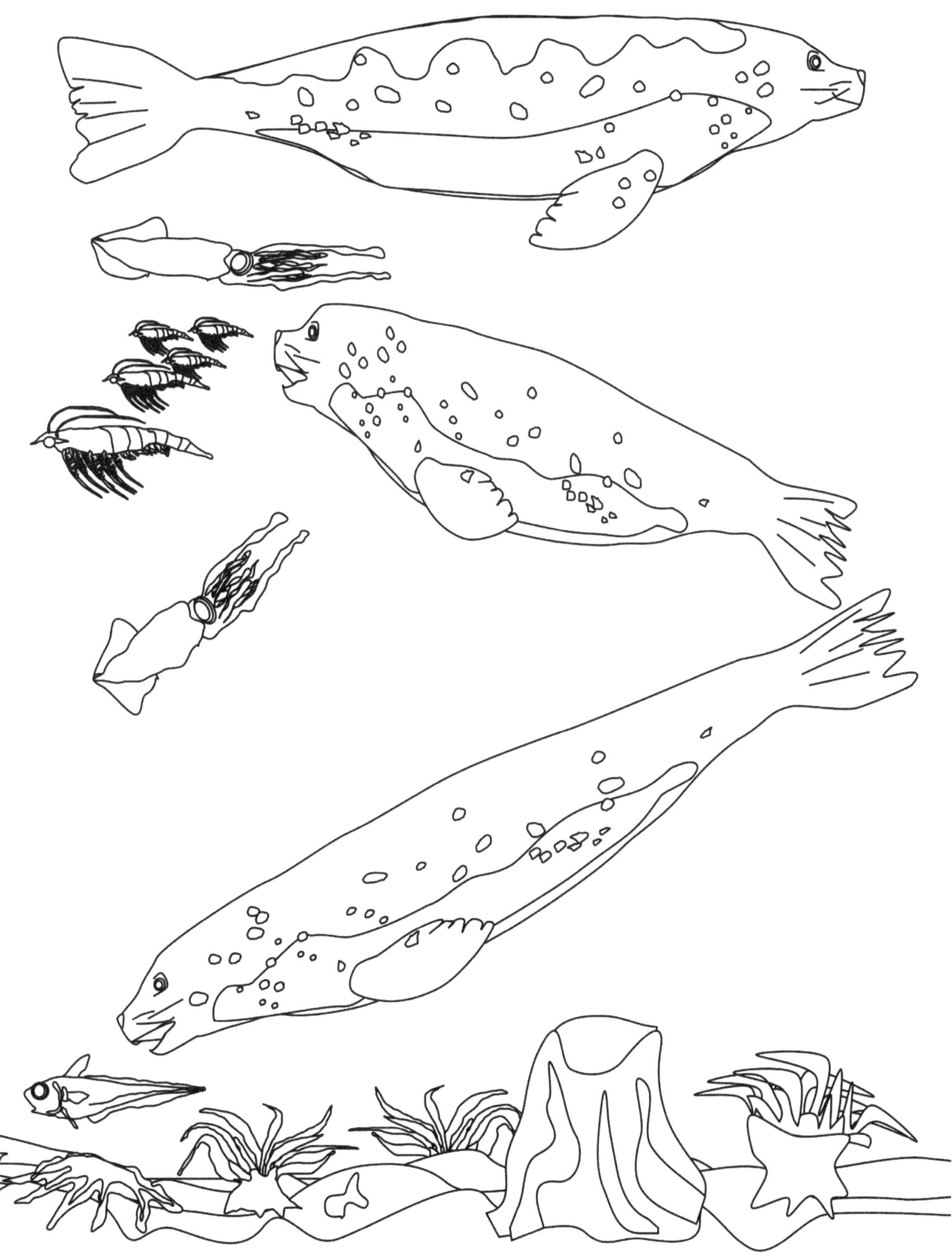

THIS PAGE LEFT INTENTIONALLY BLANK

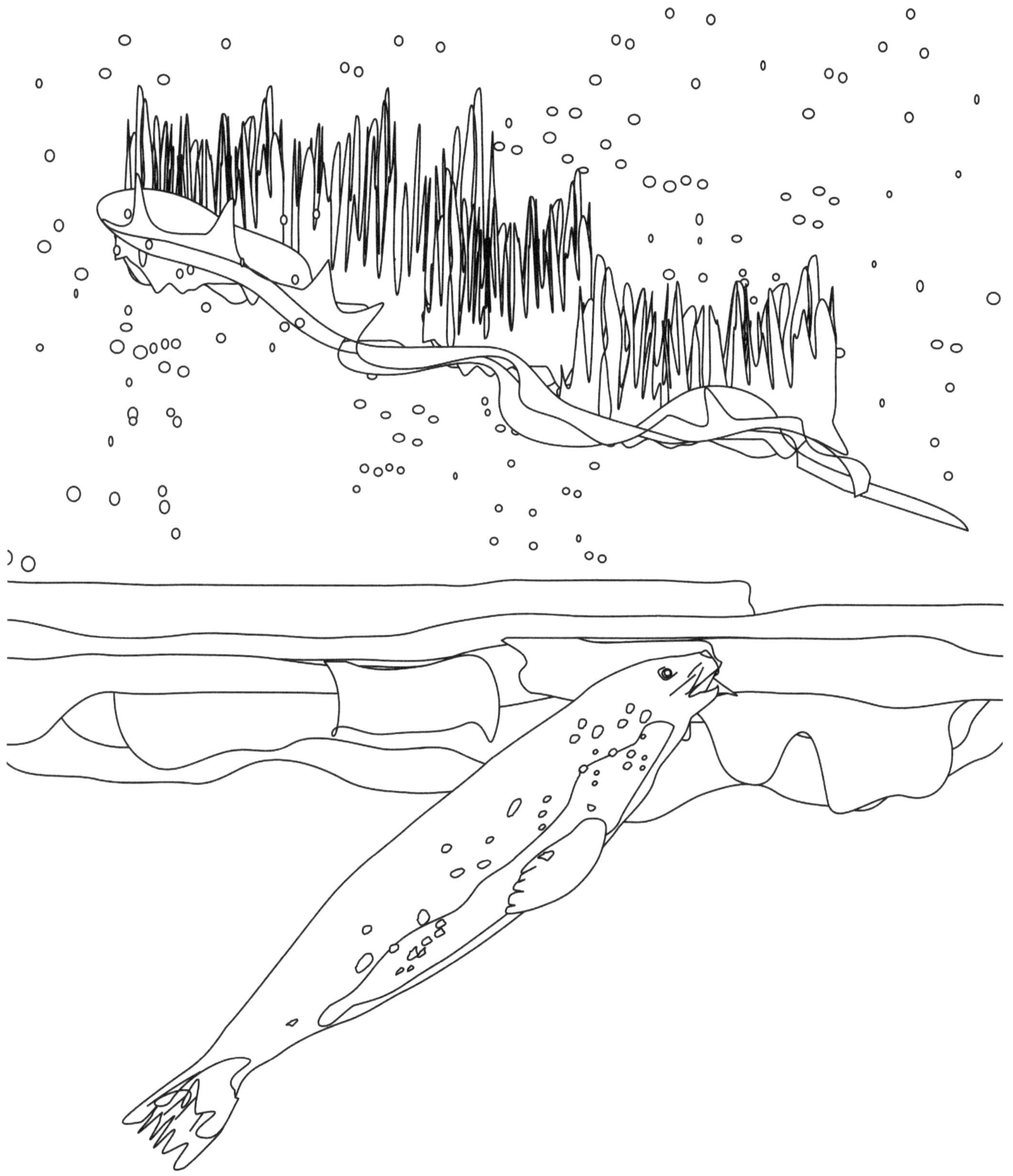

THIS PAGE LEFT INTENTIONALLY BLANK

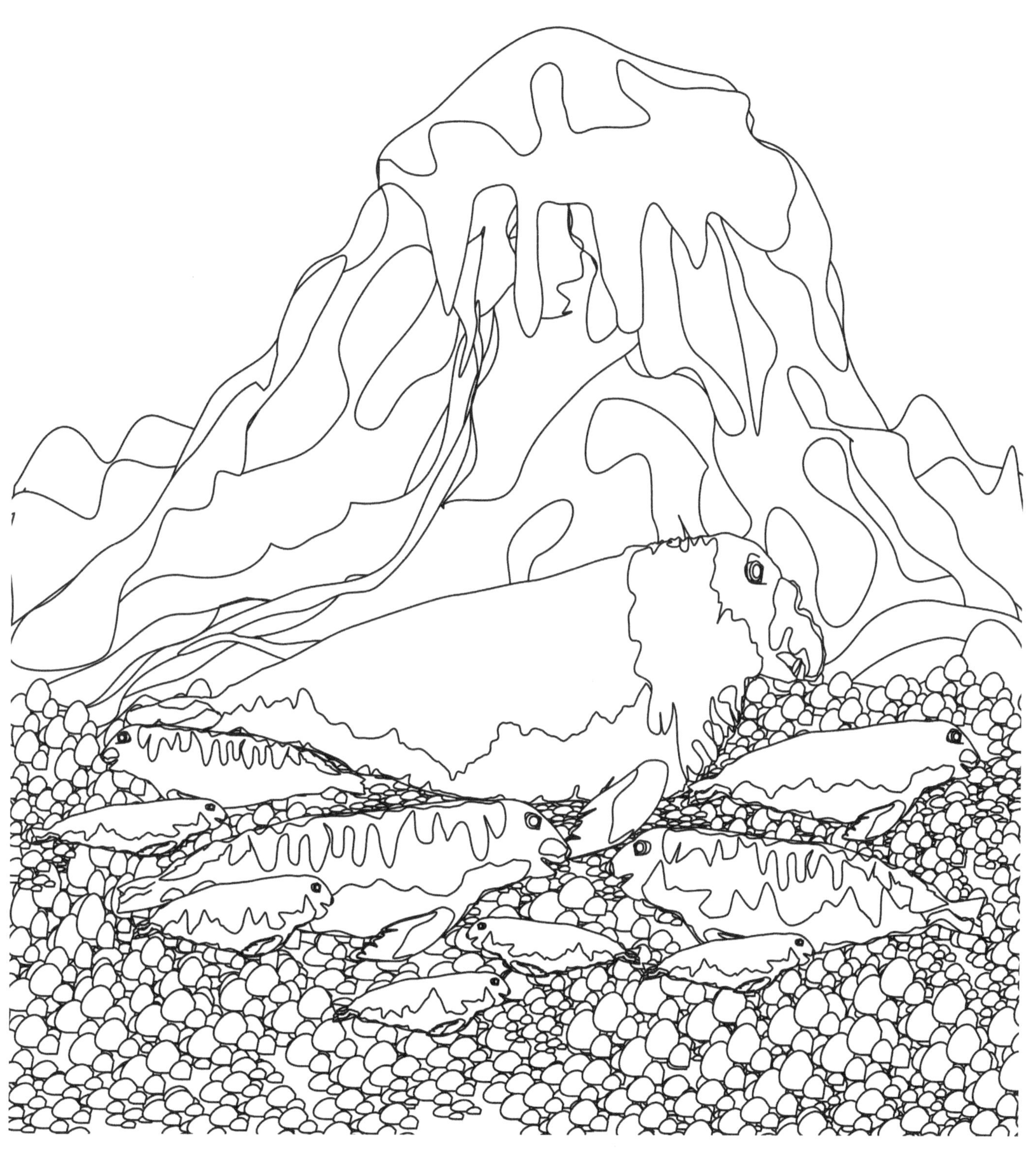

THIS PAGE LEFT INTENTIONALLY BLANK

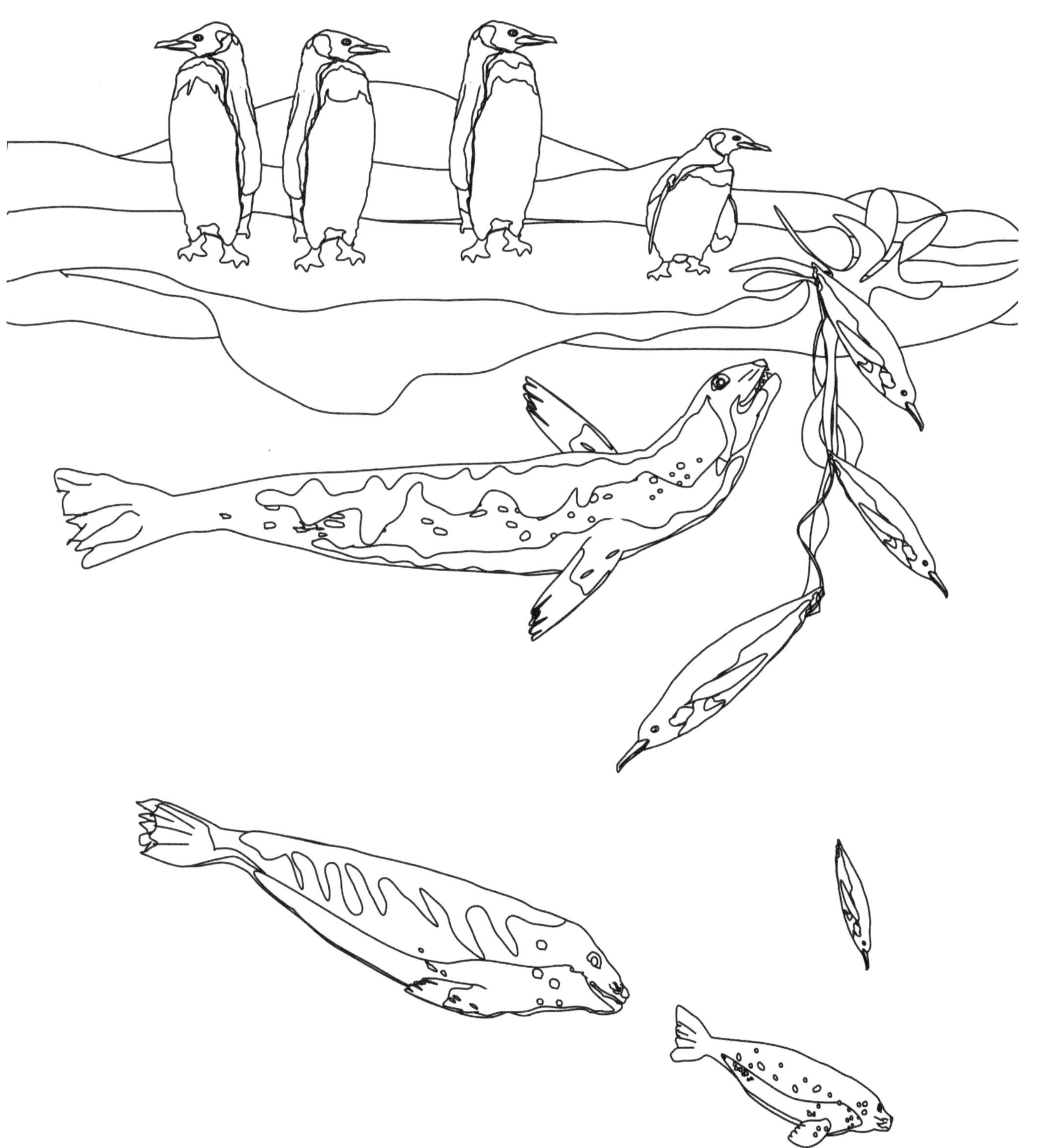

THIS PAGE LEFT INTENTIONALLY BLANK

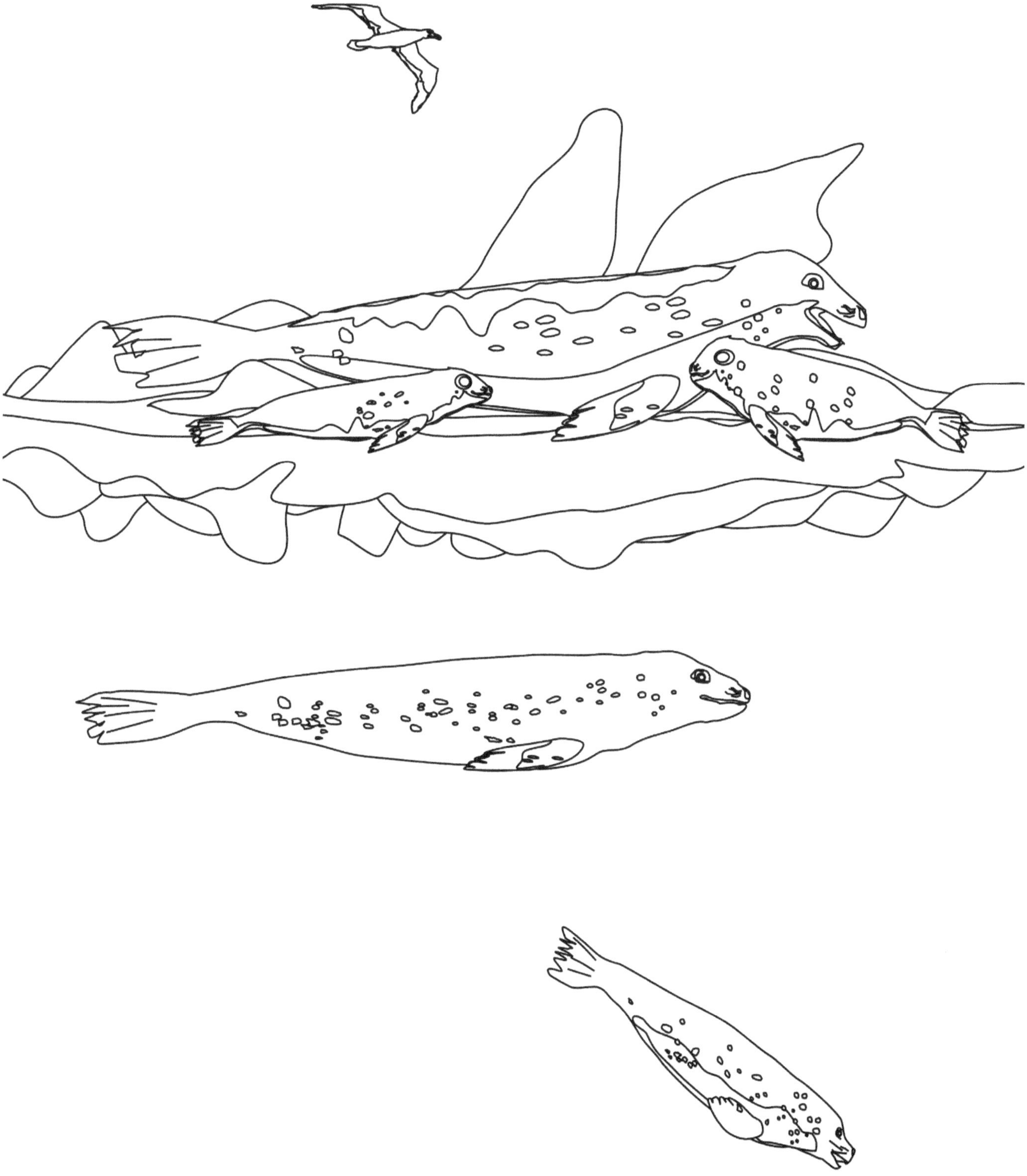

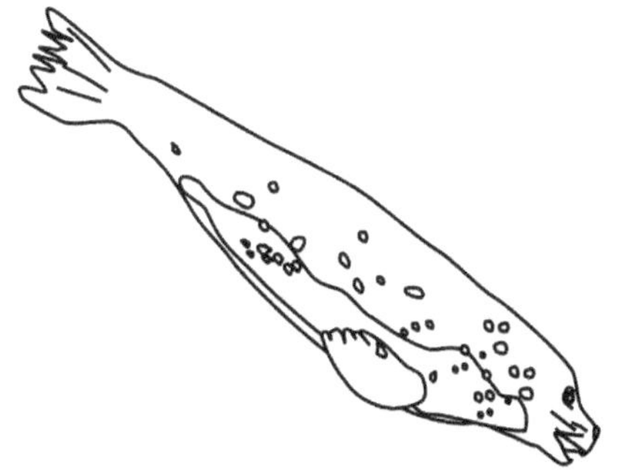

THIS PAGE LEFT INTENTIONALLY BLANK

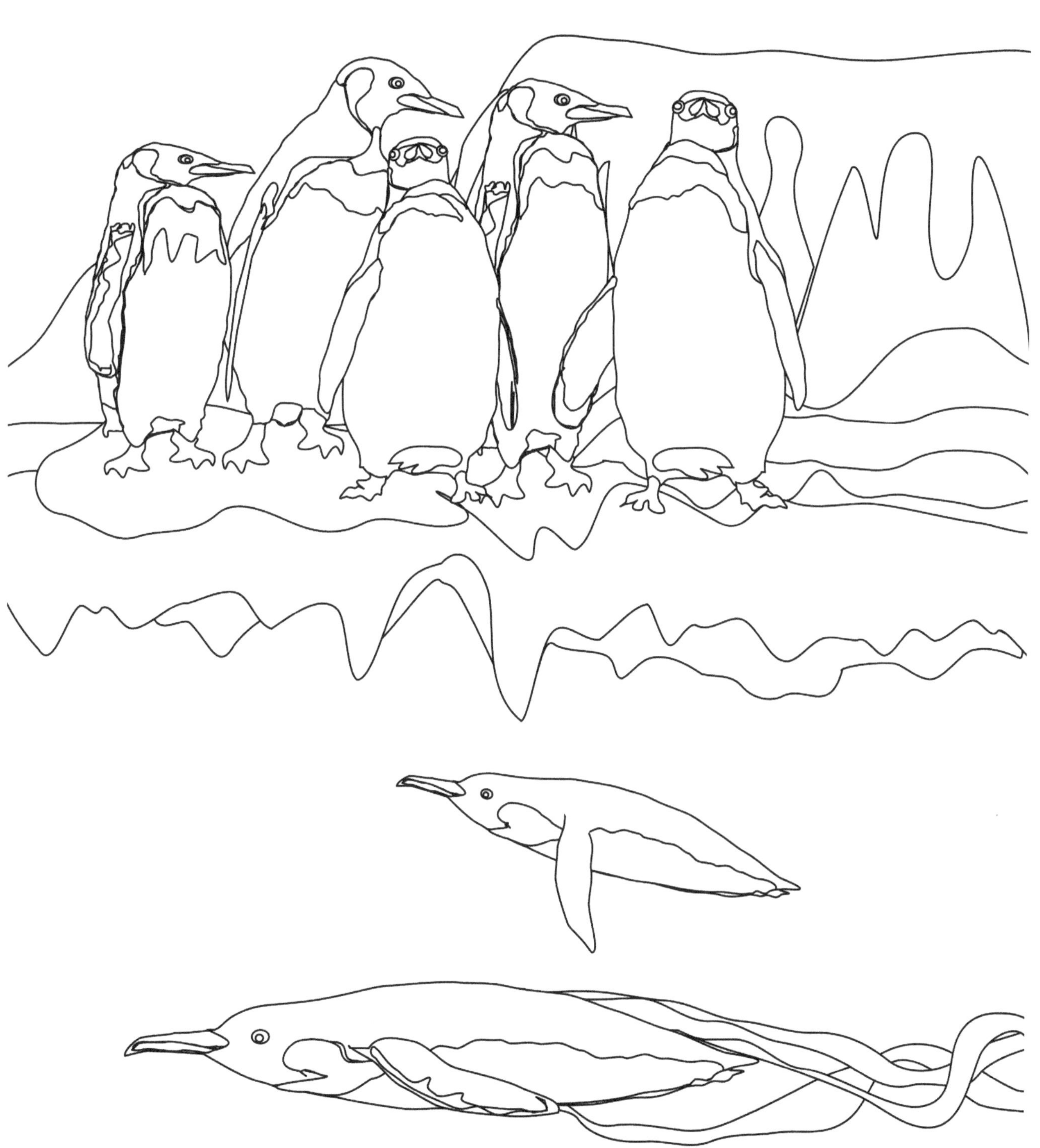

THIS PAGE LEFT INTENTIONALLY BLANK

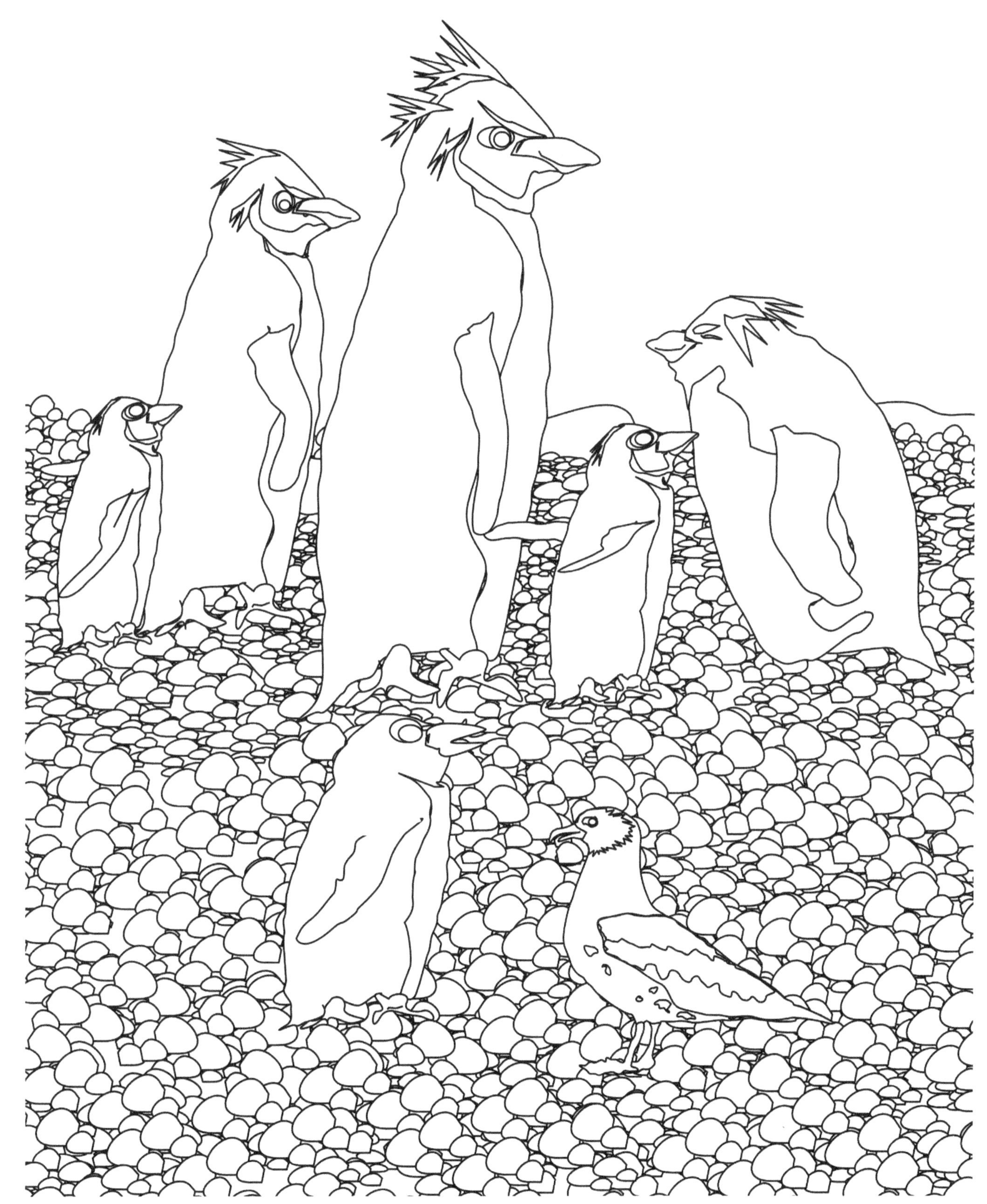

THIS PAGE LEFT INTENTIONALLY BLANK

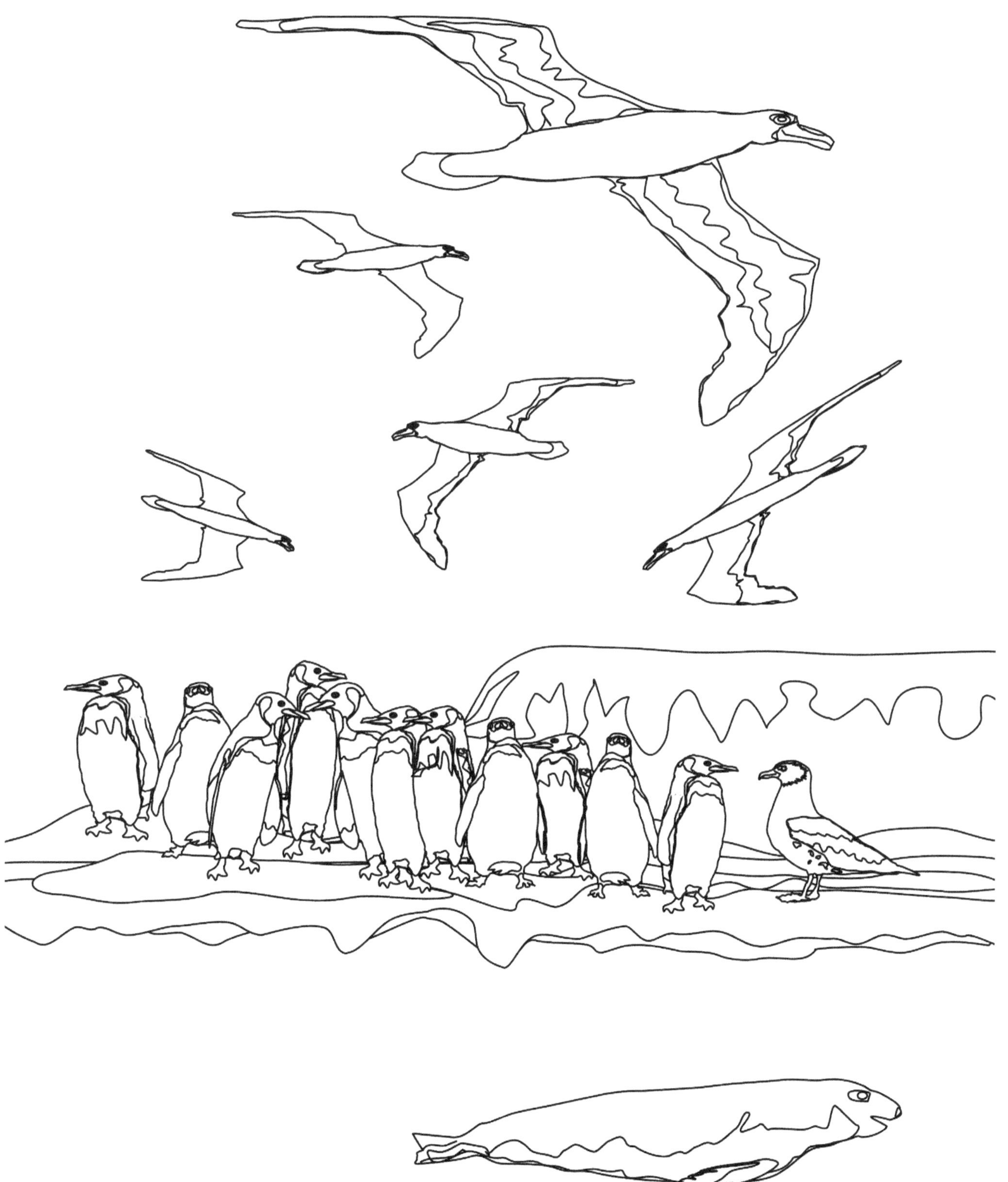

THIS PAGE LEFT INTENTIONALLY BLANK

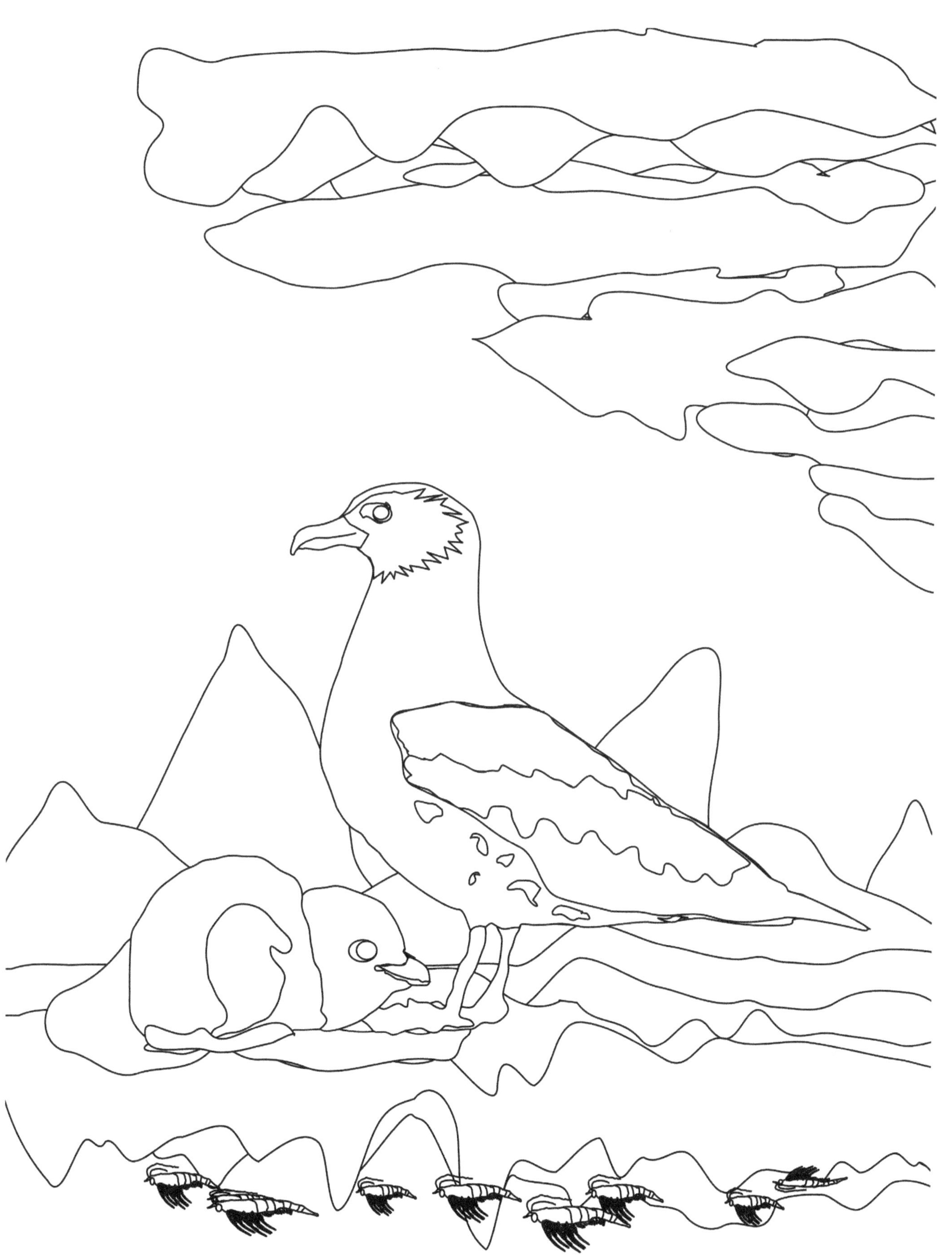

THIS PAGE LEFT INTENTIONALLY BLANK

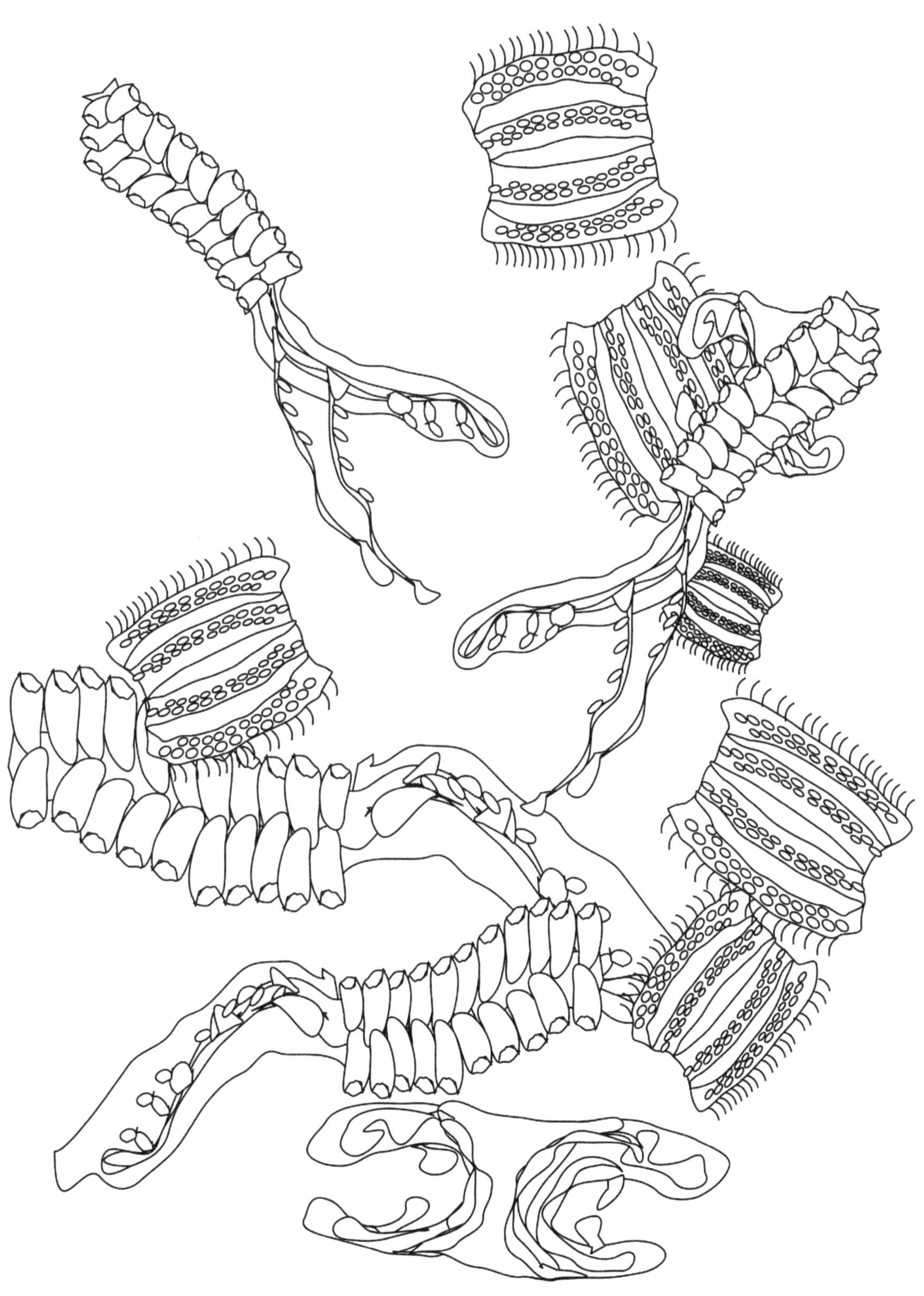

THIS PAGE LEFT INTENTIONALLY BLANK

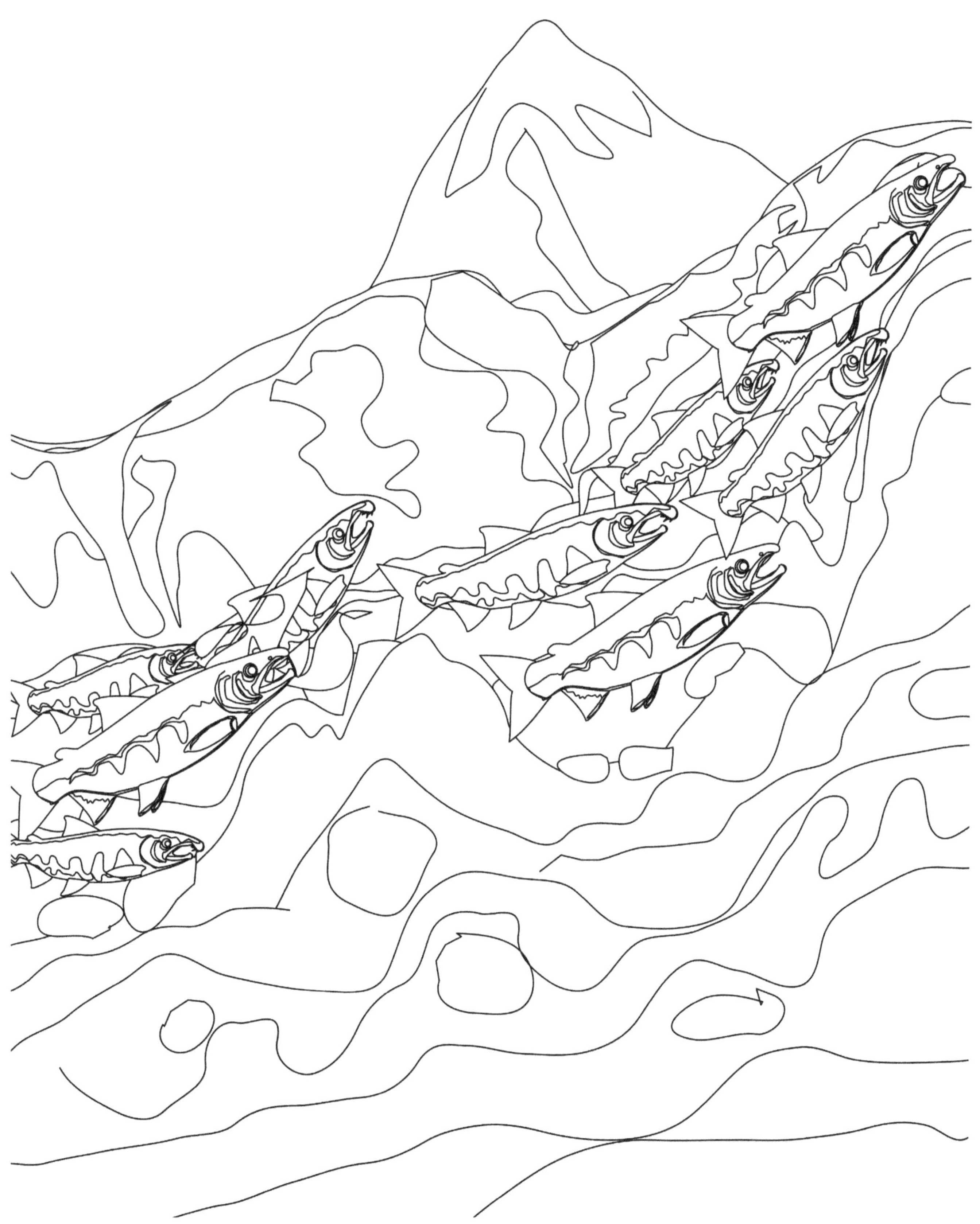

THIS PAGE LEFT INTENTIONALLY BLANK

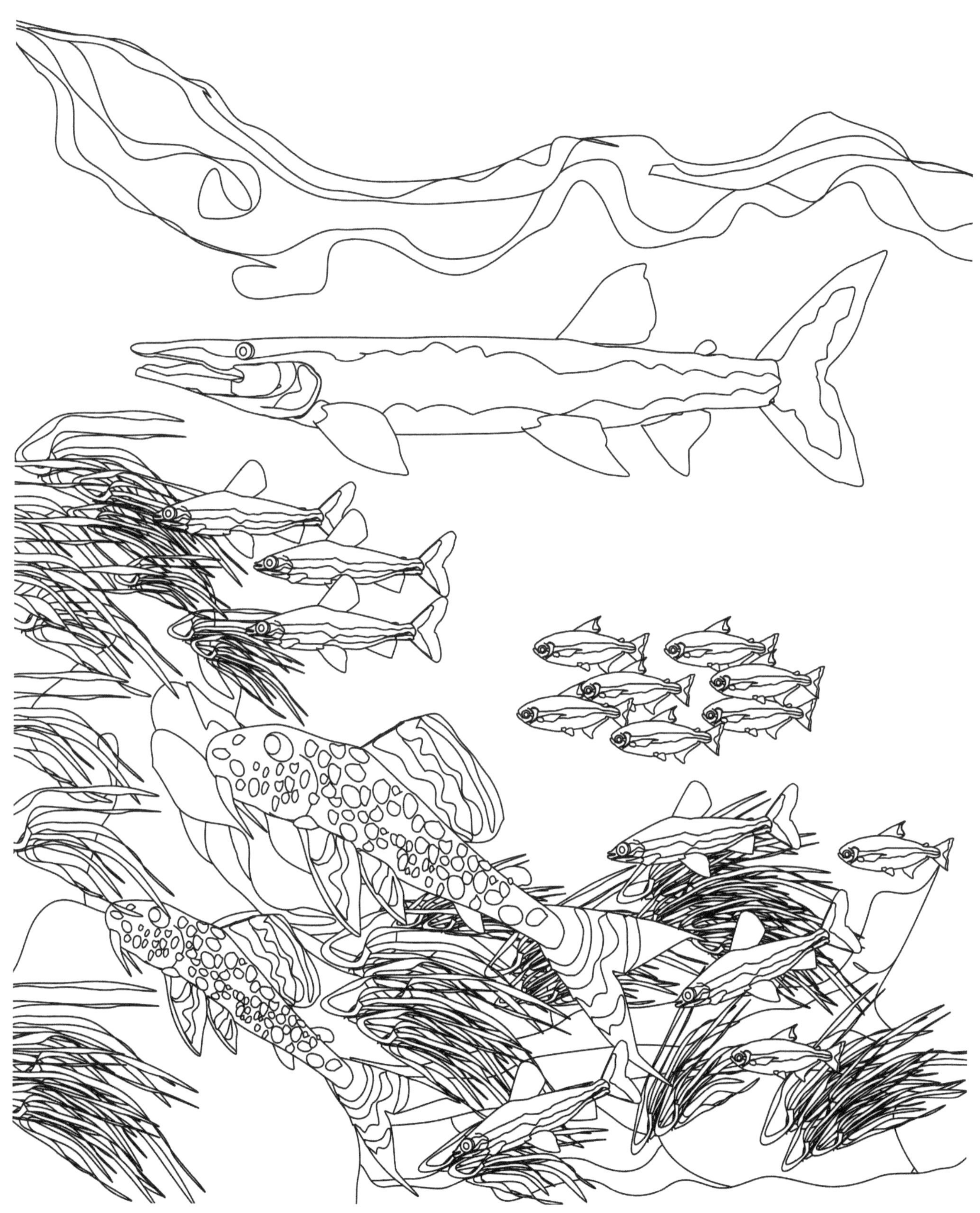

THIS PAGE LEFT INTENTIONALLY BLANK

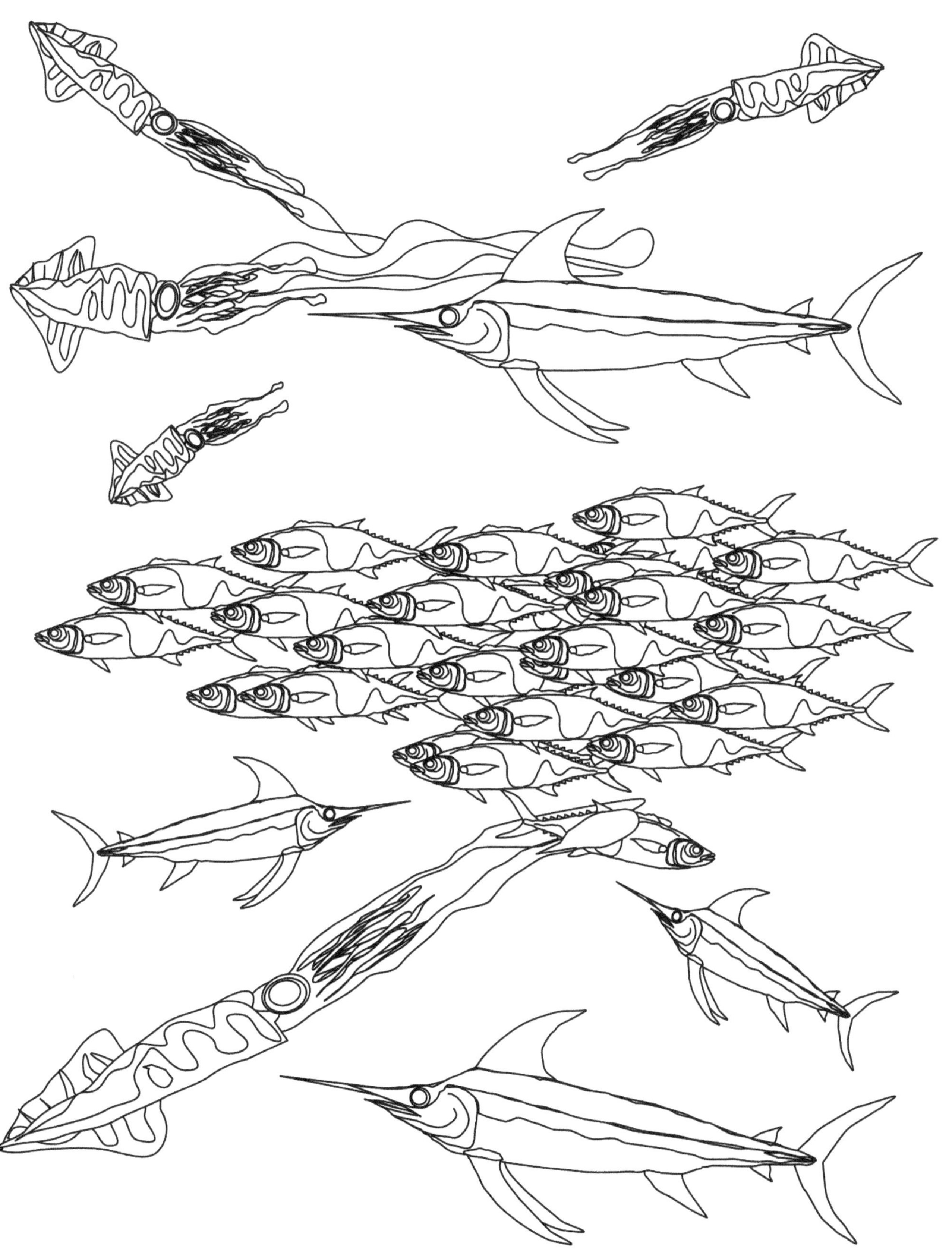

THIS PAGE LEFT INTENTIONALLY BLANK

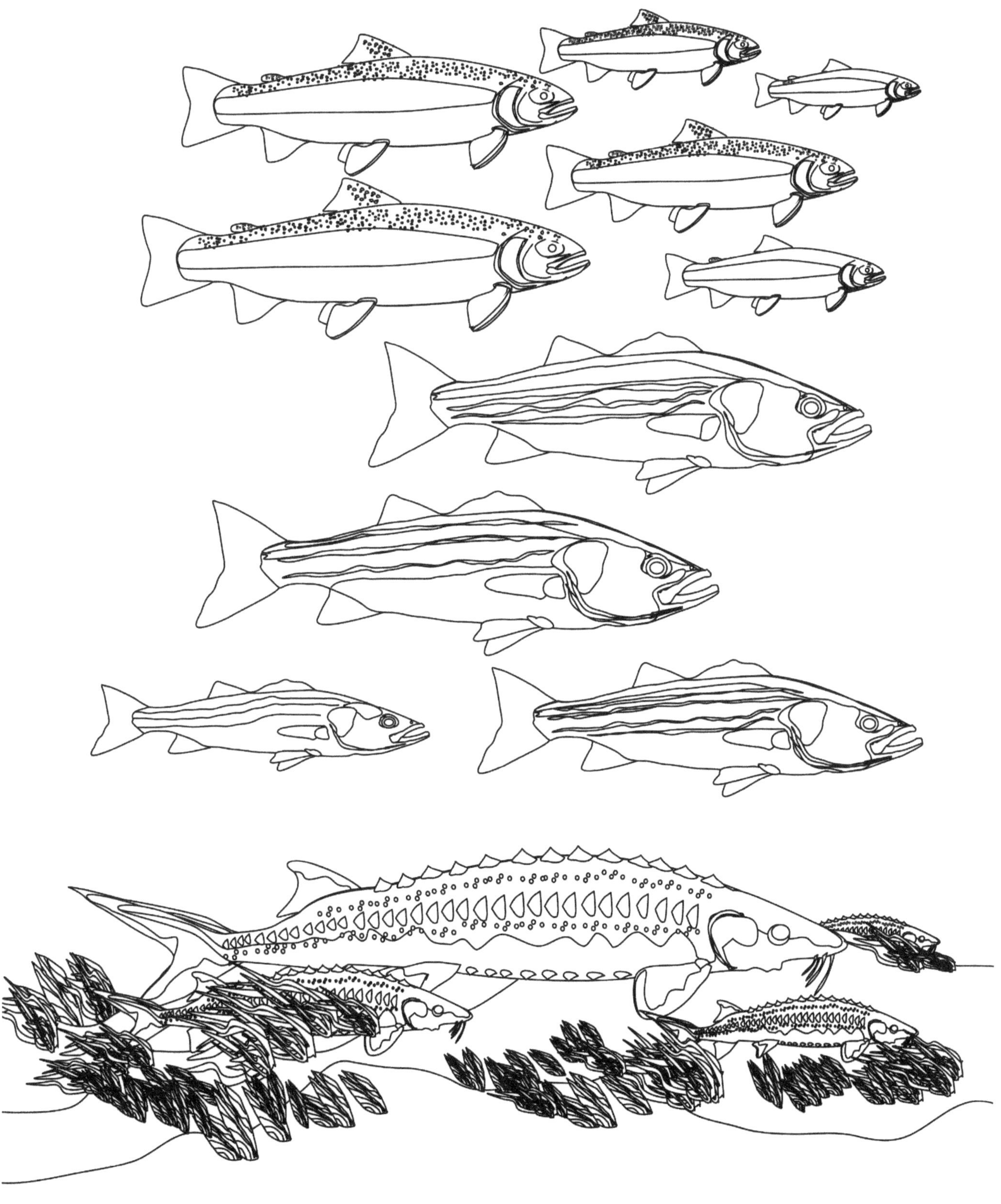

THIS PAGE LEFT INTENTIONALLY BLANK

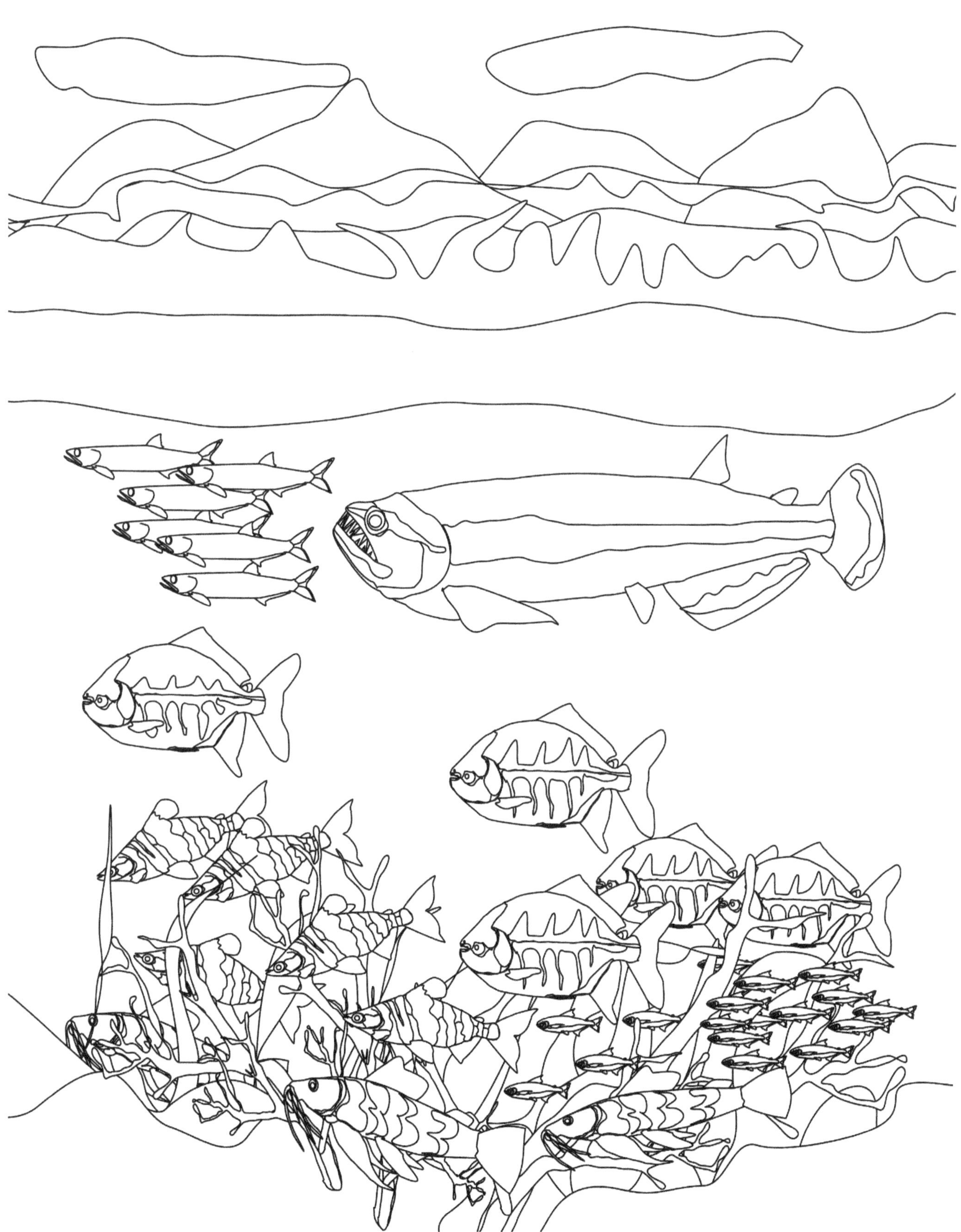

THIS PAGE LEFT INTENTIONALLY BLANK

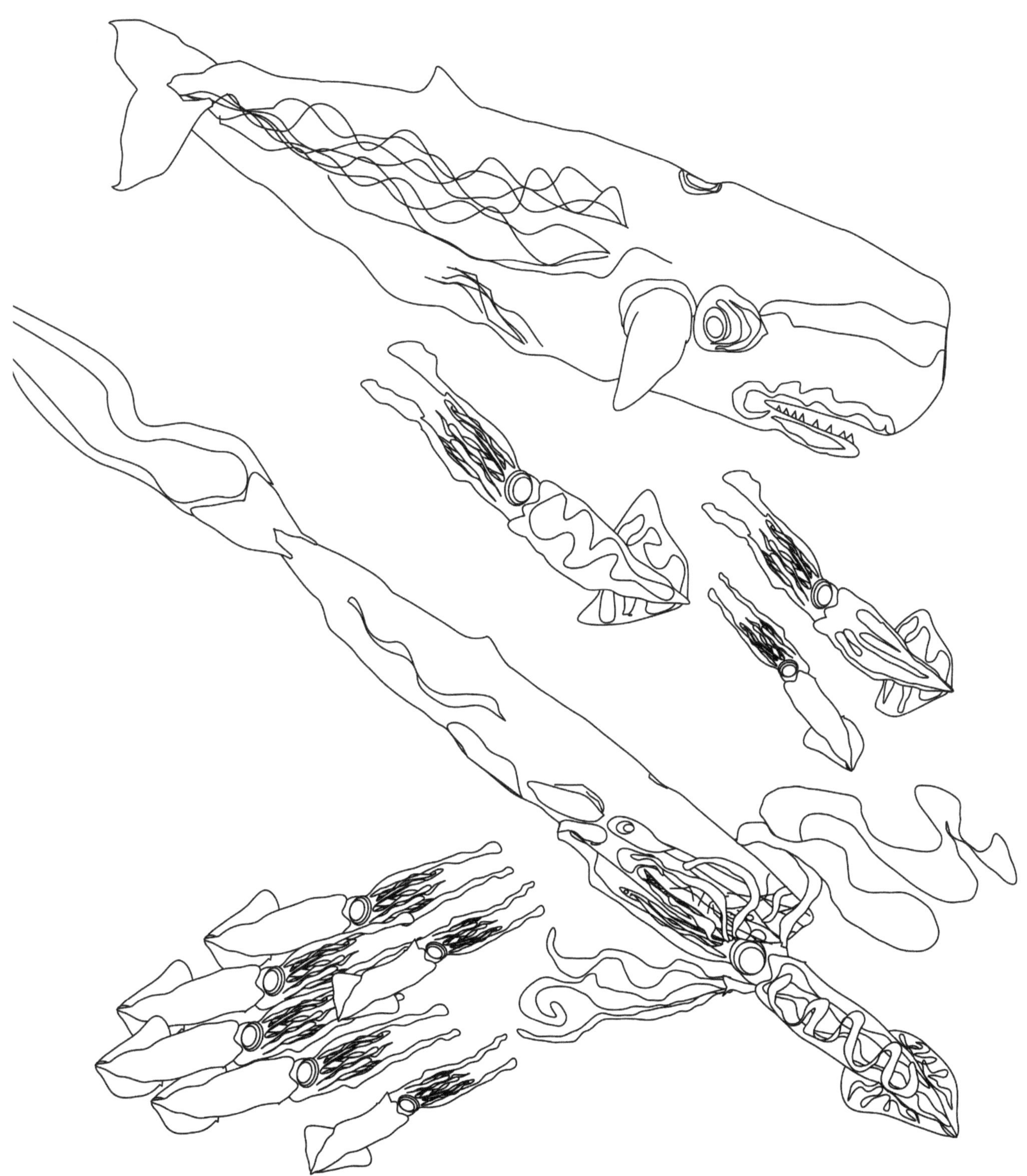

THIS PAGE LEFT INTENTIONALLY BLANK

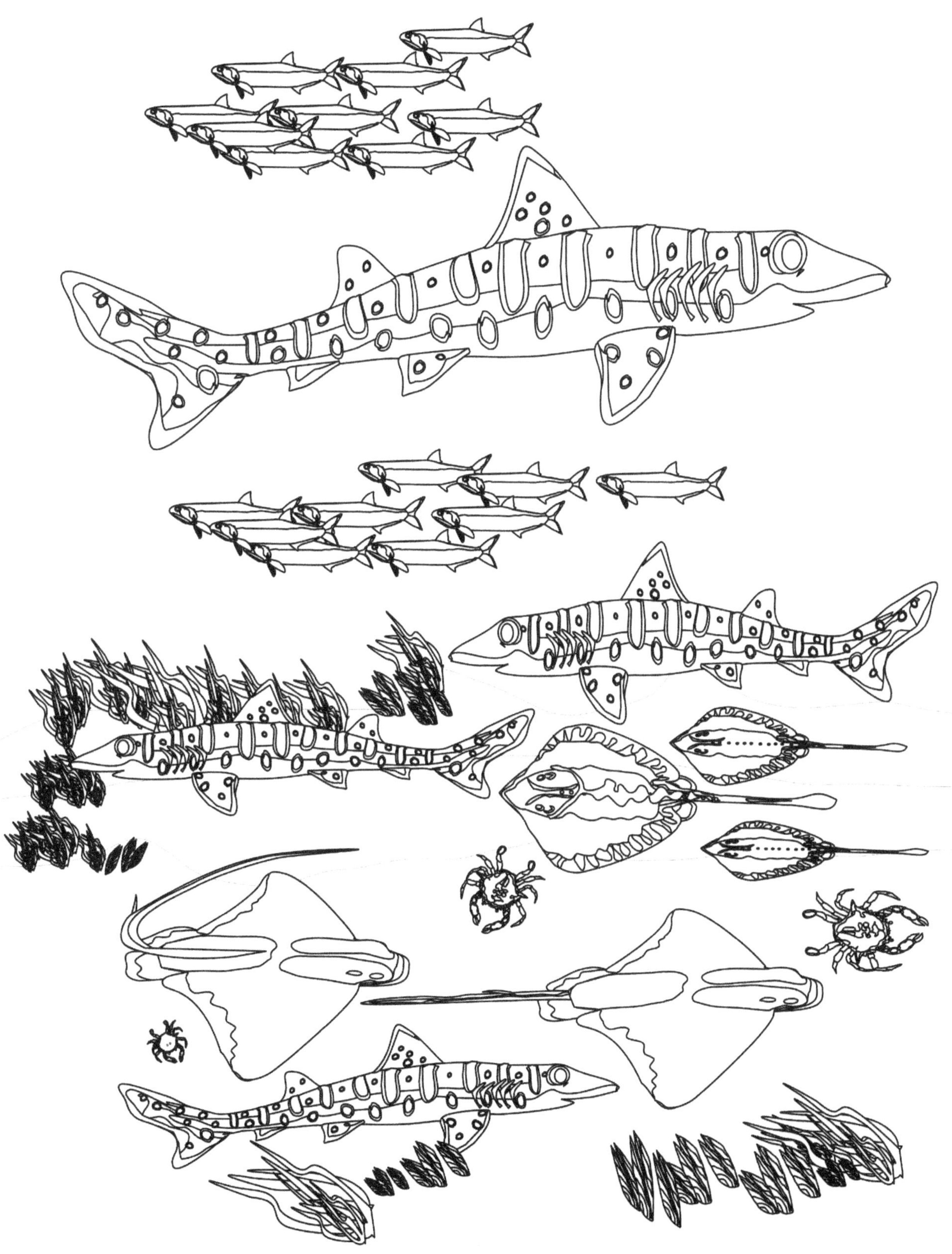

THIS PAGE LEFT INTENTIONALLY BLANK

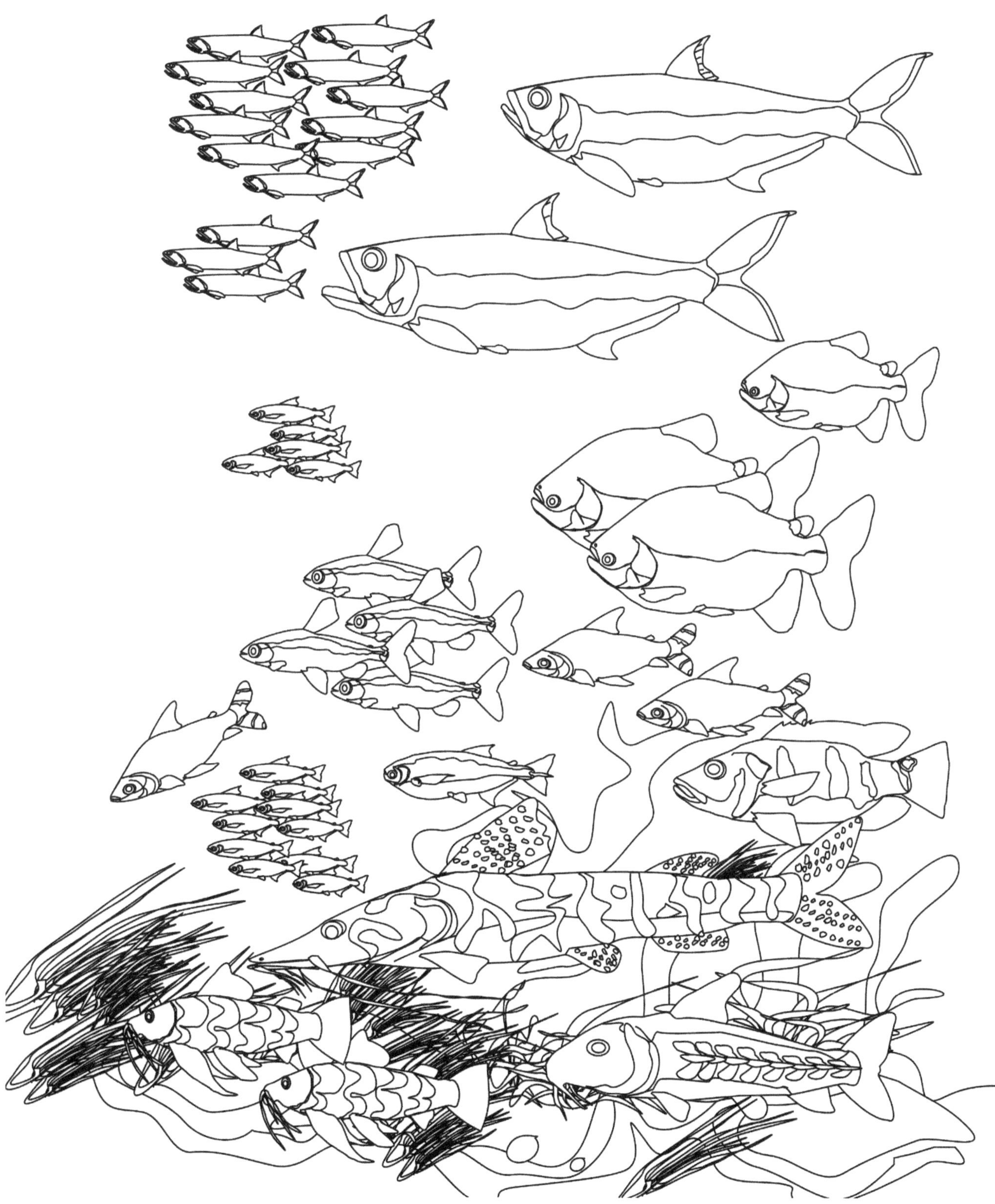

THIS PAGE LEFT INTENTIONALLY BLANK

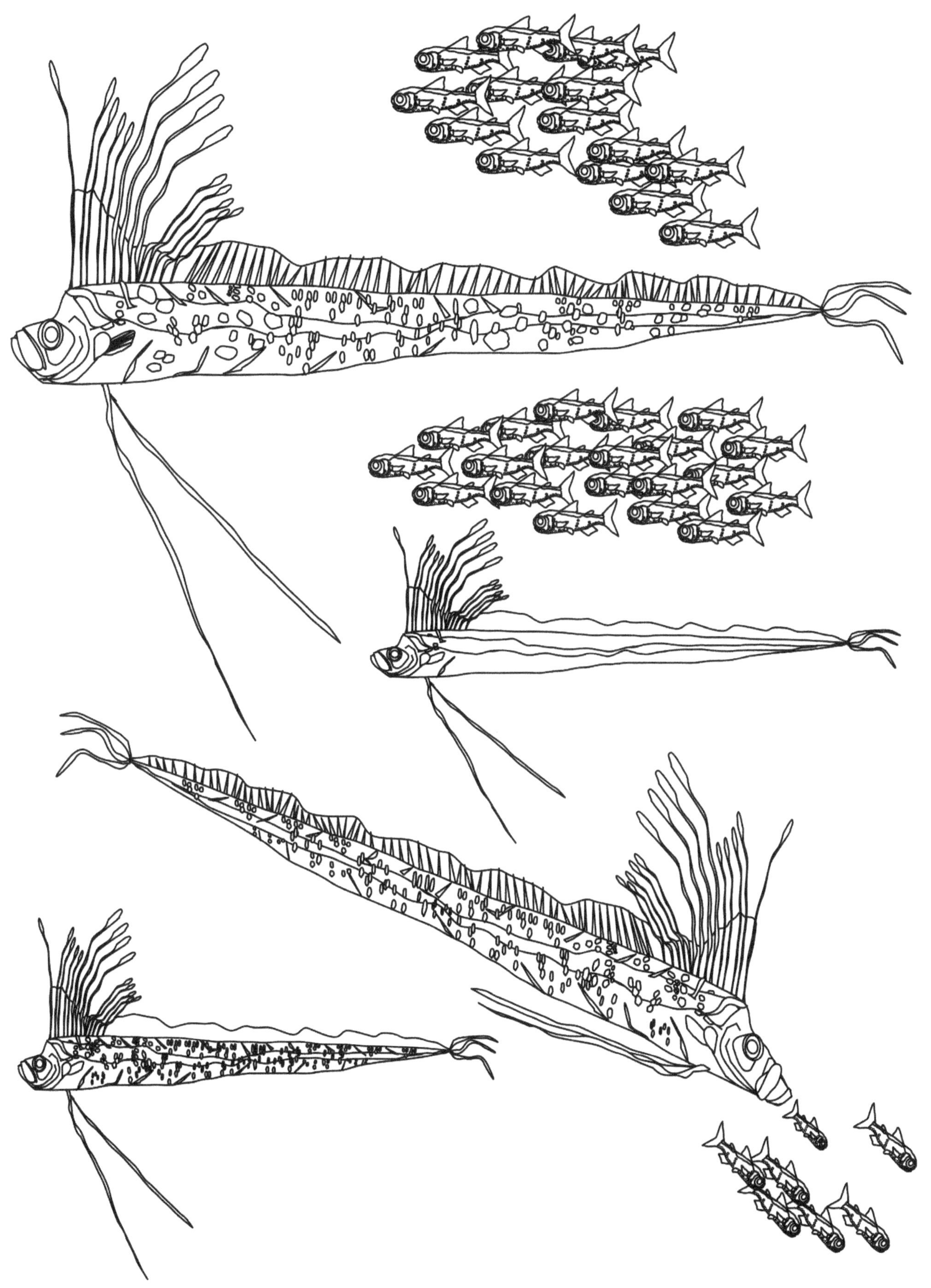

THIS PAGE LEFT INTENTIONALLY BLANK

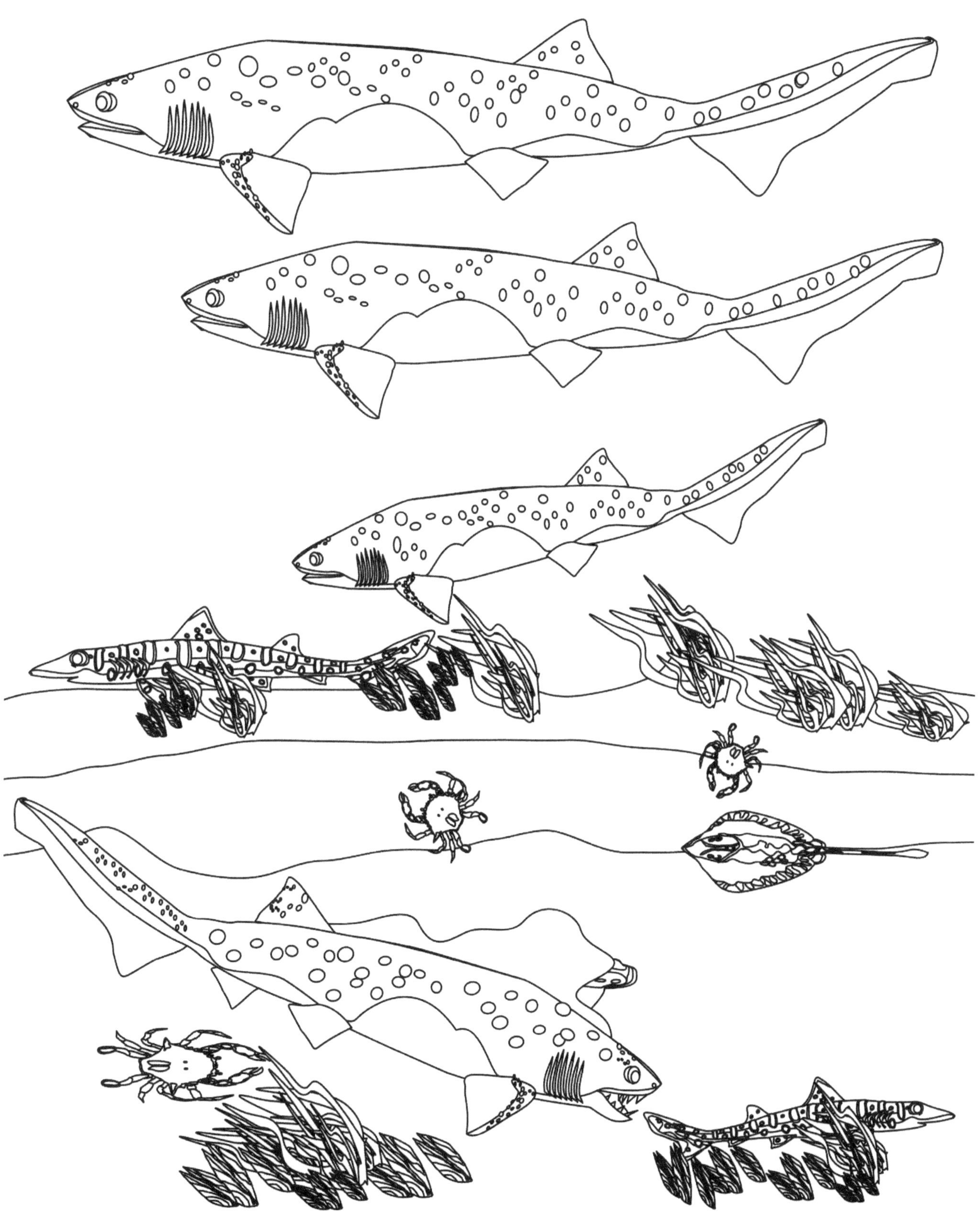

THIS PAGE LEFT INTENTIONALLY BLANK

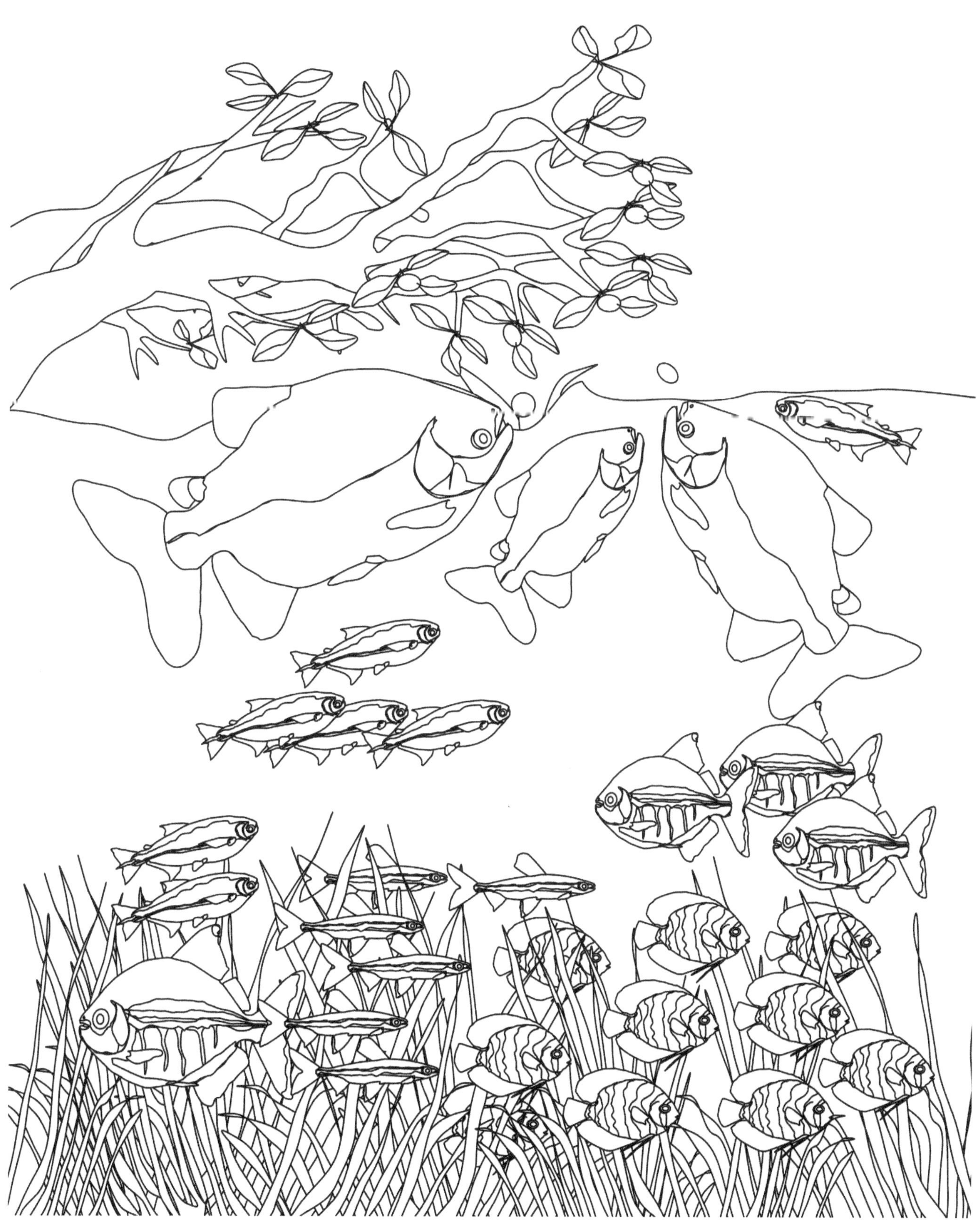

THIS PAGE LEFT INTENTIONALLY BLANK

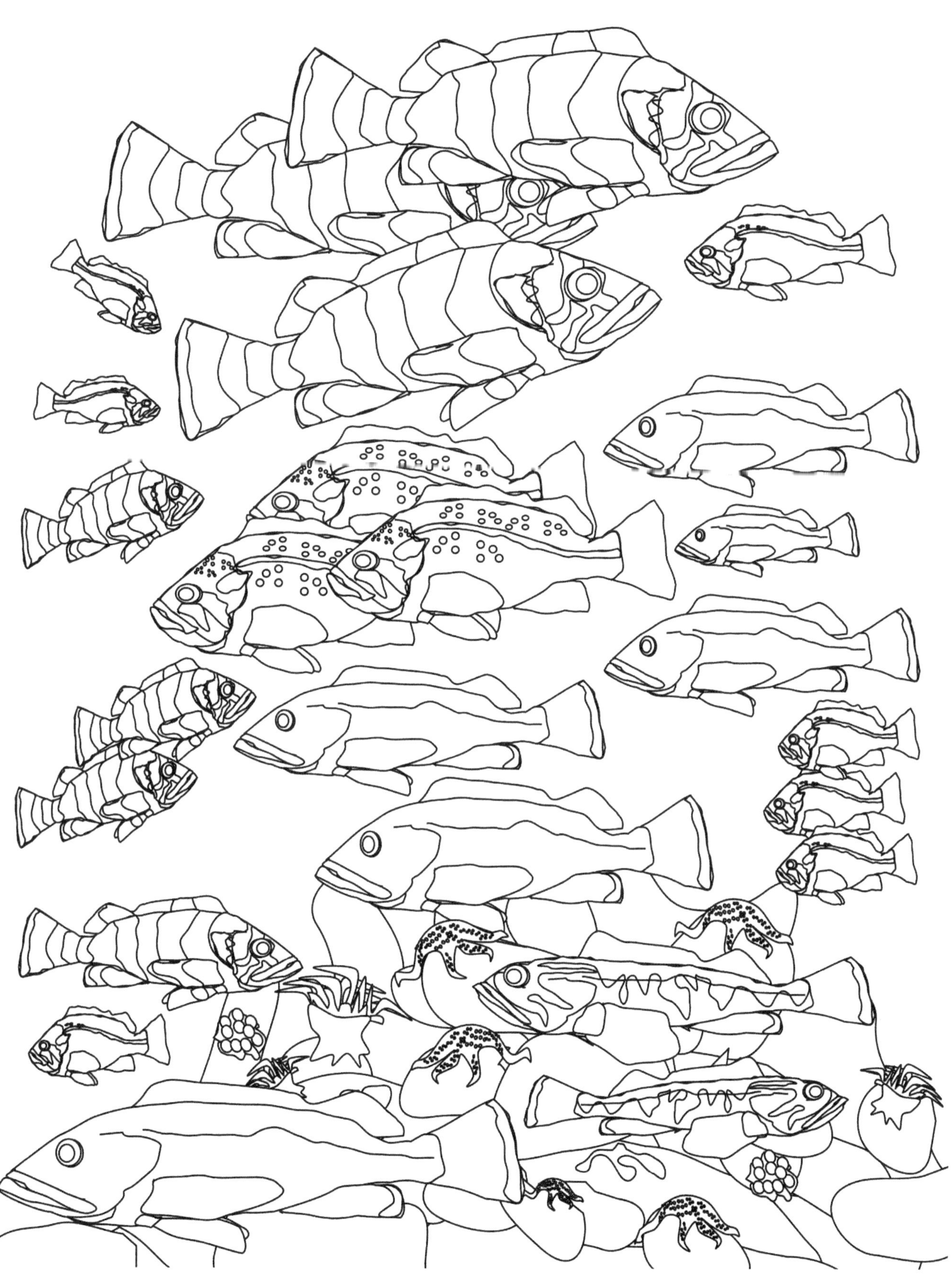

THIS PAGE LEFT INTENTIONALLY BLANK

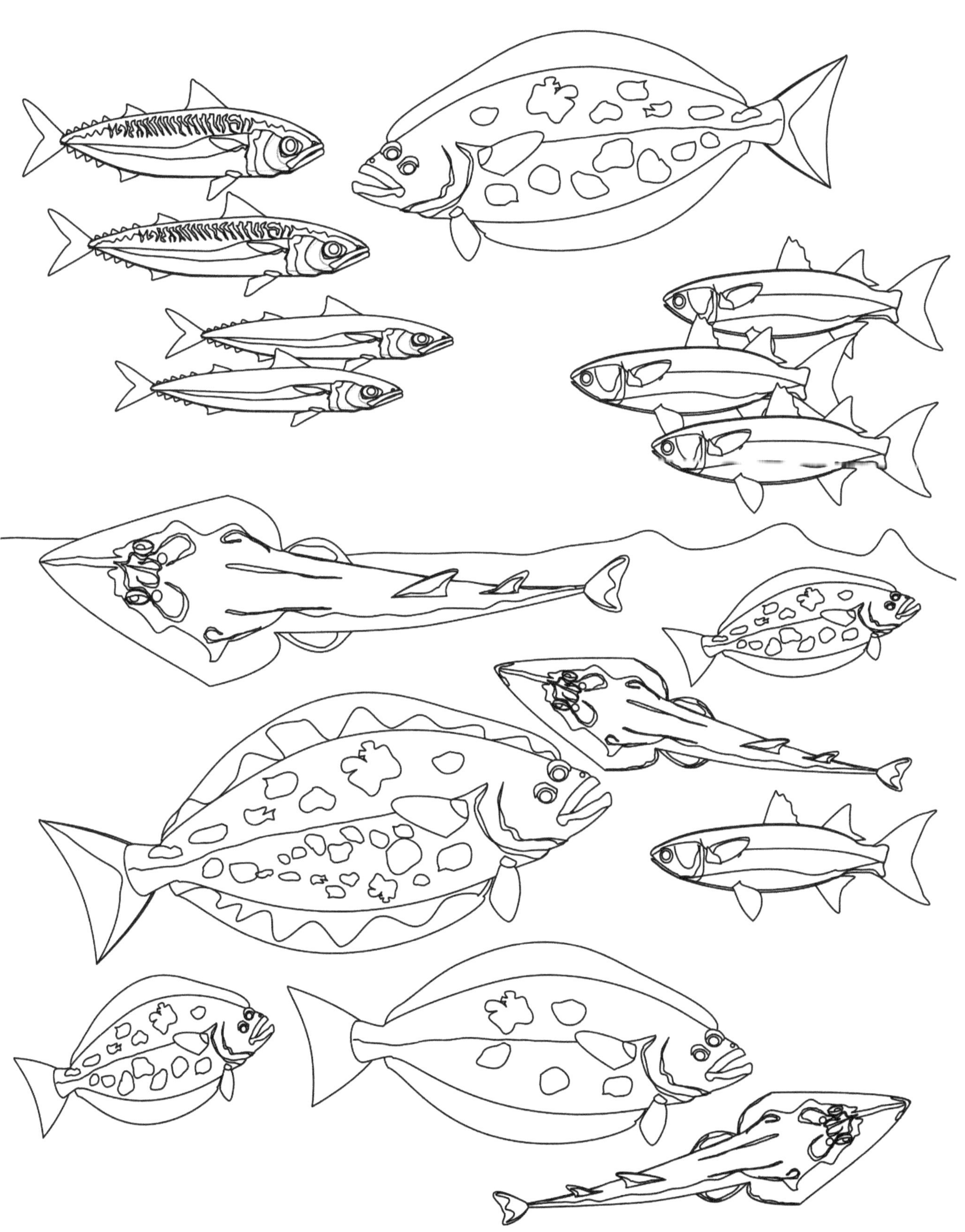

THIS PAGE LEFT INTENTIONALLY BLANK

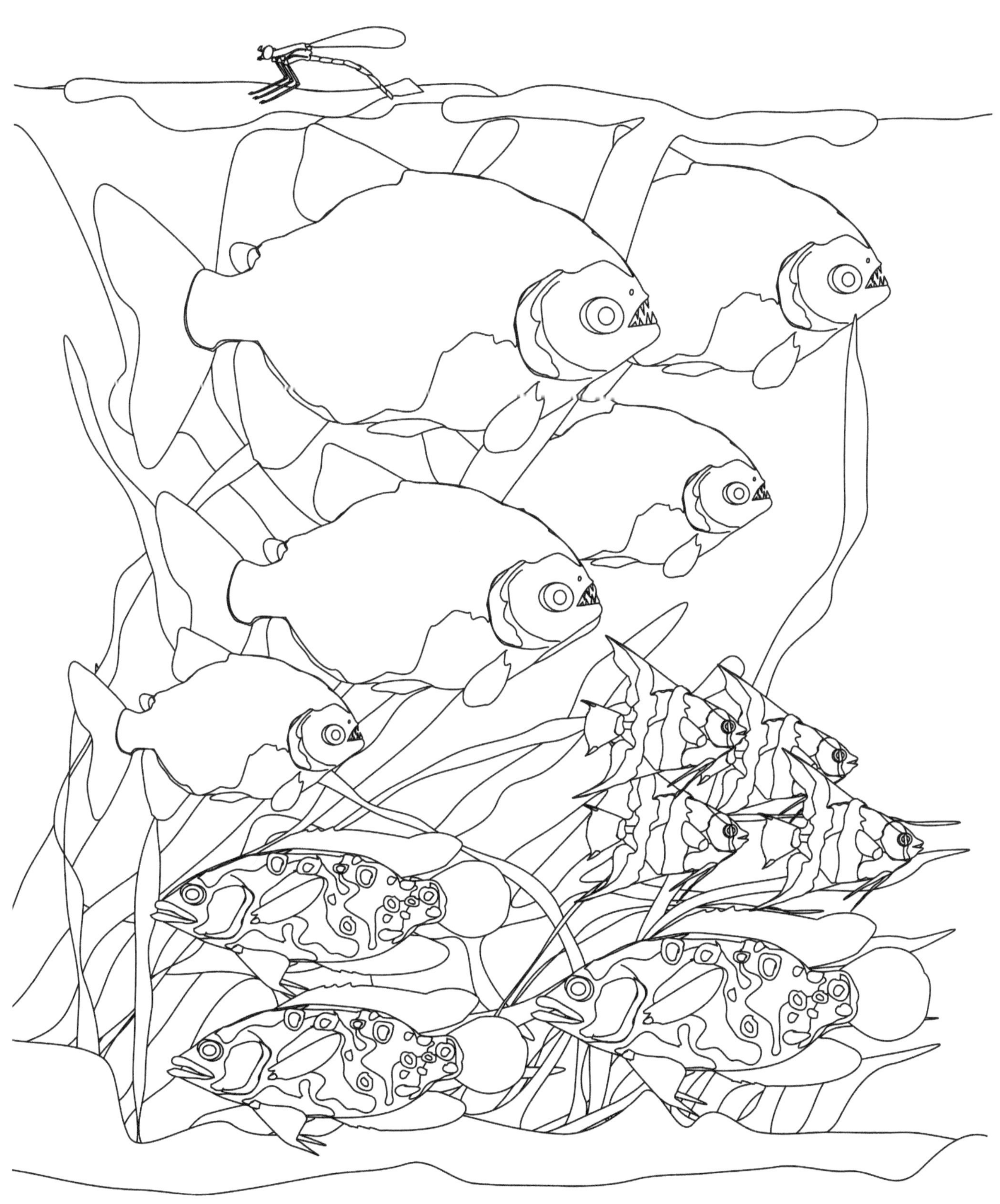

THIS PAGE LEFT INTENTIONALLY BLANK

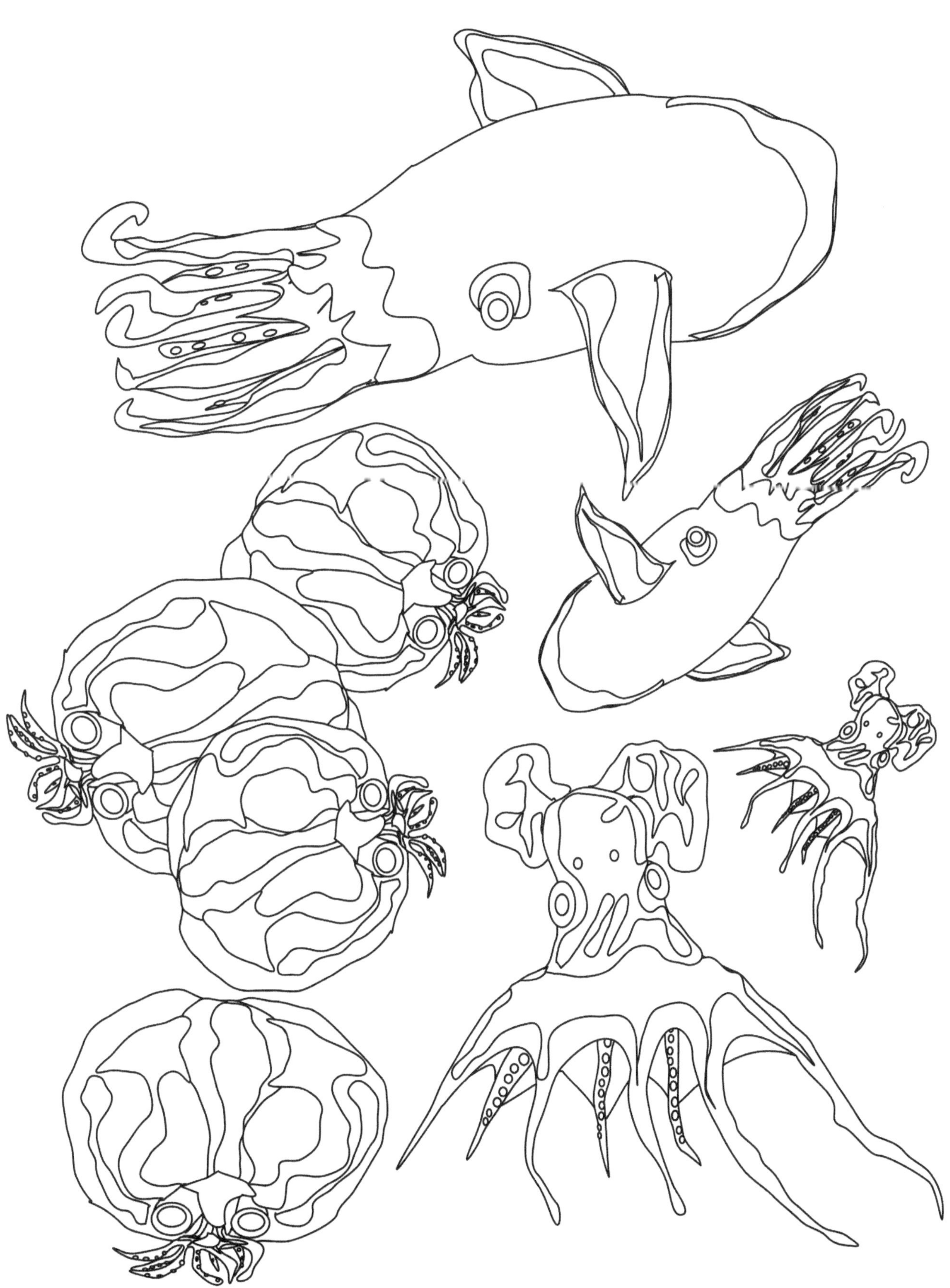

THIS PAGE LEFT INTENTIONALLY BLANK

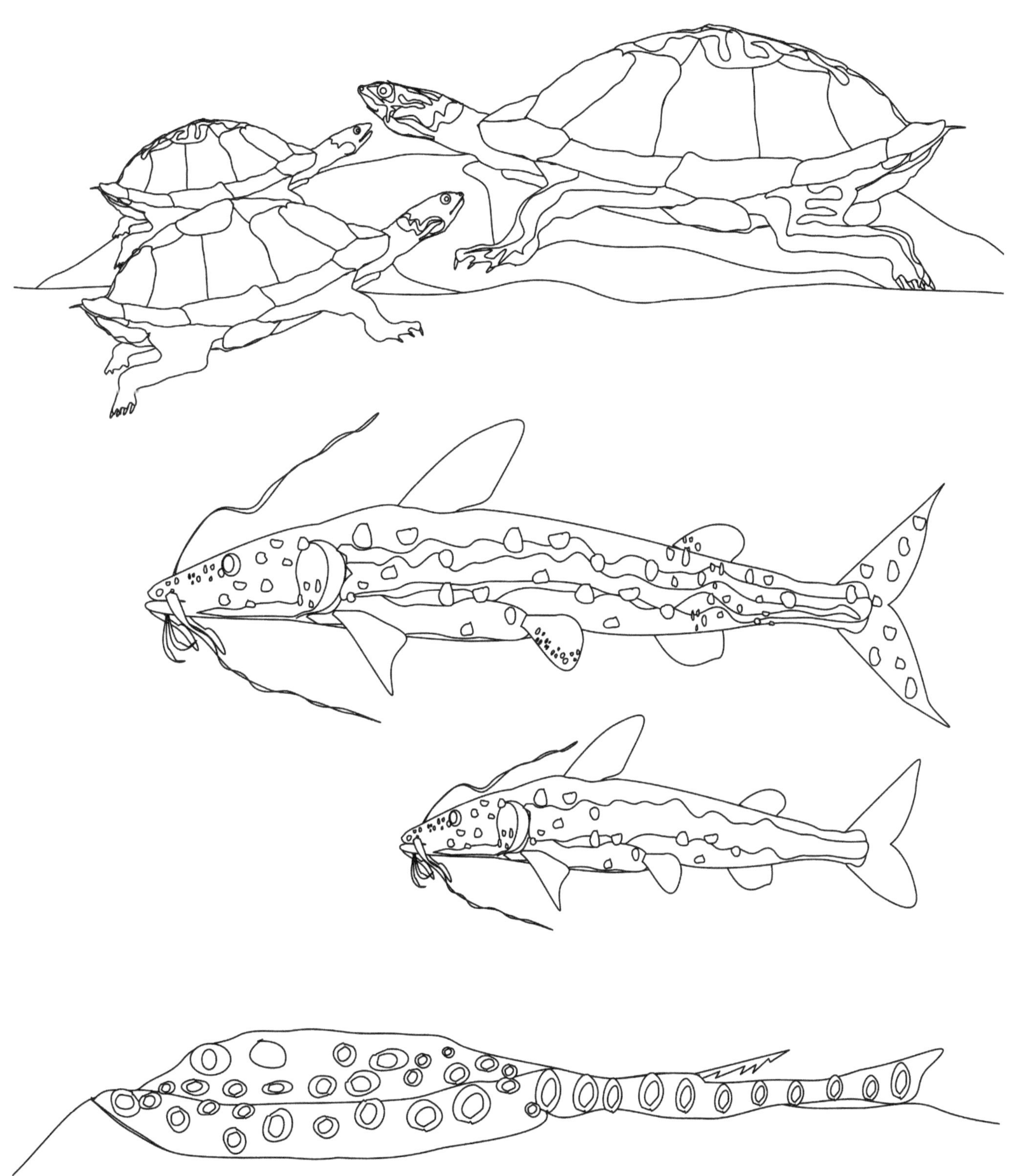

THIS PAGE LEFT INTENTIONALLY BLANK

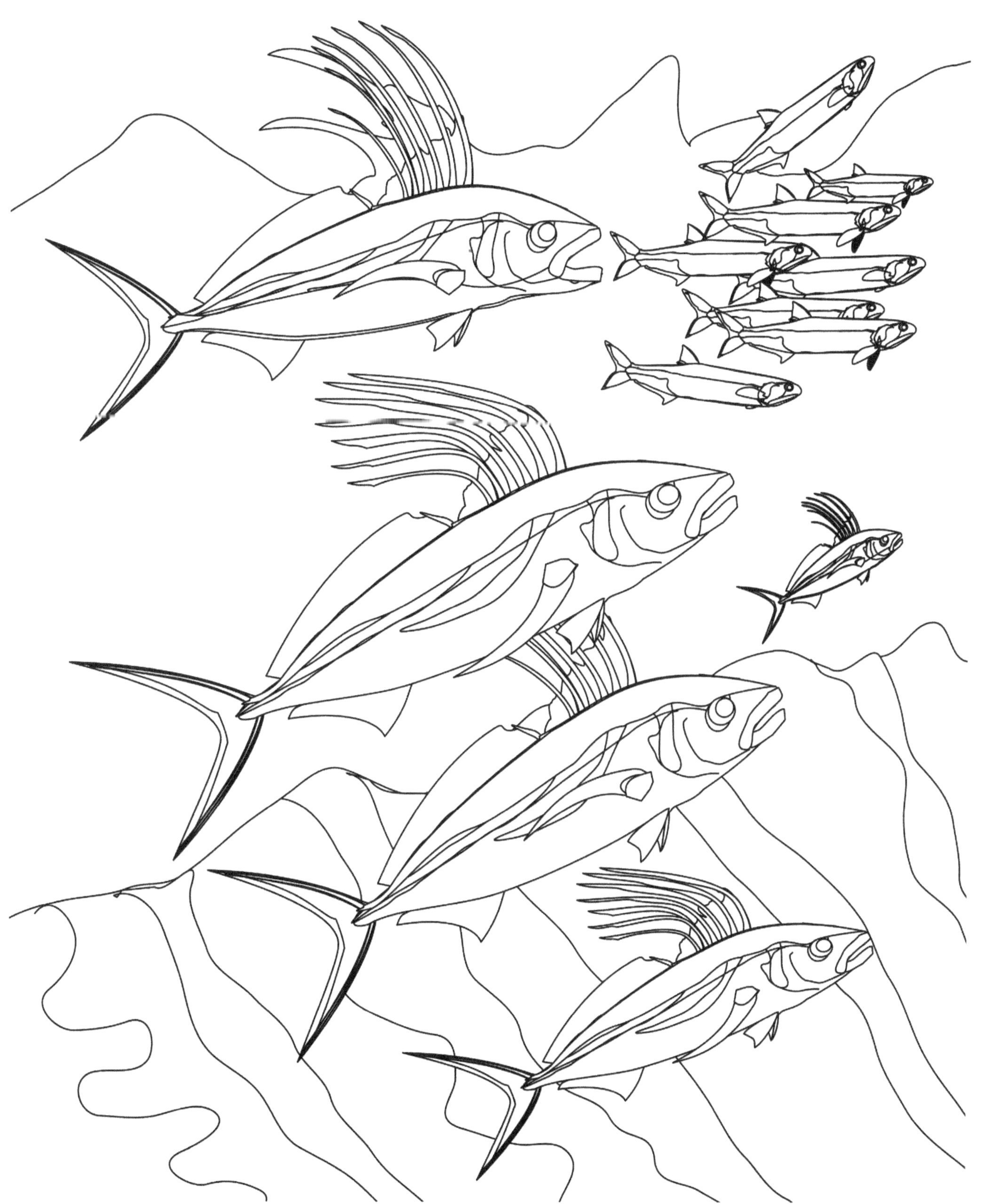

THIS PAGE LEFT INTENTIONALLY BLANK

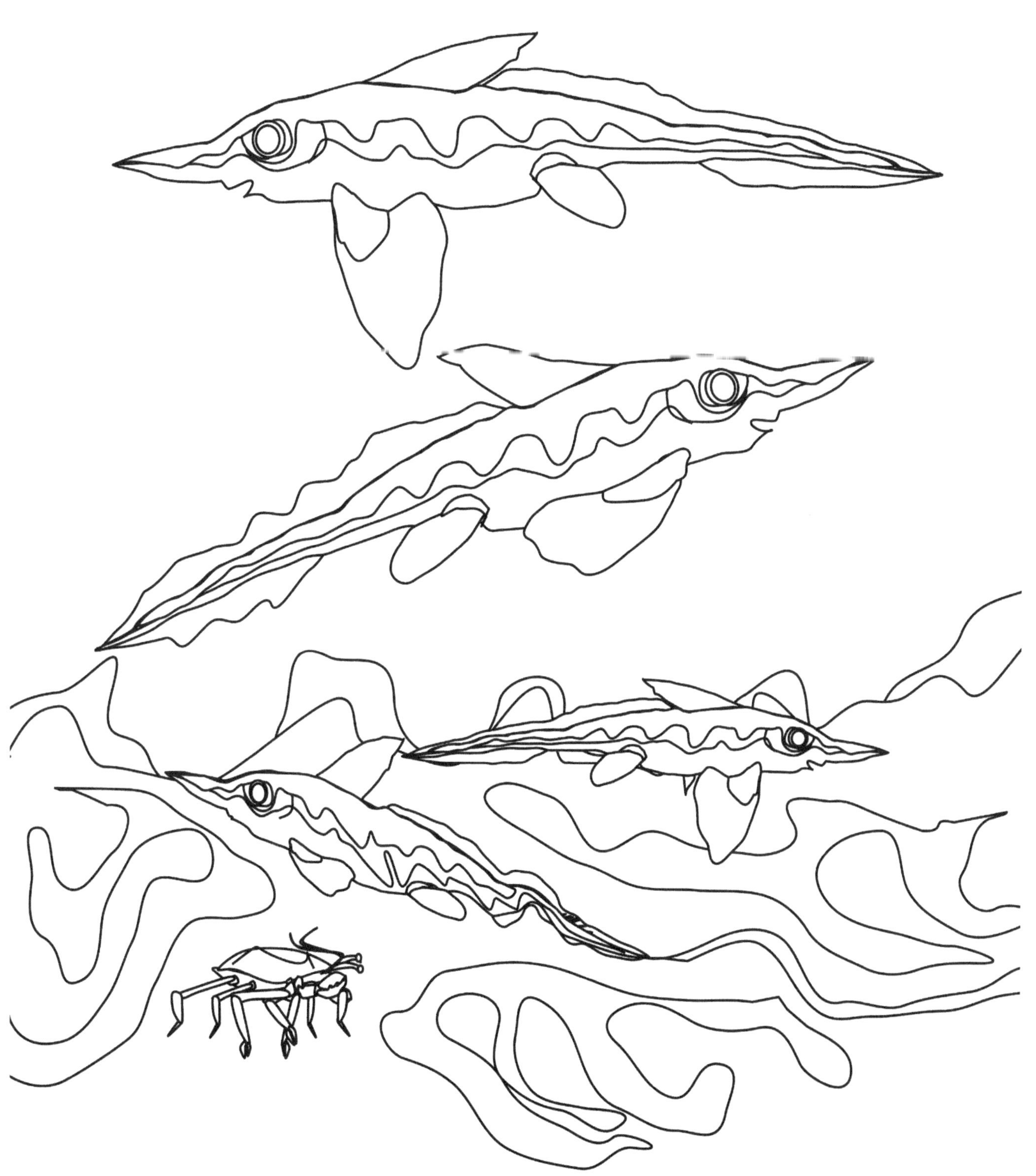

THIS PAGE LEFT INTENTIONALLY BLANK

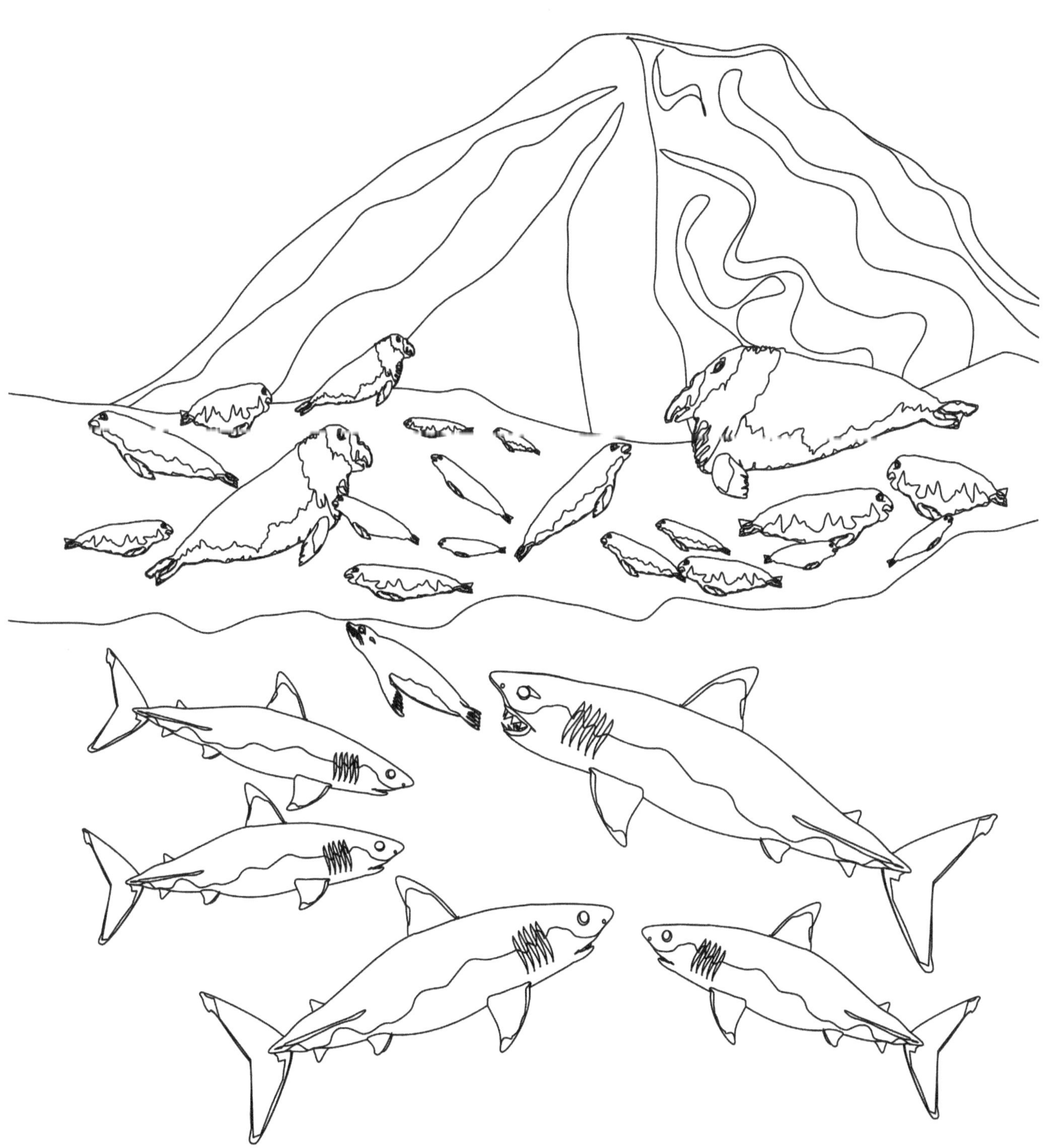

THIS PAGE LEFT INTENTIONALLY BLANK

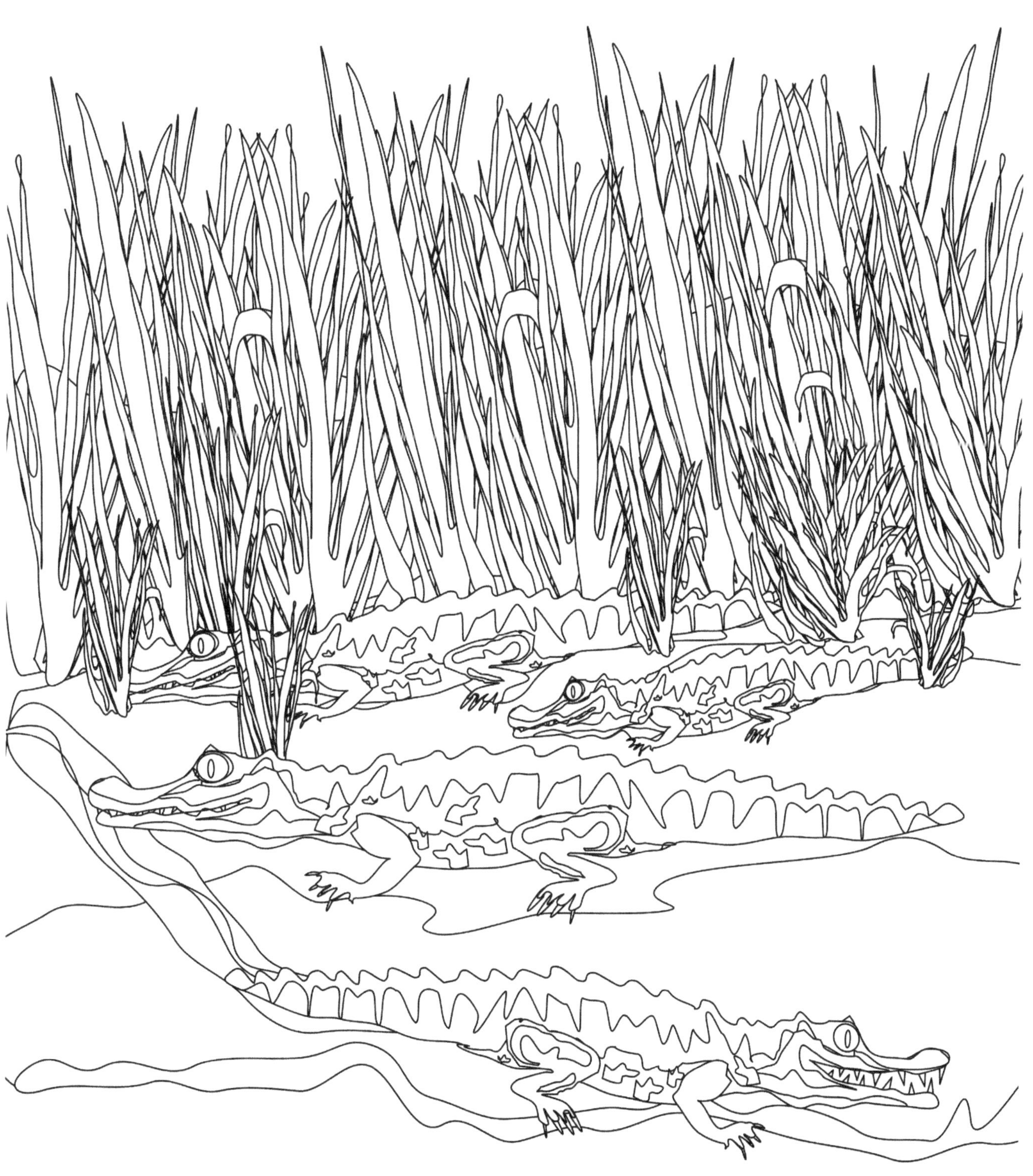

THIS PAGE LEFT INTENTIONALLY BLANK

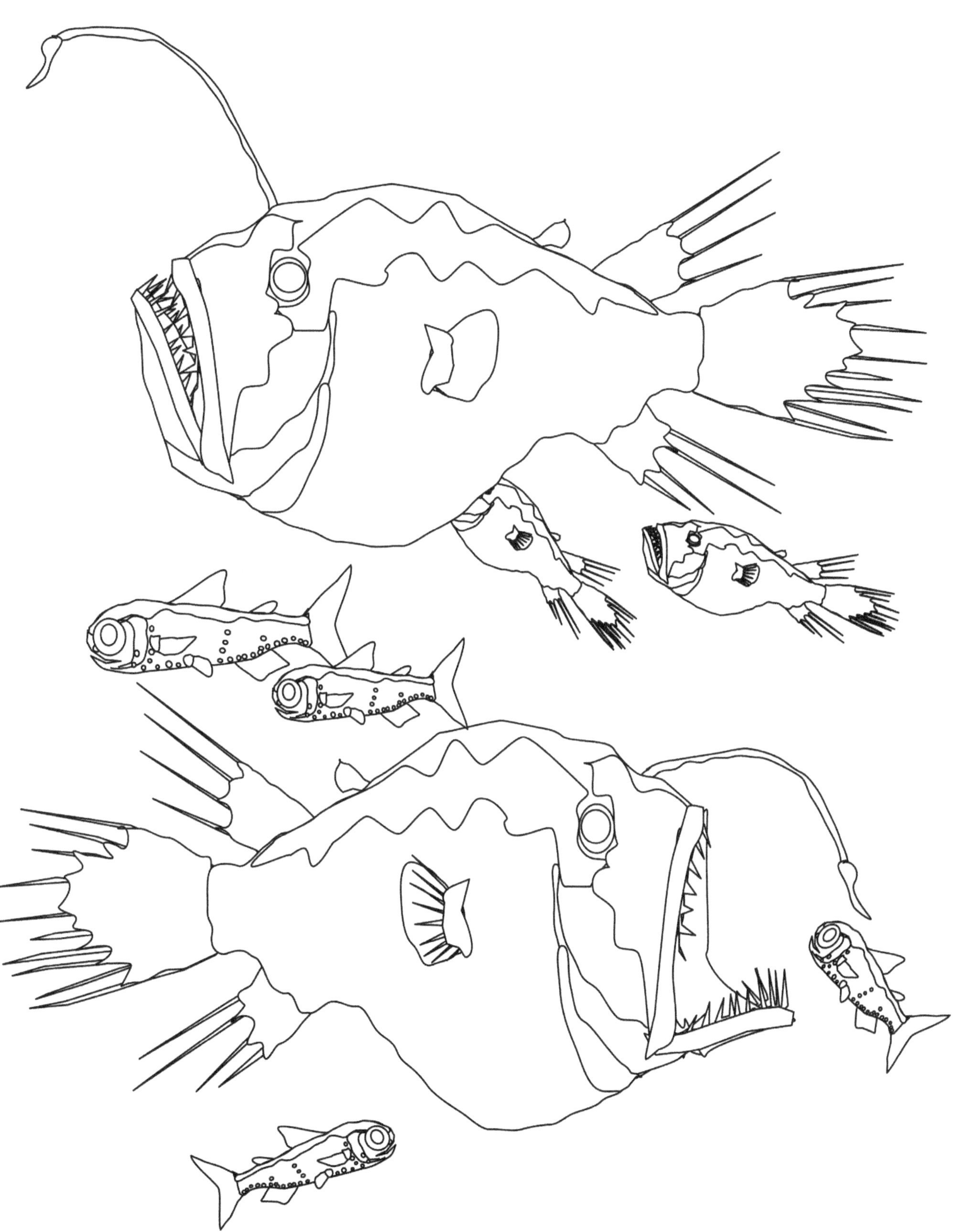

THIS PAGE LEFT INTENTIONALLY BLANK

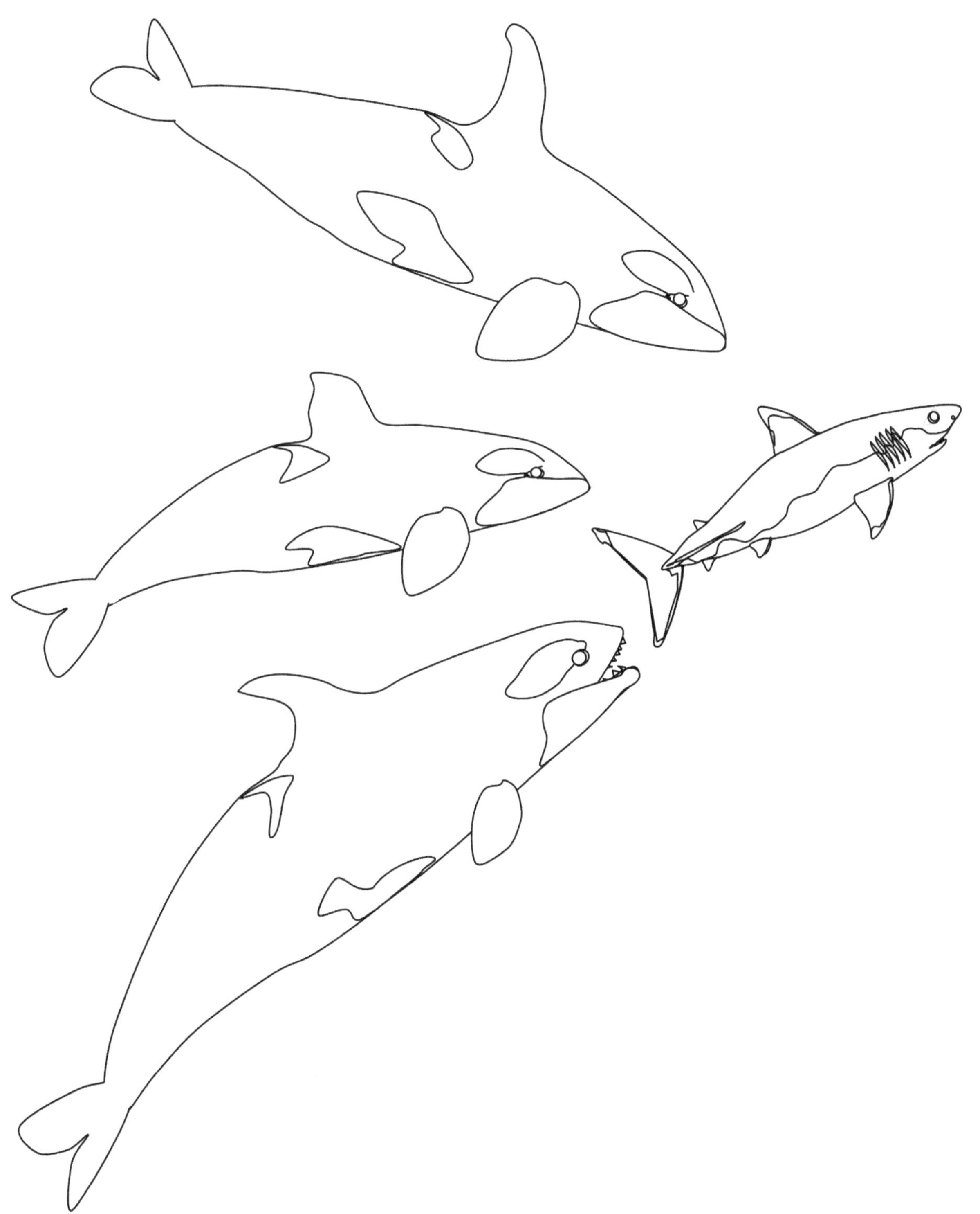

THIS PAGE LEFT INTENTIONALLY BLANK

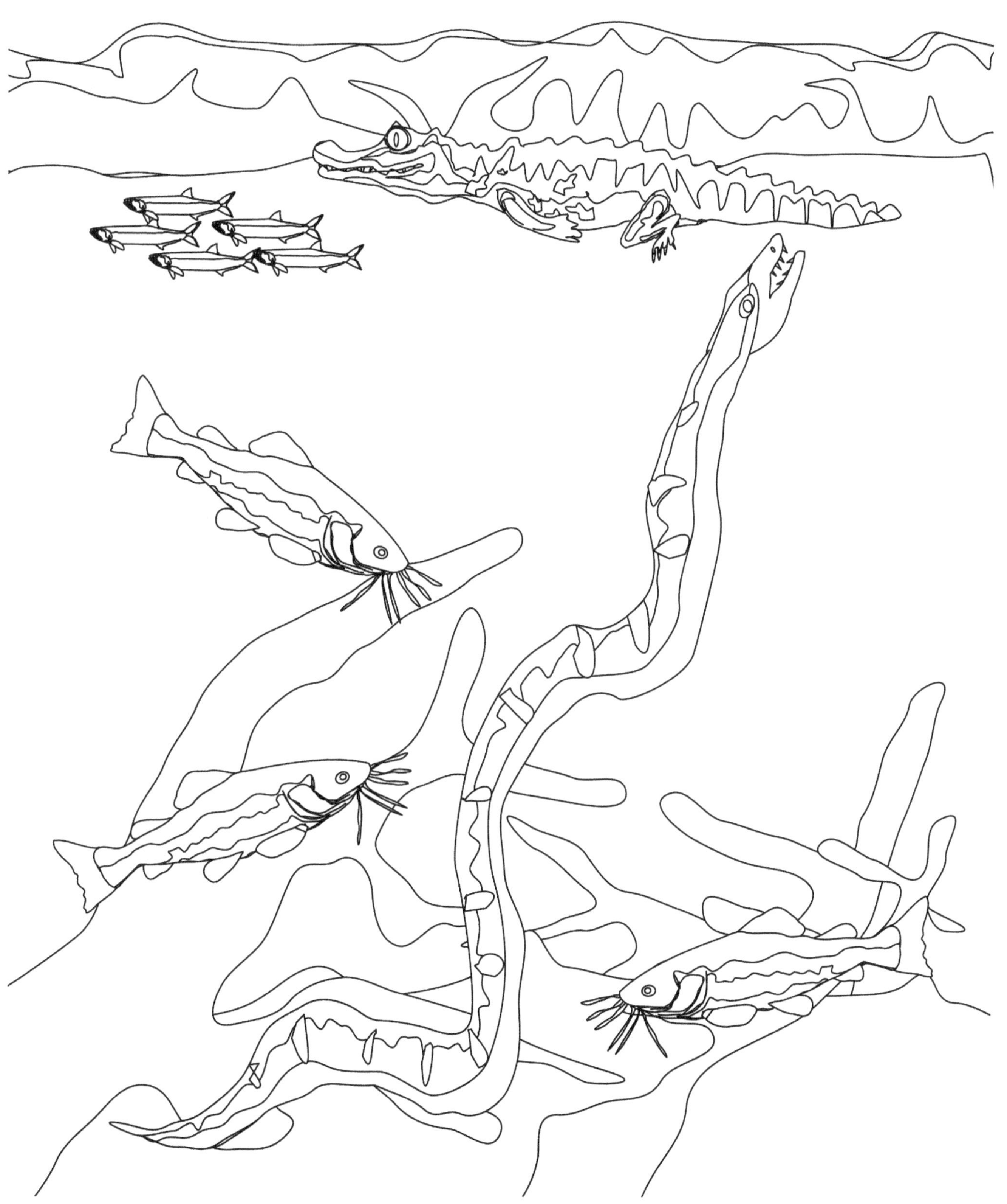

THIS PAGE LEFT INTENTIONALLY BLANK

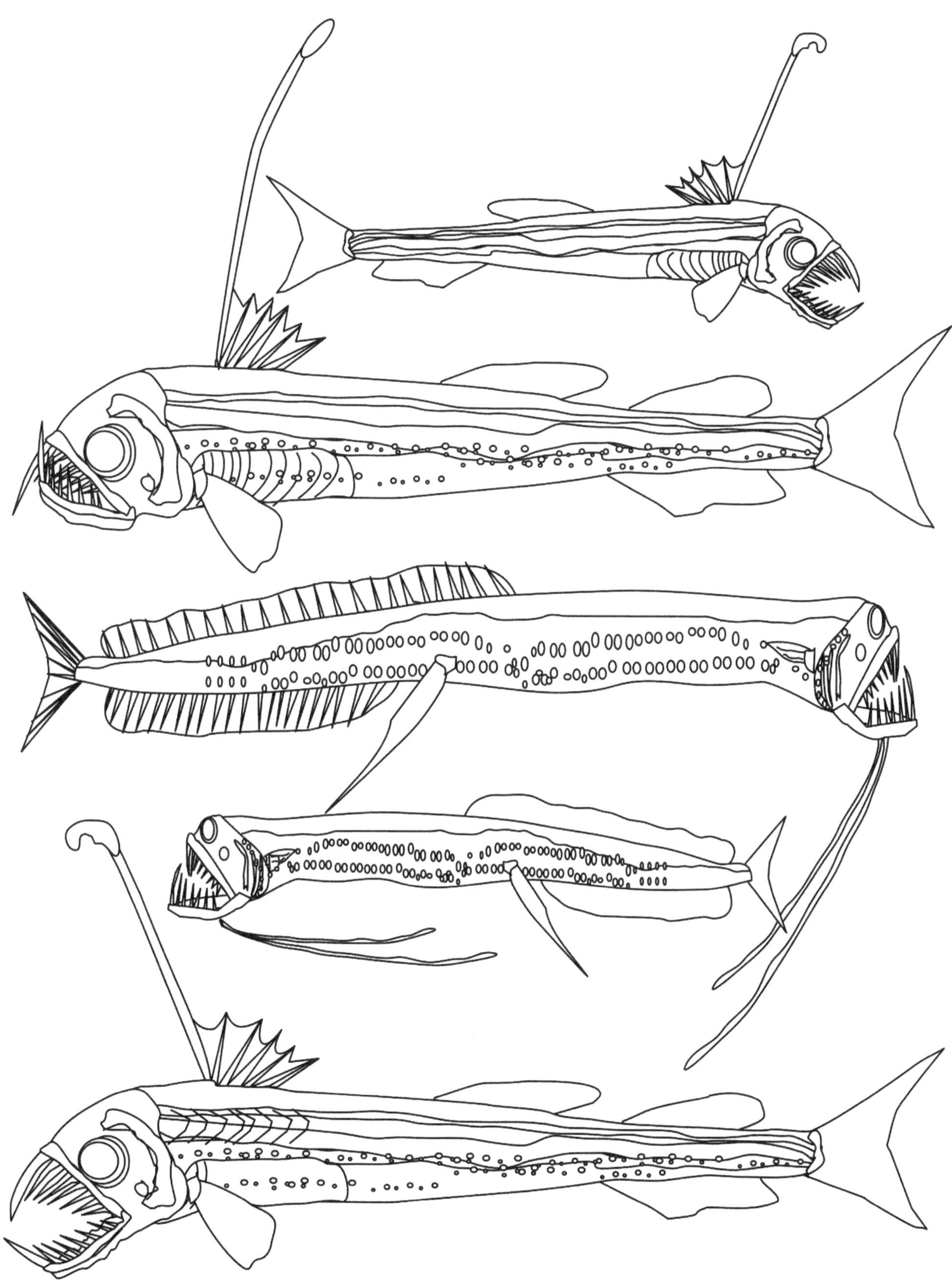

THIS PAGE LEFT INTENTIONALLY BLANK

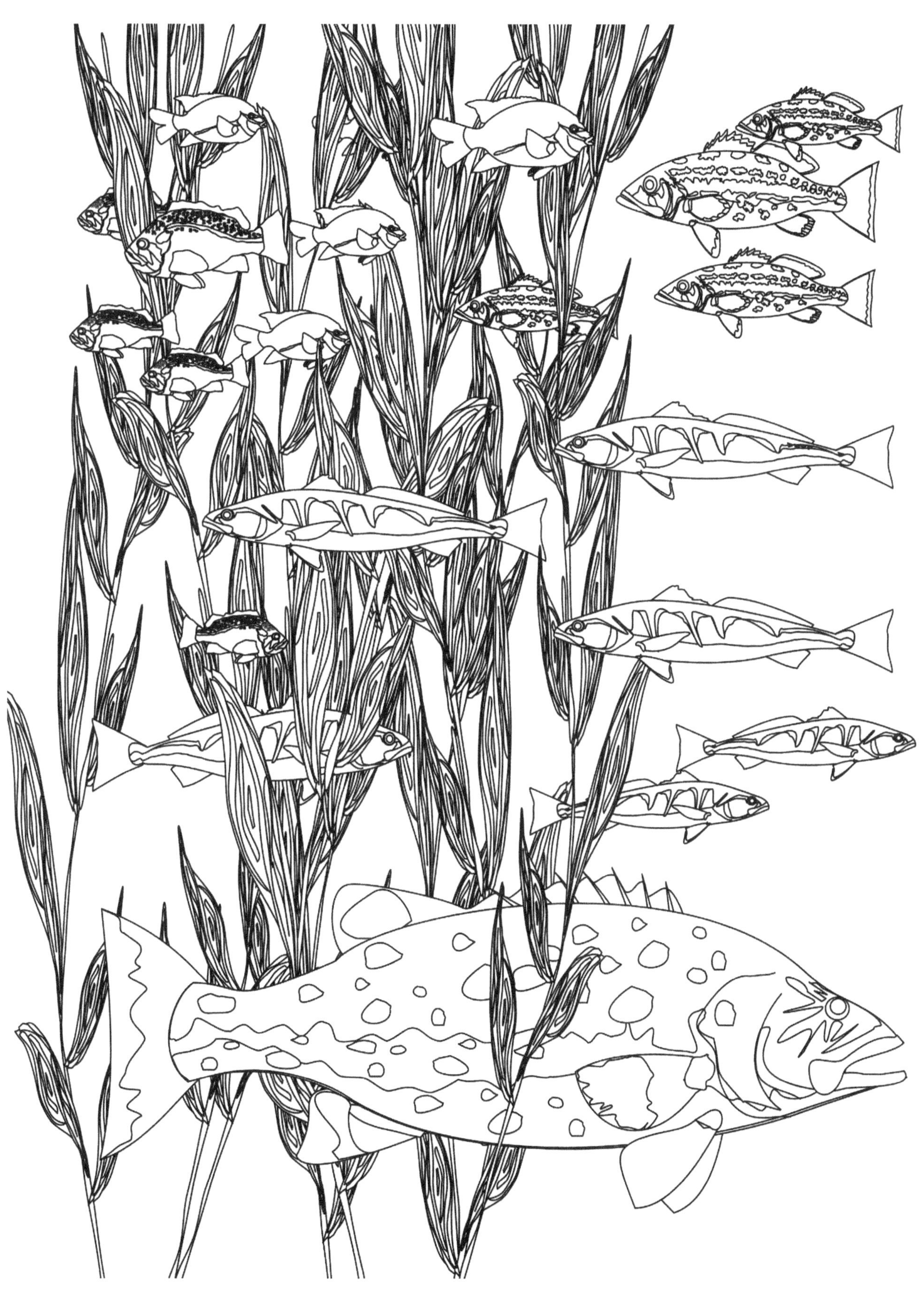

THIS PAGE LEFT INTENTIONALLY BLANK

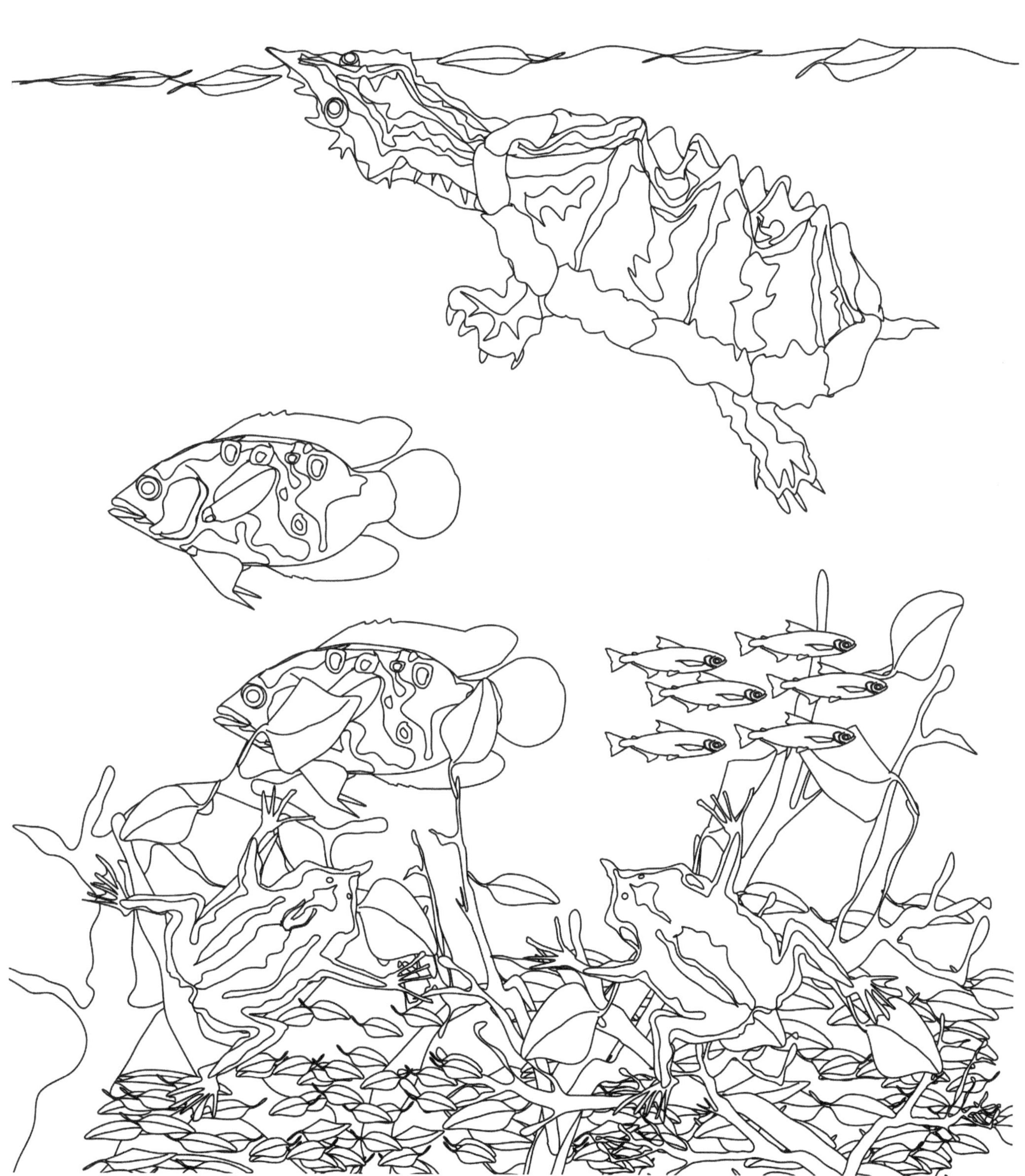

THIS PAGE LEFT INTENTIONALLY BLANK

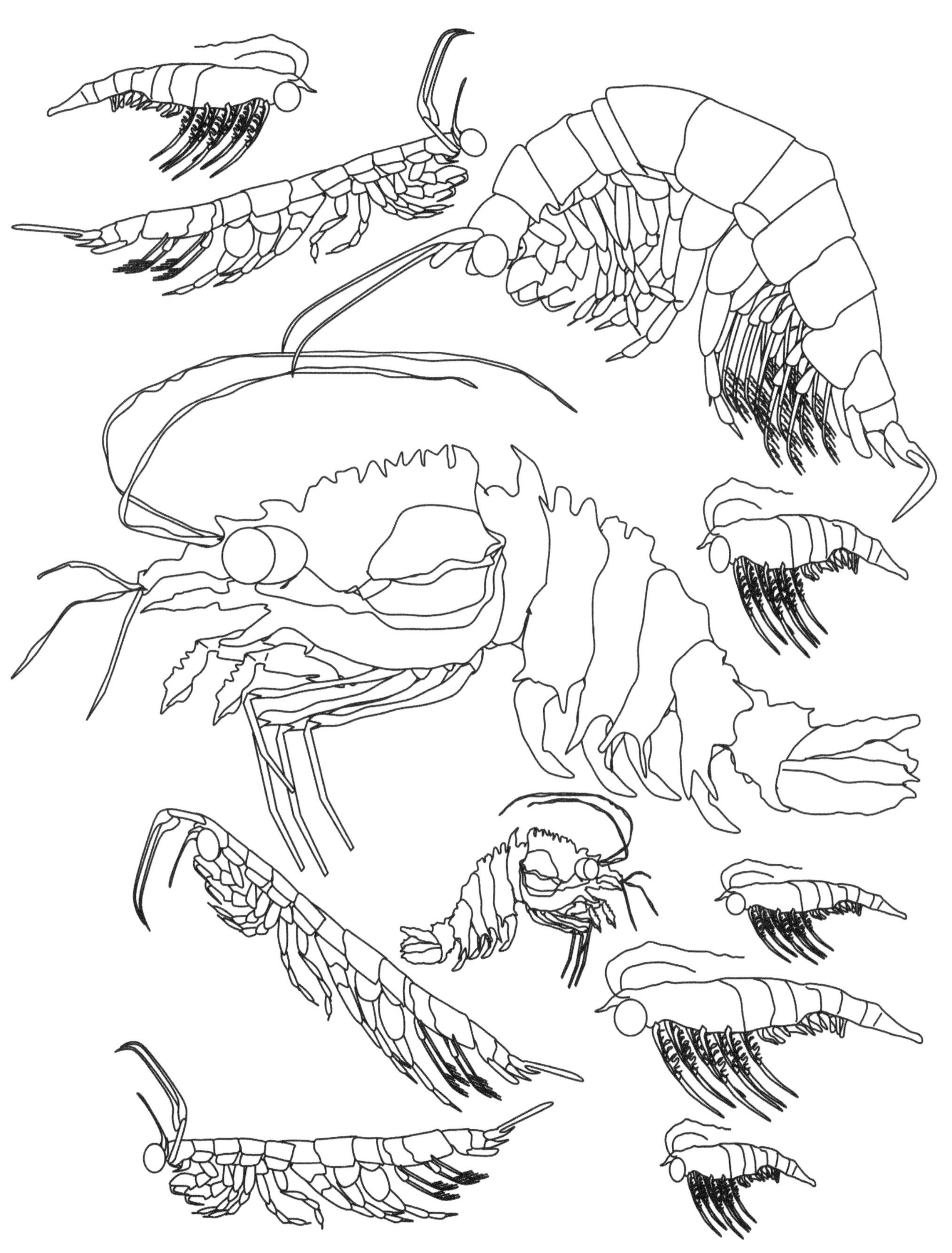

THIS PAGE LEFT INTENTIONALLY BLANK

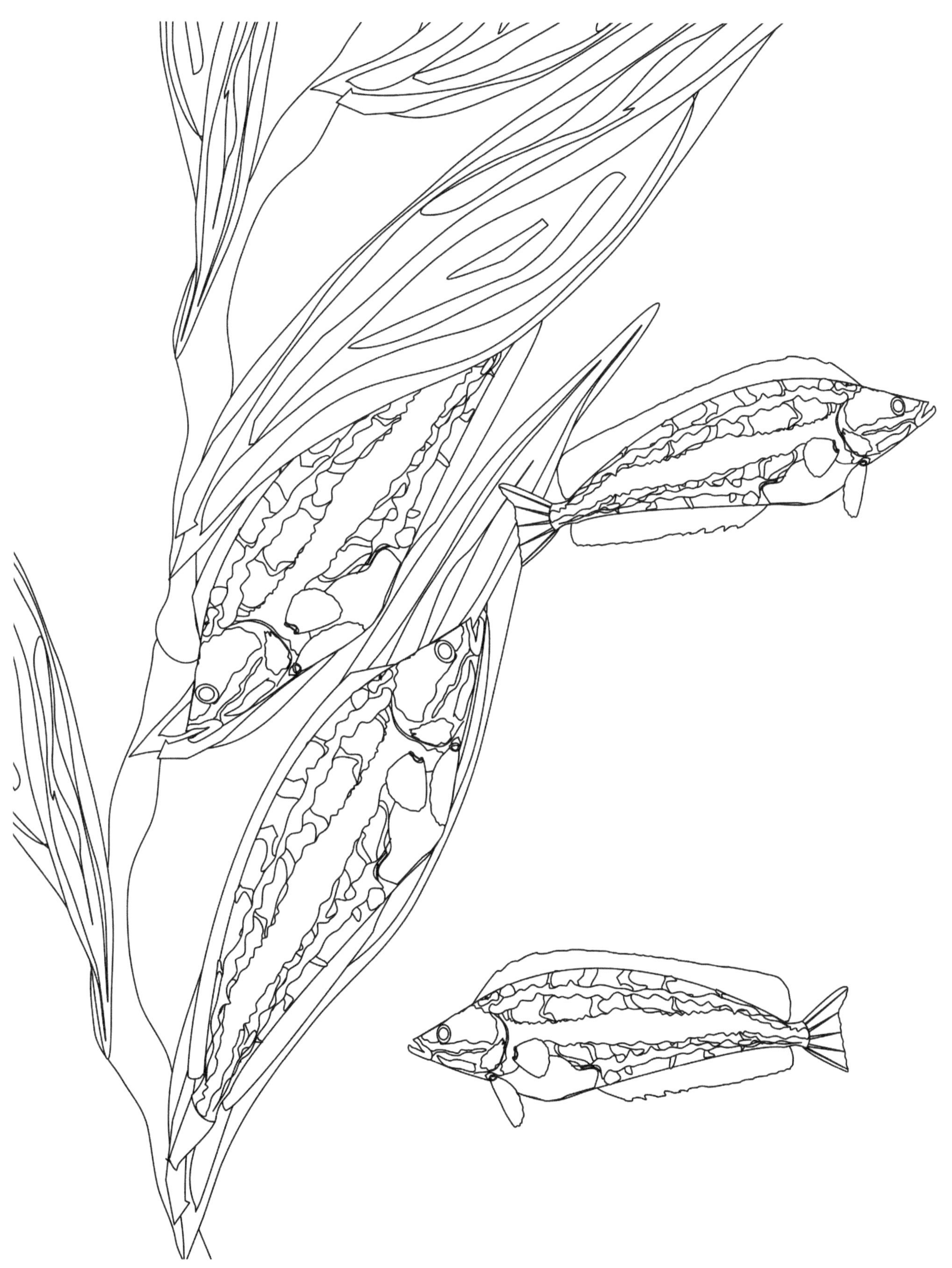

THIS PAGE LEFT INTENTIONALLY BLANK

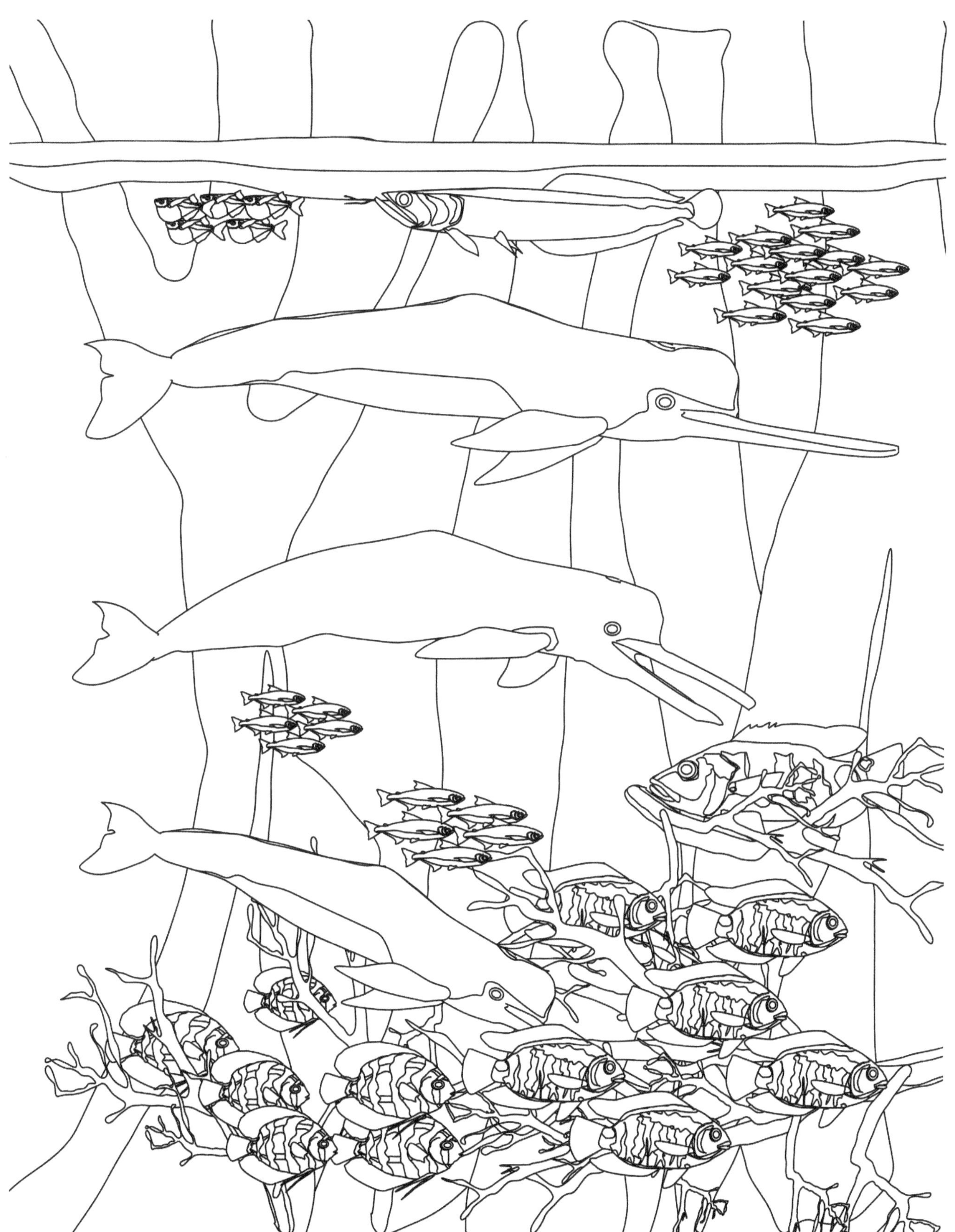

THIS PAGE LEFT INTENTIONALLY BLANK

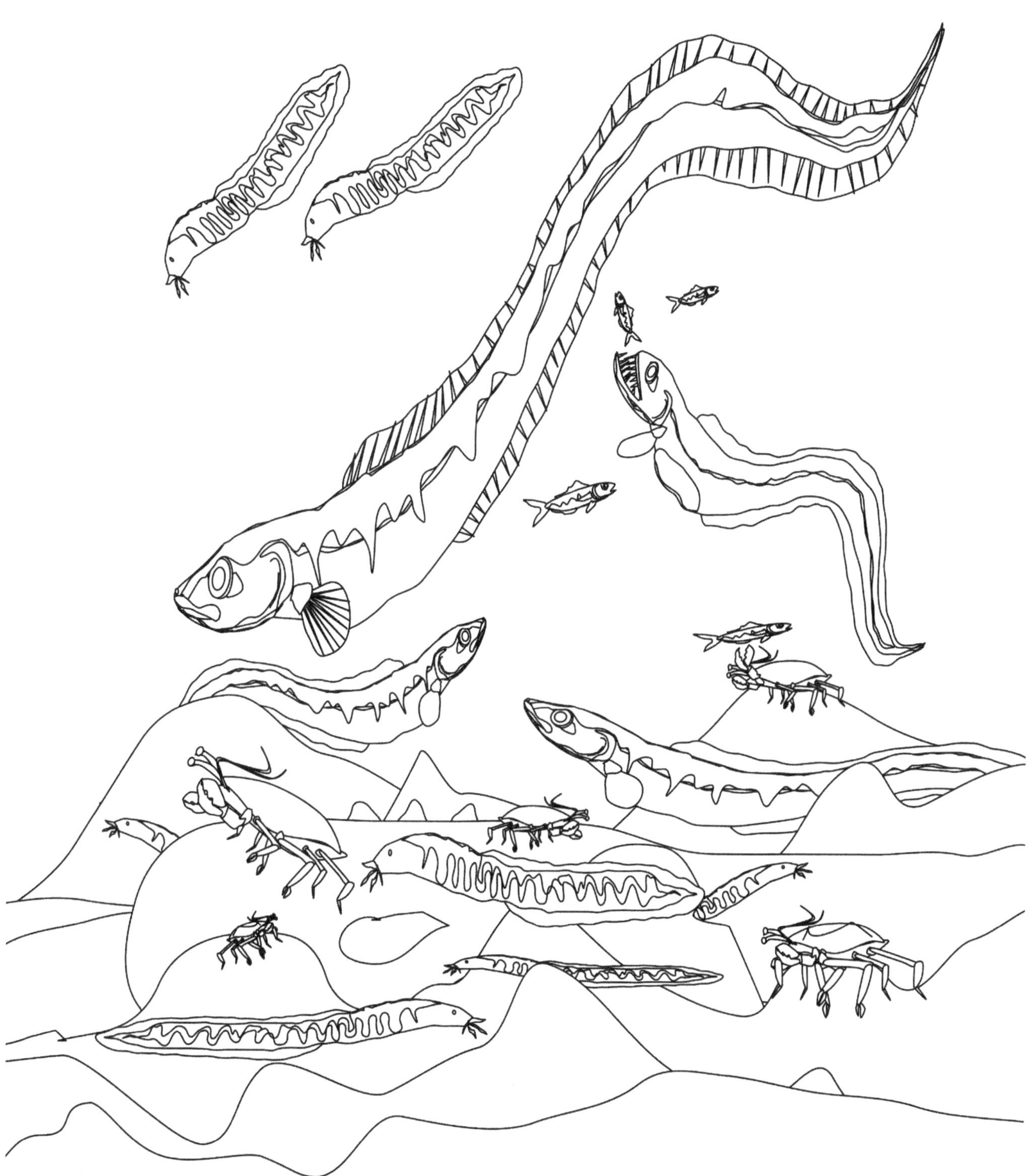

THIS PAGE LEFT INTENTIONALLY BLANK

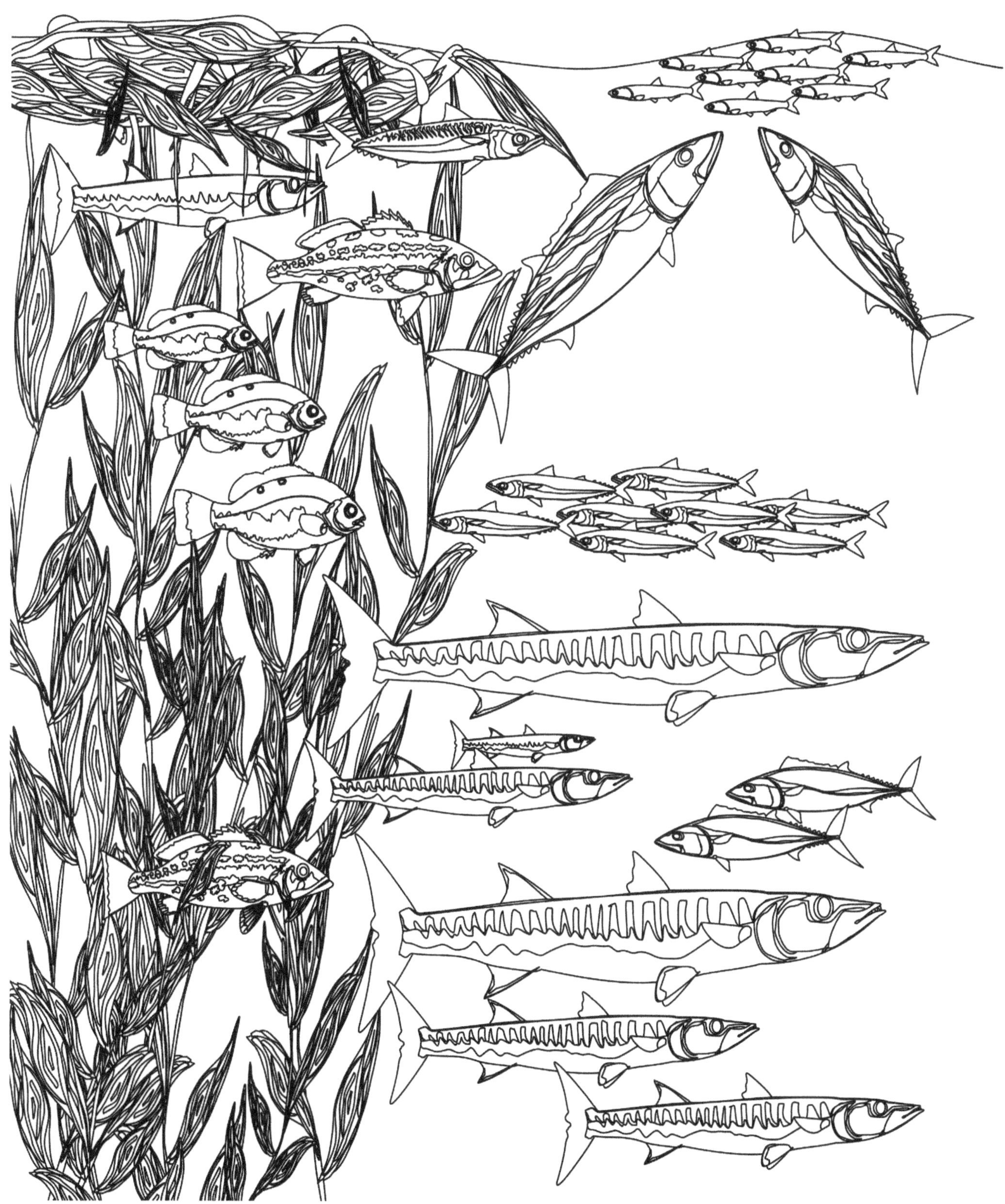

THIS PAGE LEFT INTENTIONALLY BLANK

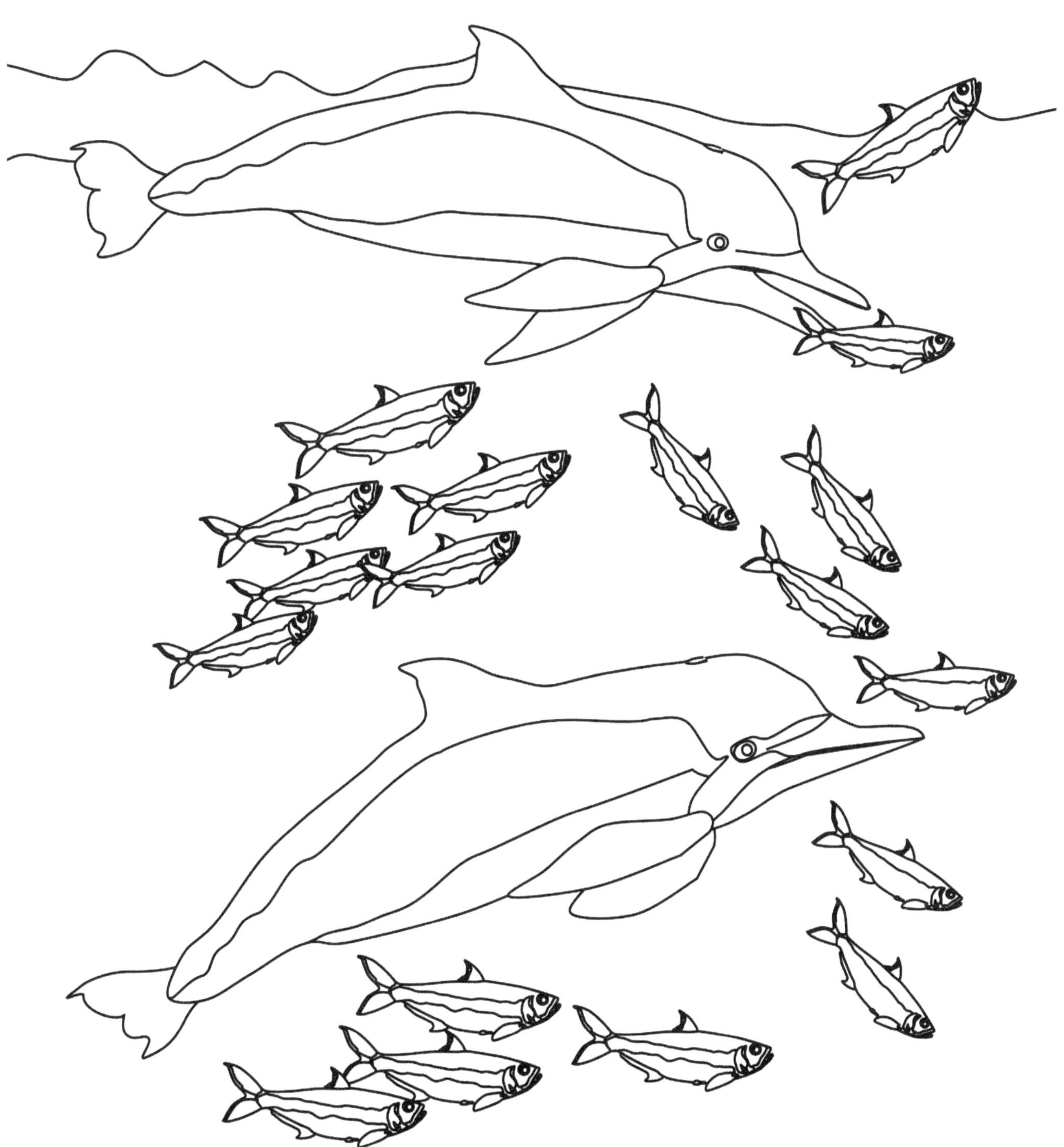

THIS PAGE LEFT INTENTIONALLY BLANK

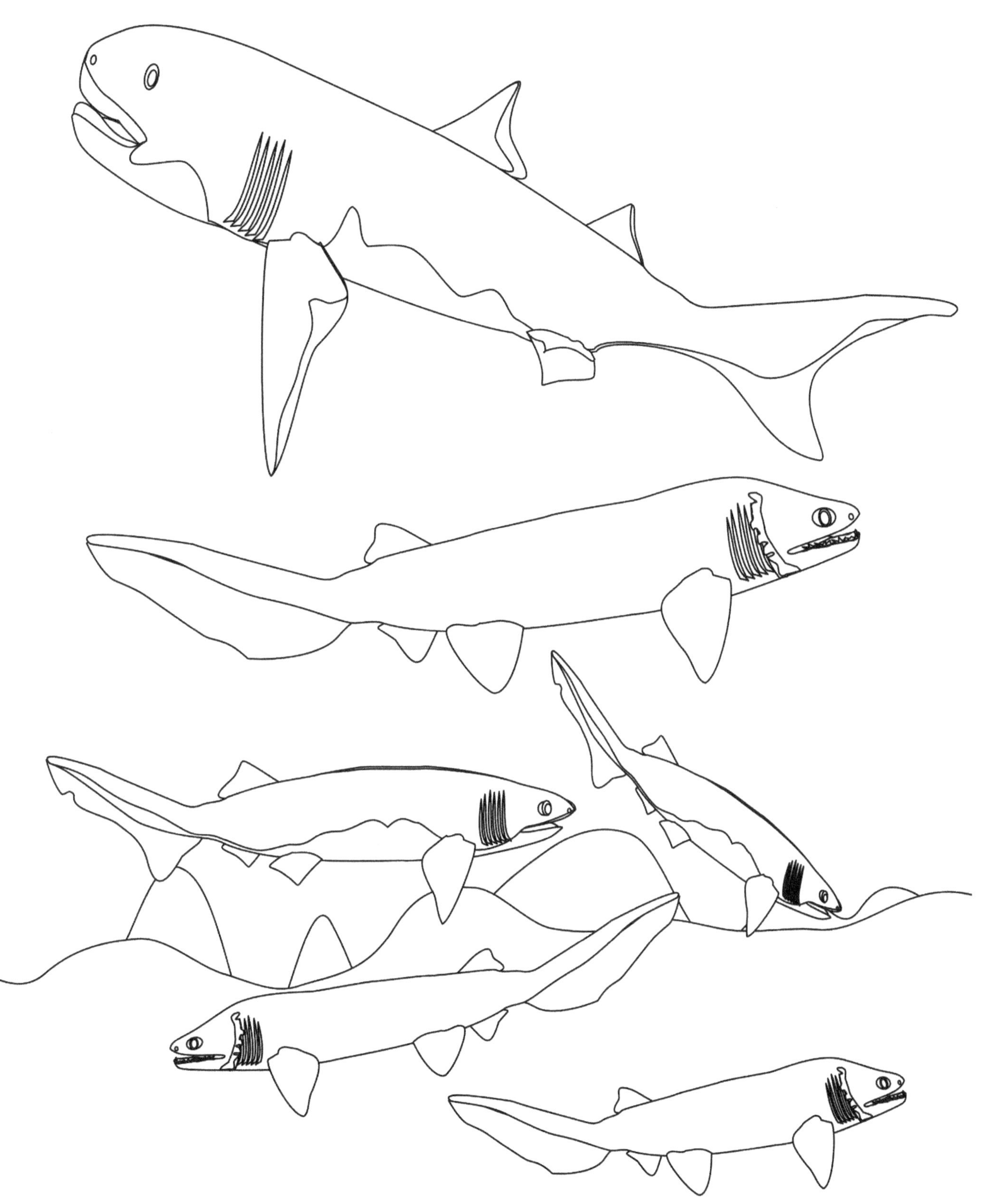

THIS PAGE LEFT INTENTIONALLY BLANK

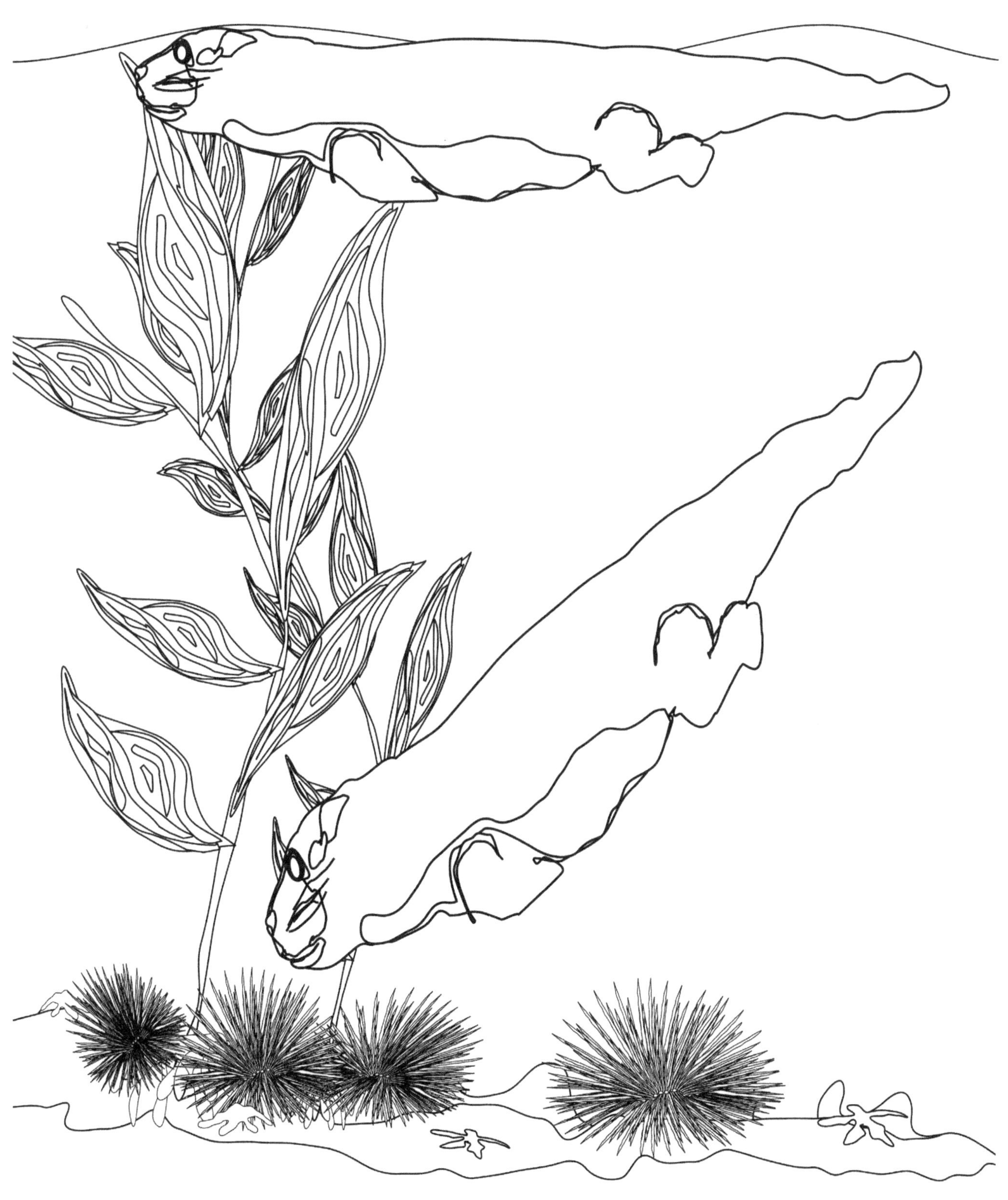

THIS PAGE LEFT INTENTIONALLY BLANK

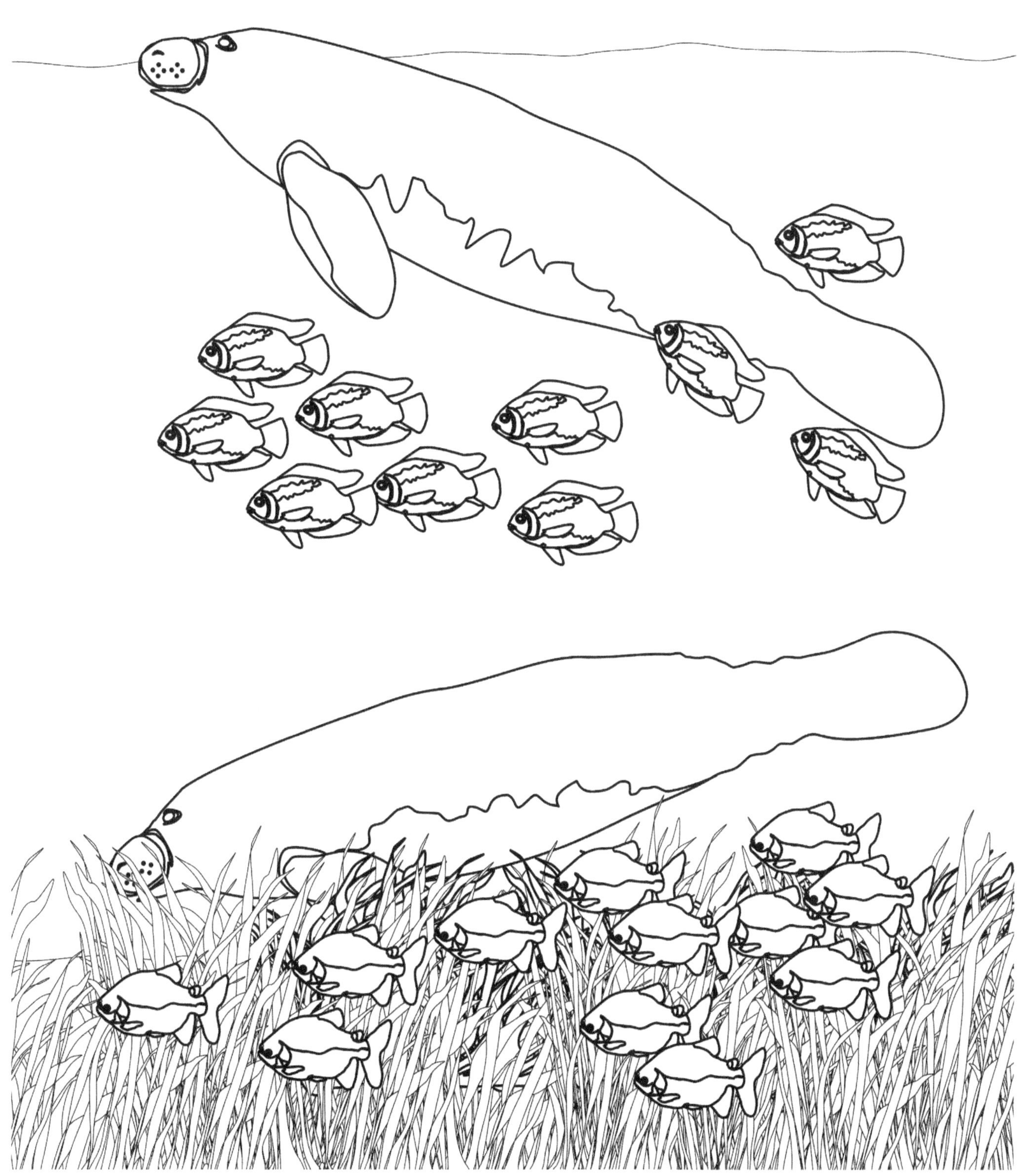

THIS PAGE LEFT INTENTIONALLY BLANK

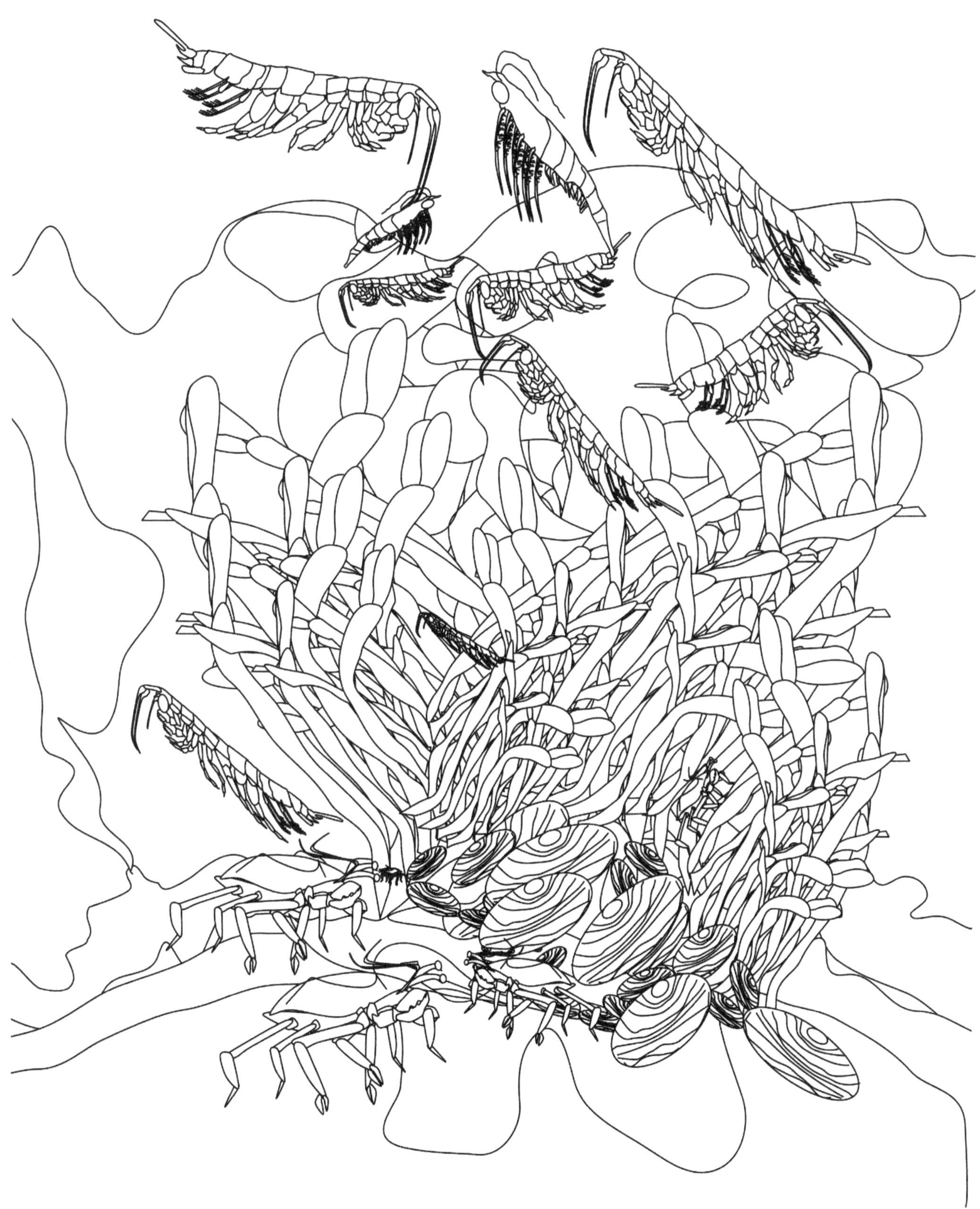

THIS PAGE LEFT INTENTIONALLY BLANK

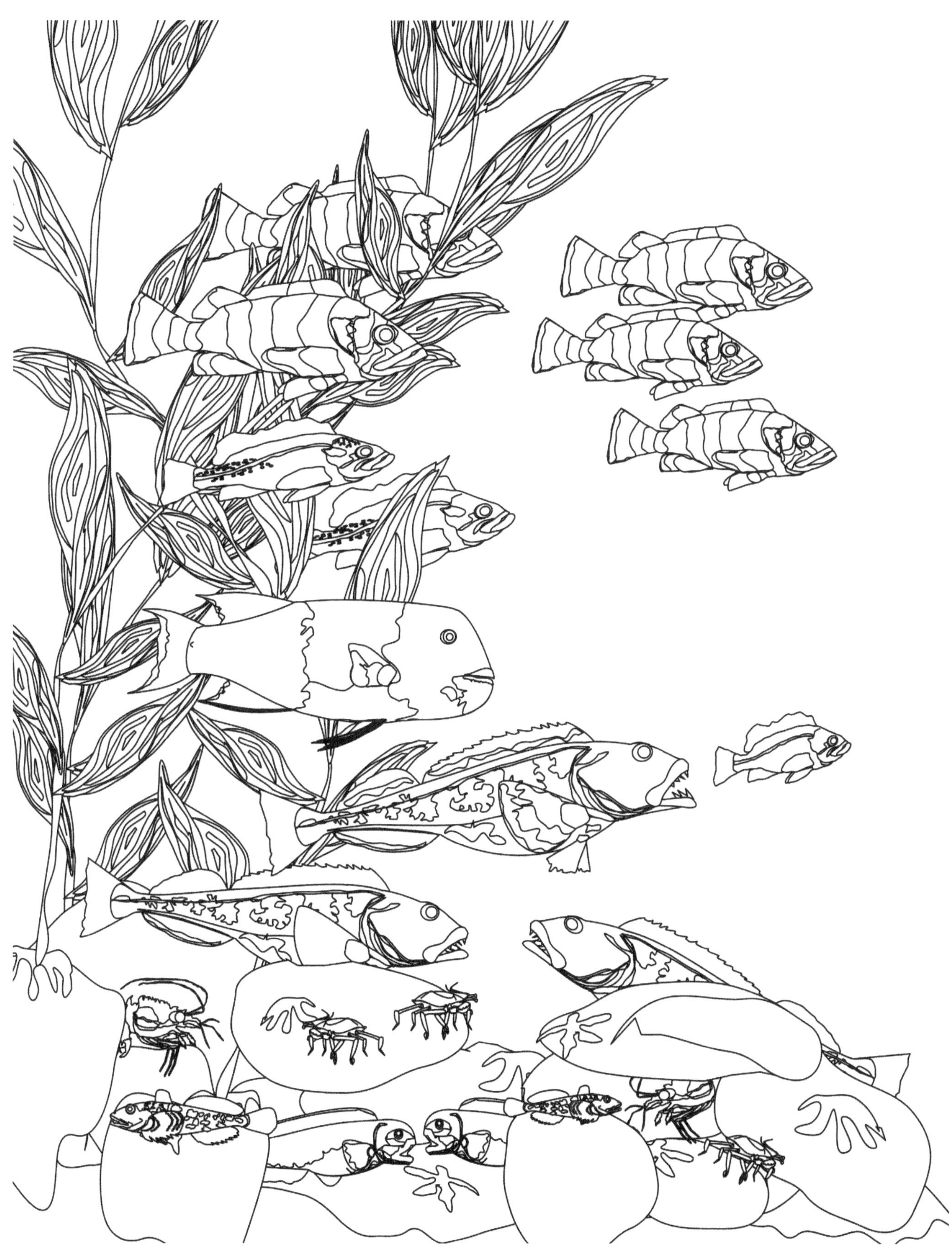

THIS PAGE LEFT INTENTIONALLY BLANK

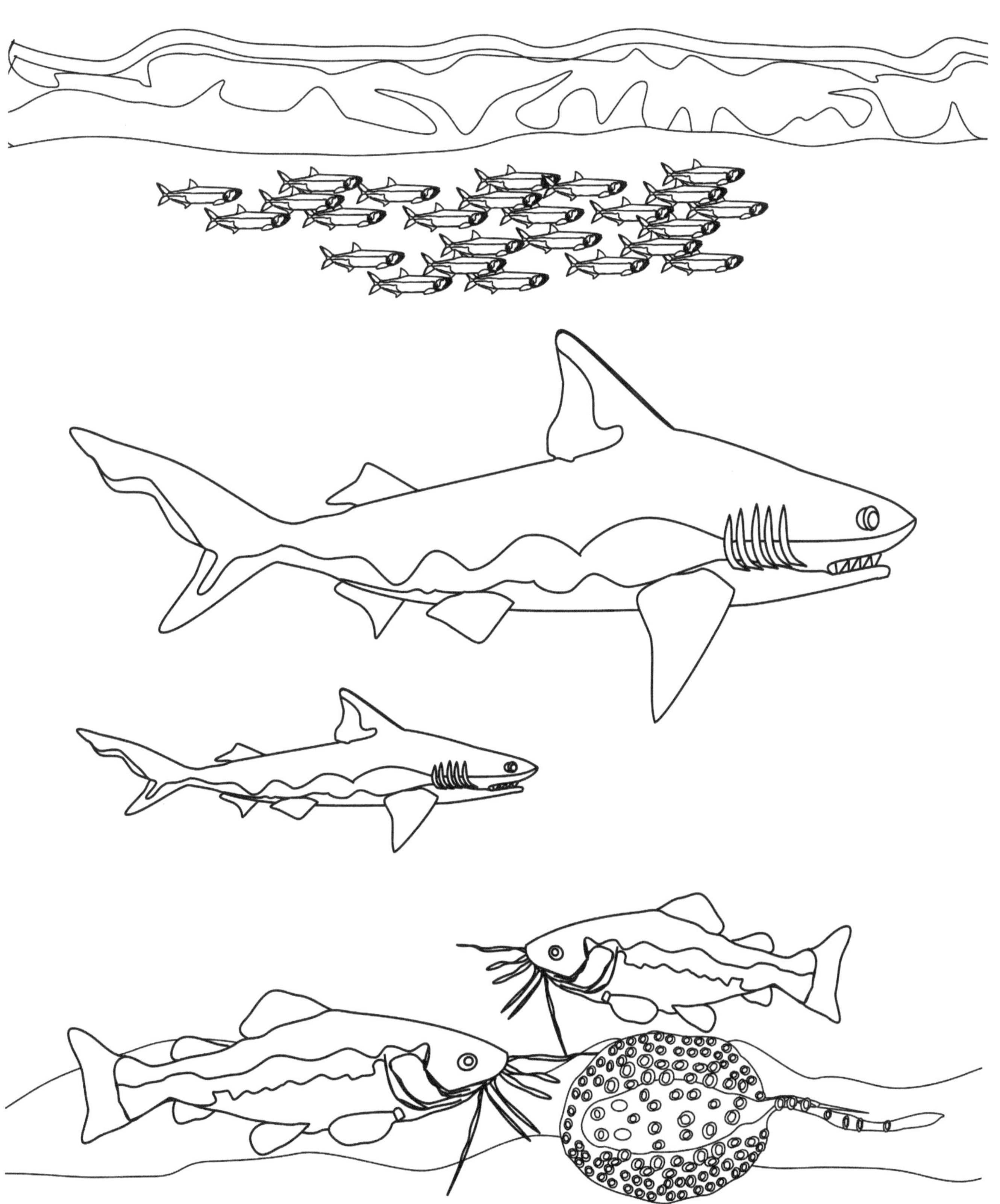

THIS PAGE LEFT INTENTIONALLY BLANK

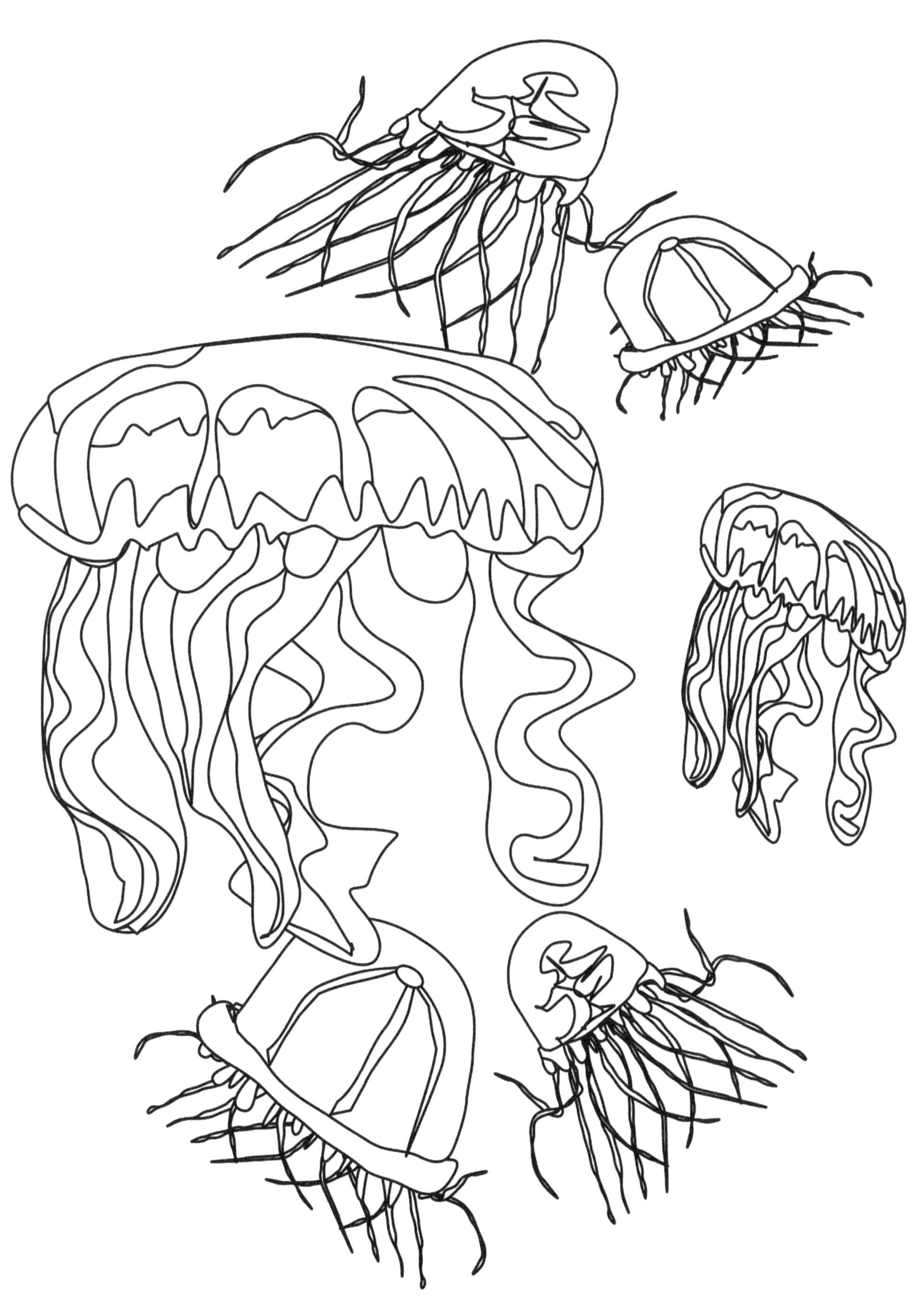

THIS PAGE LEFT INTENTIONALLY BLANK

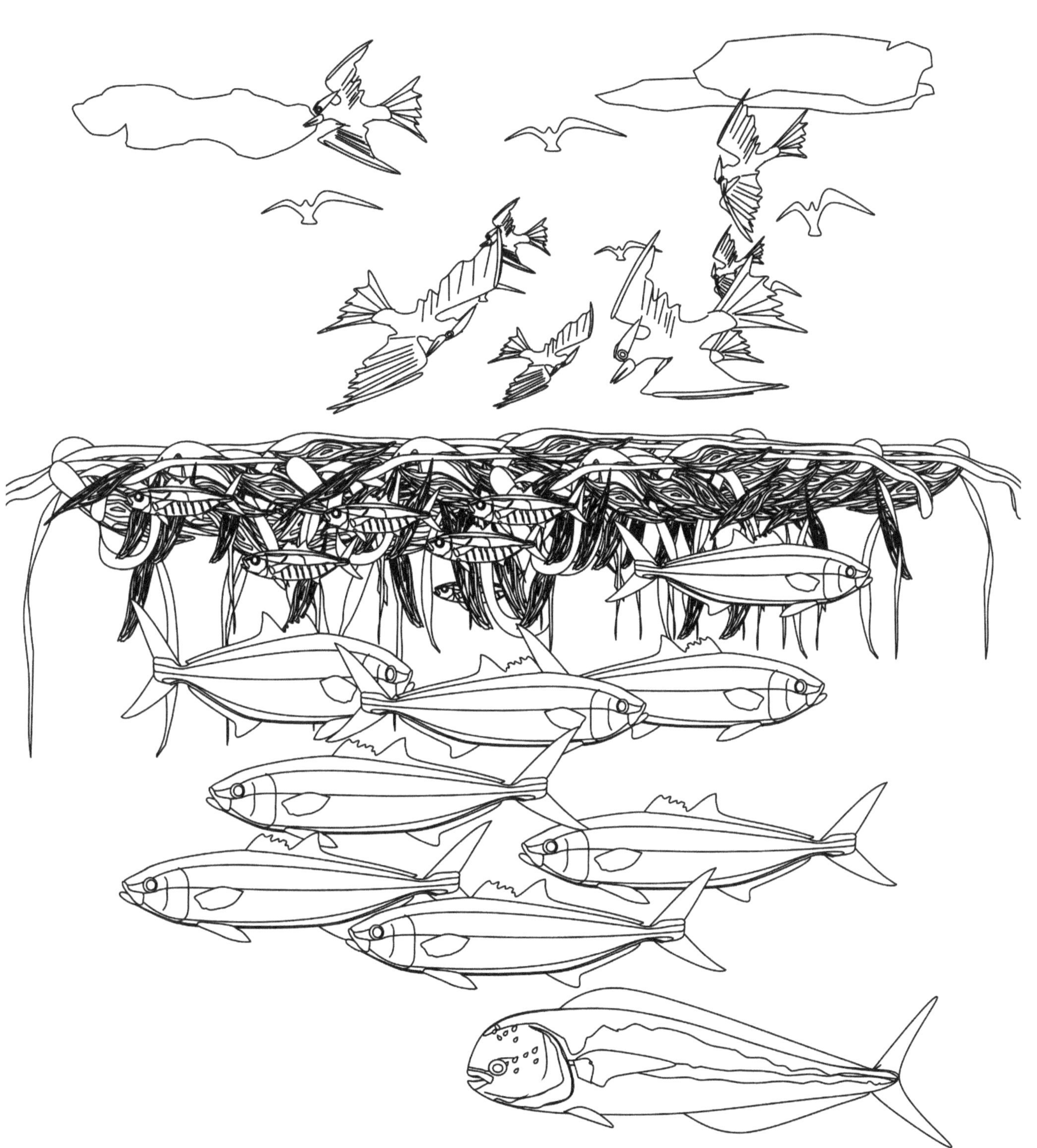

THIS PAGE LEFT INTENTIONALLY BLANK

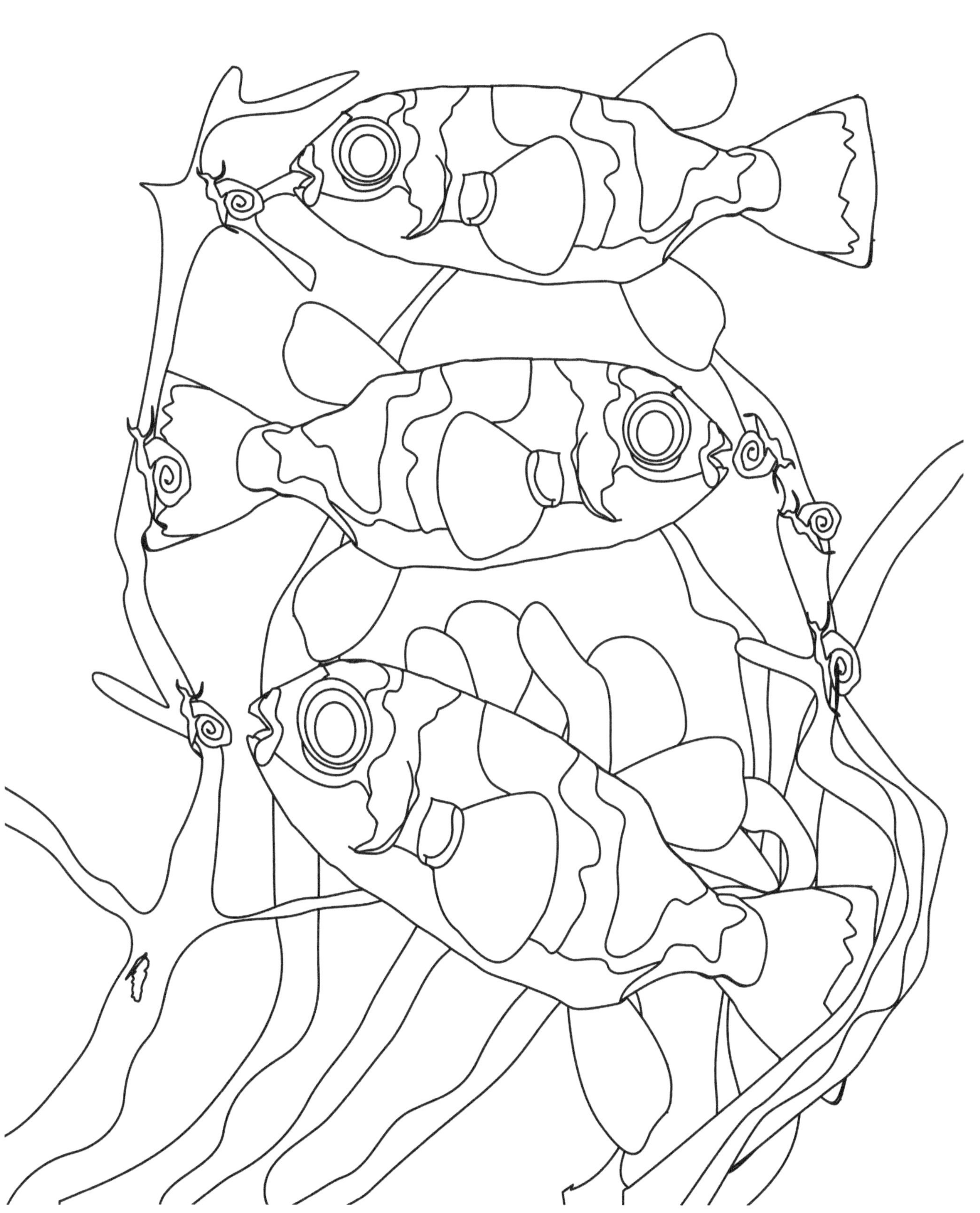

THIS PAGE LEFT INTENTIONALLY BLANK

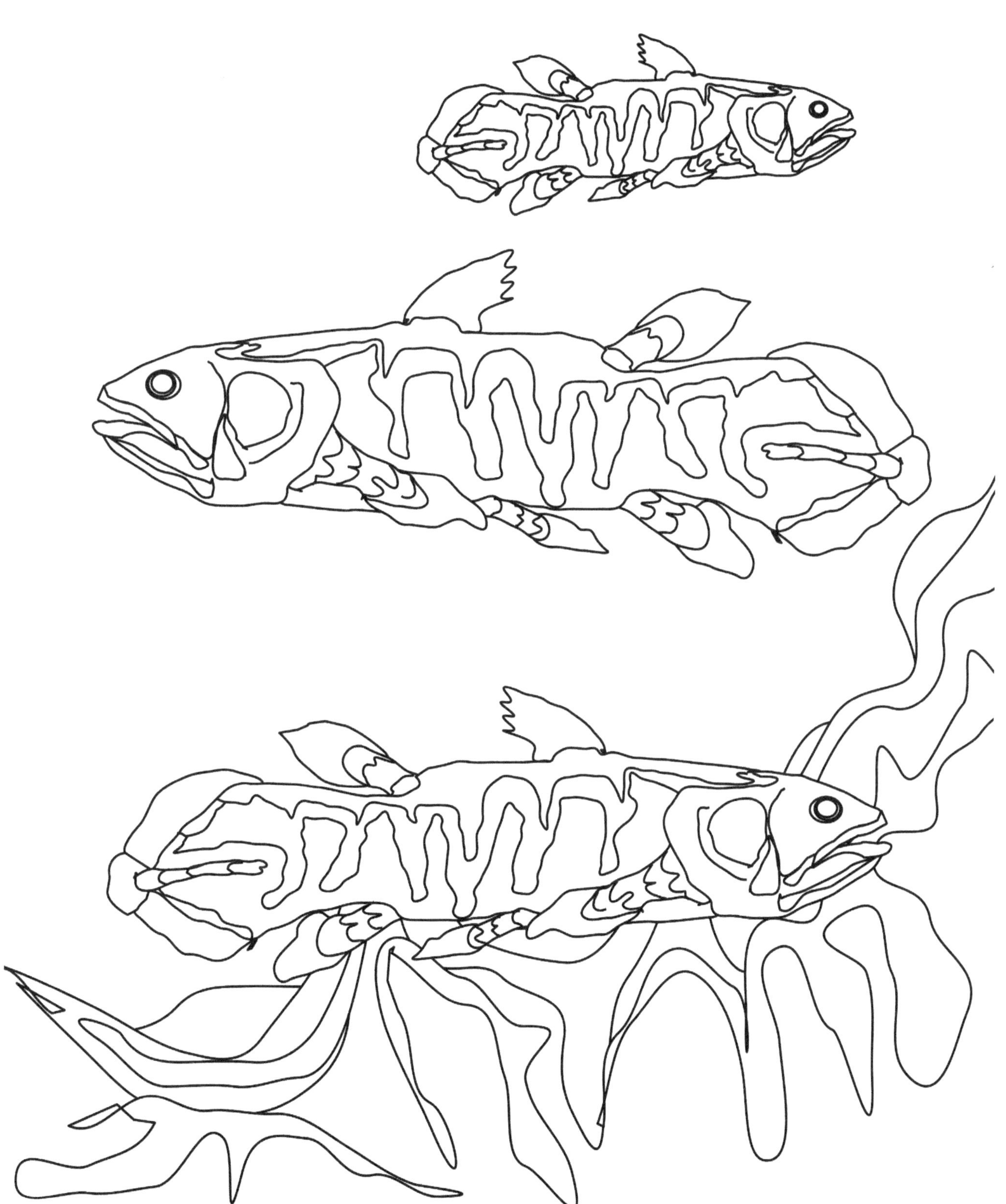

THIS PAGE LEFT INTENTIONALLY BLANK

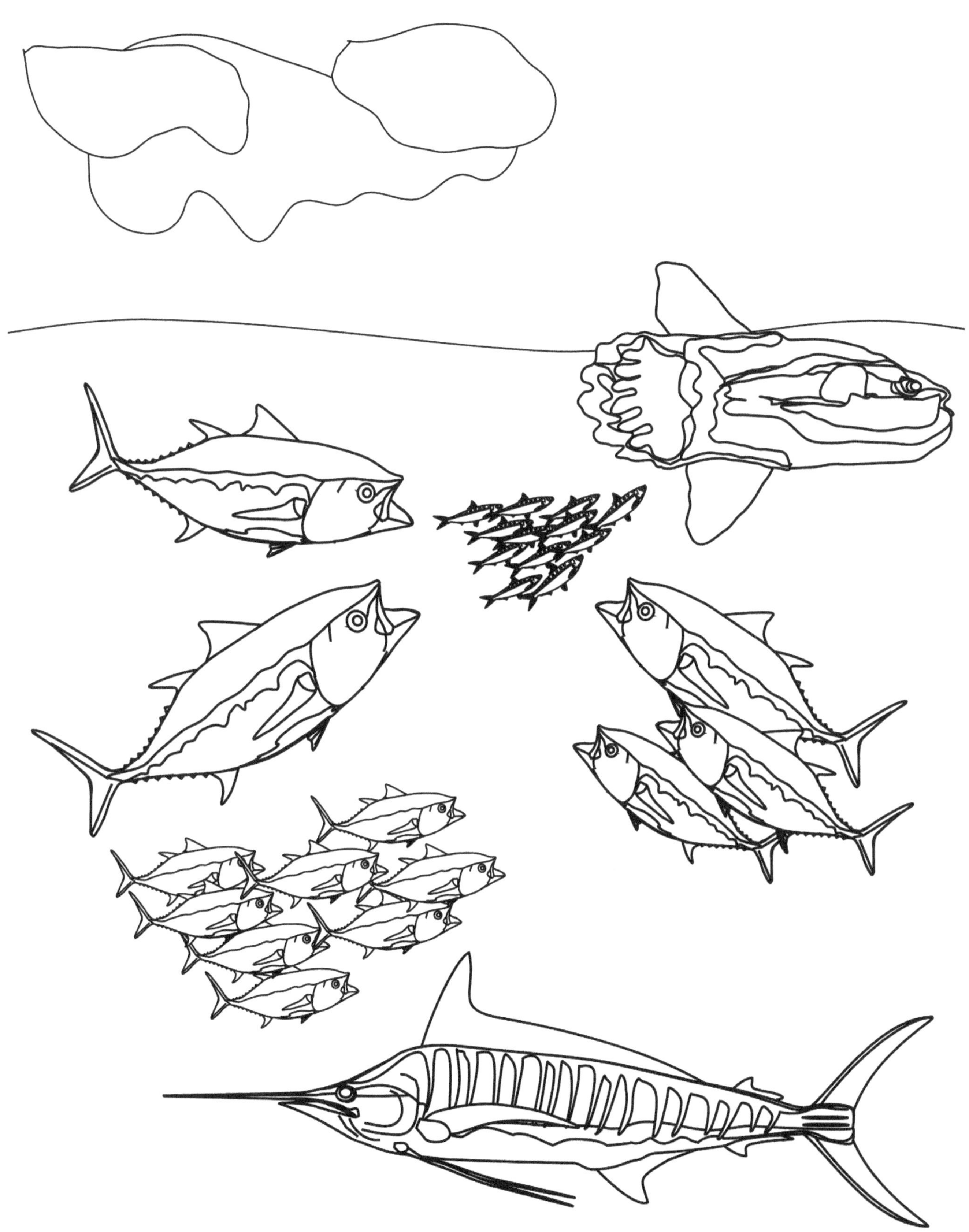

THIS PAGE LEFT INTENTIONALLY BLANK

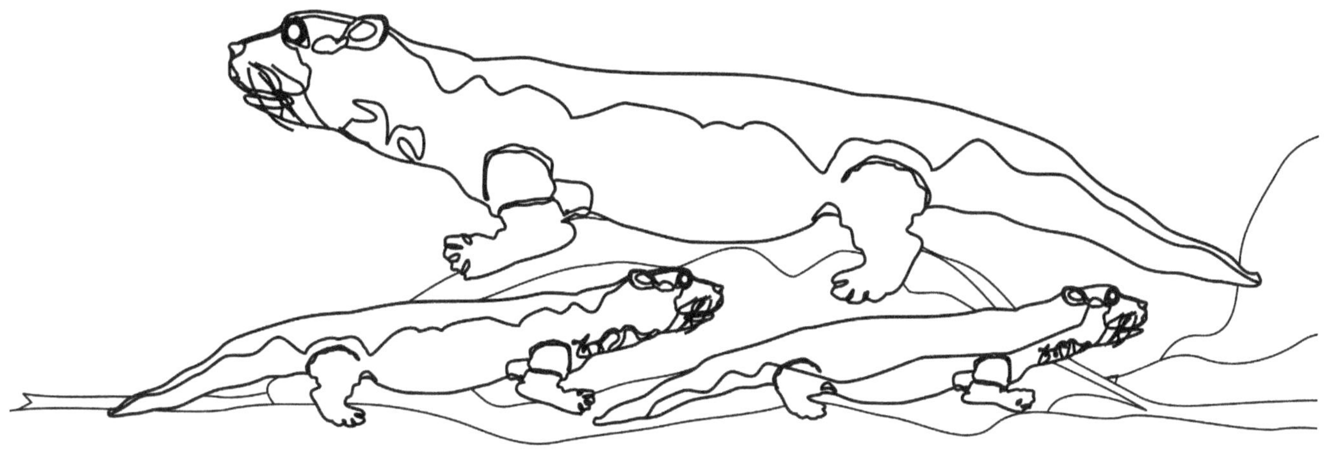

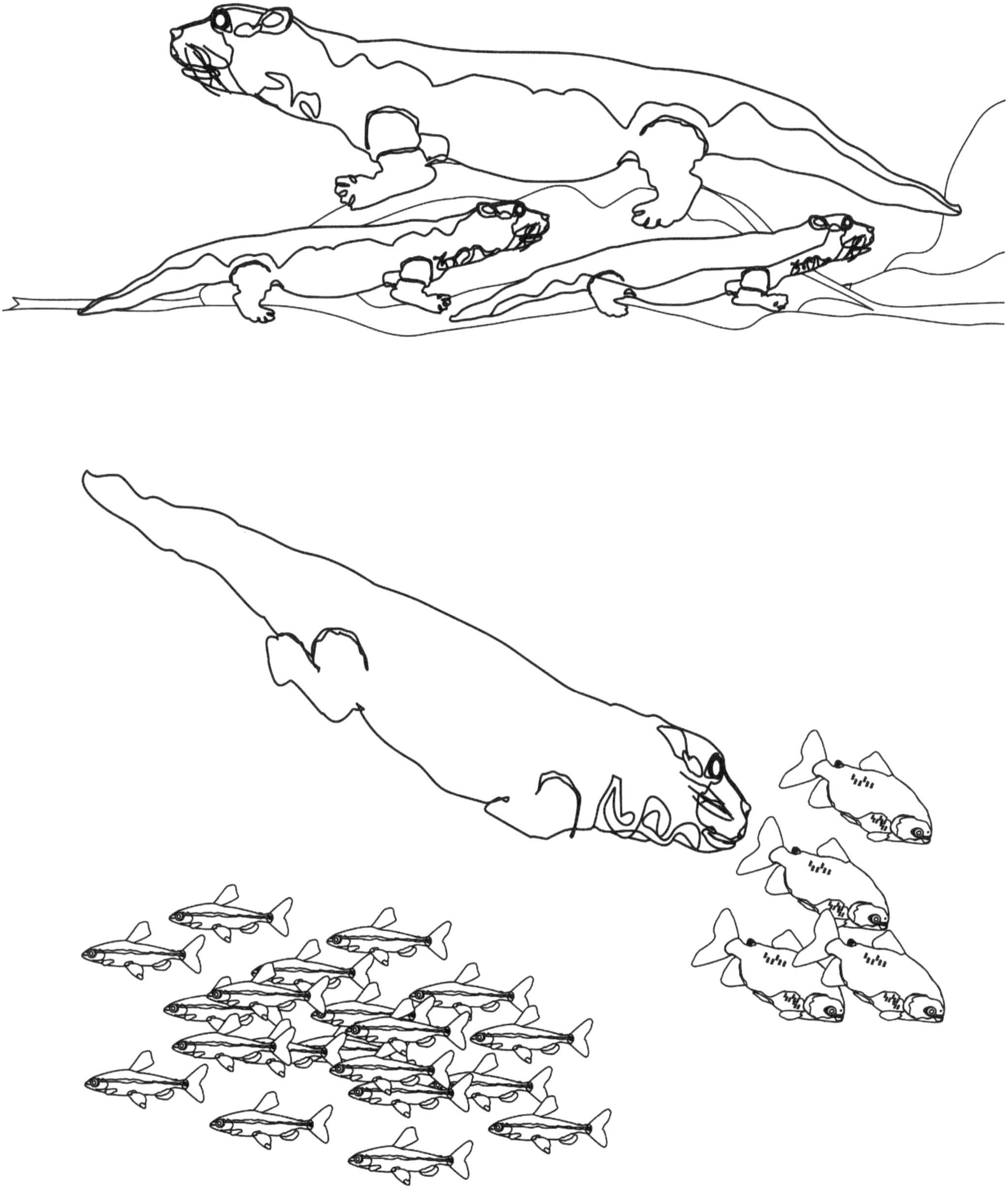

THIS PAGE LEFT INTENTIONALLY BLANK

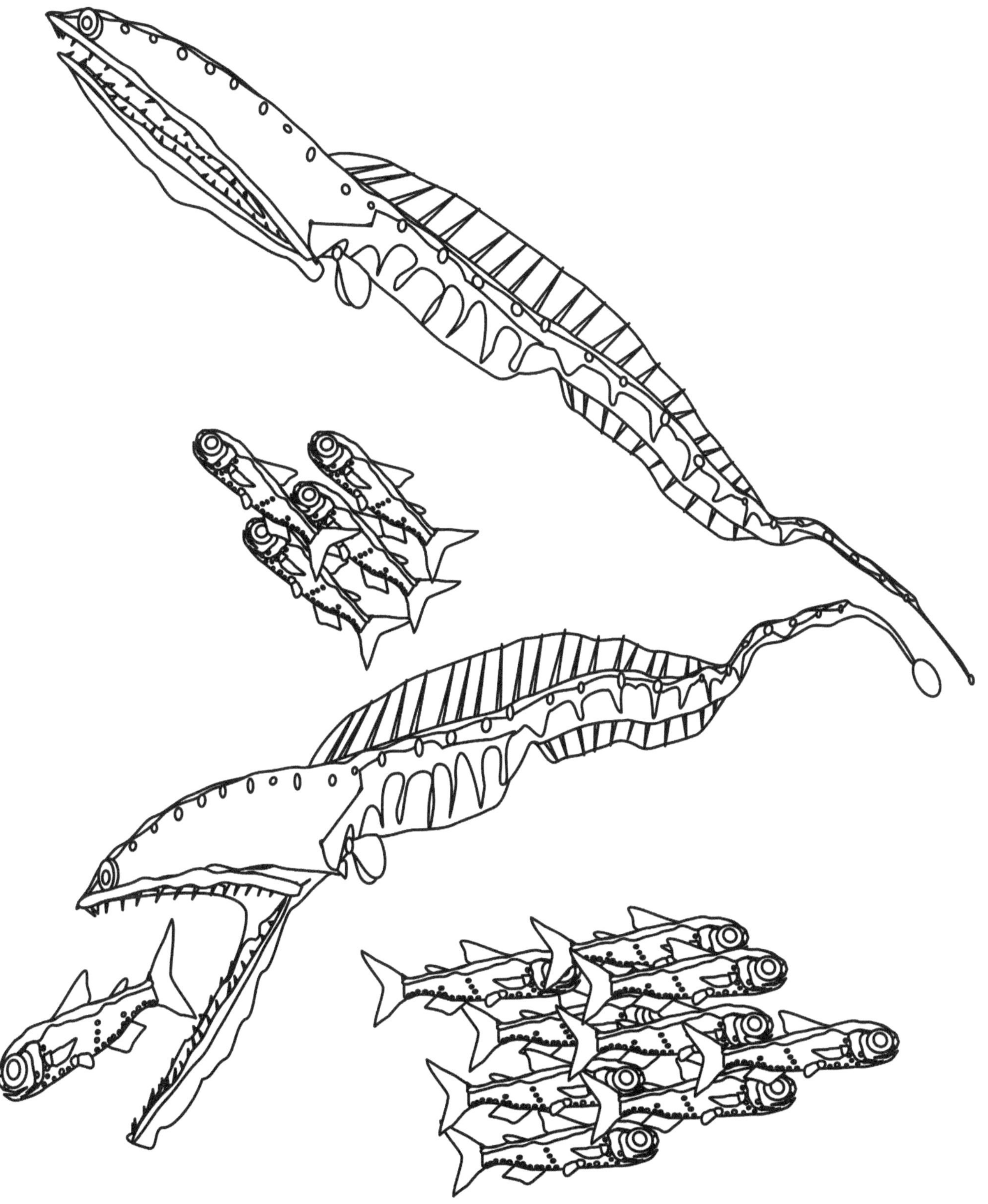

THIS PAGE LEFT INTENTIONALLY BLANK

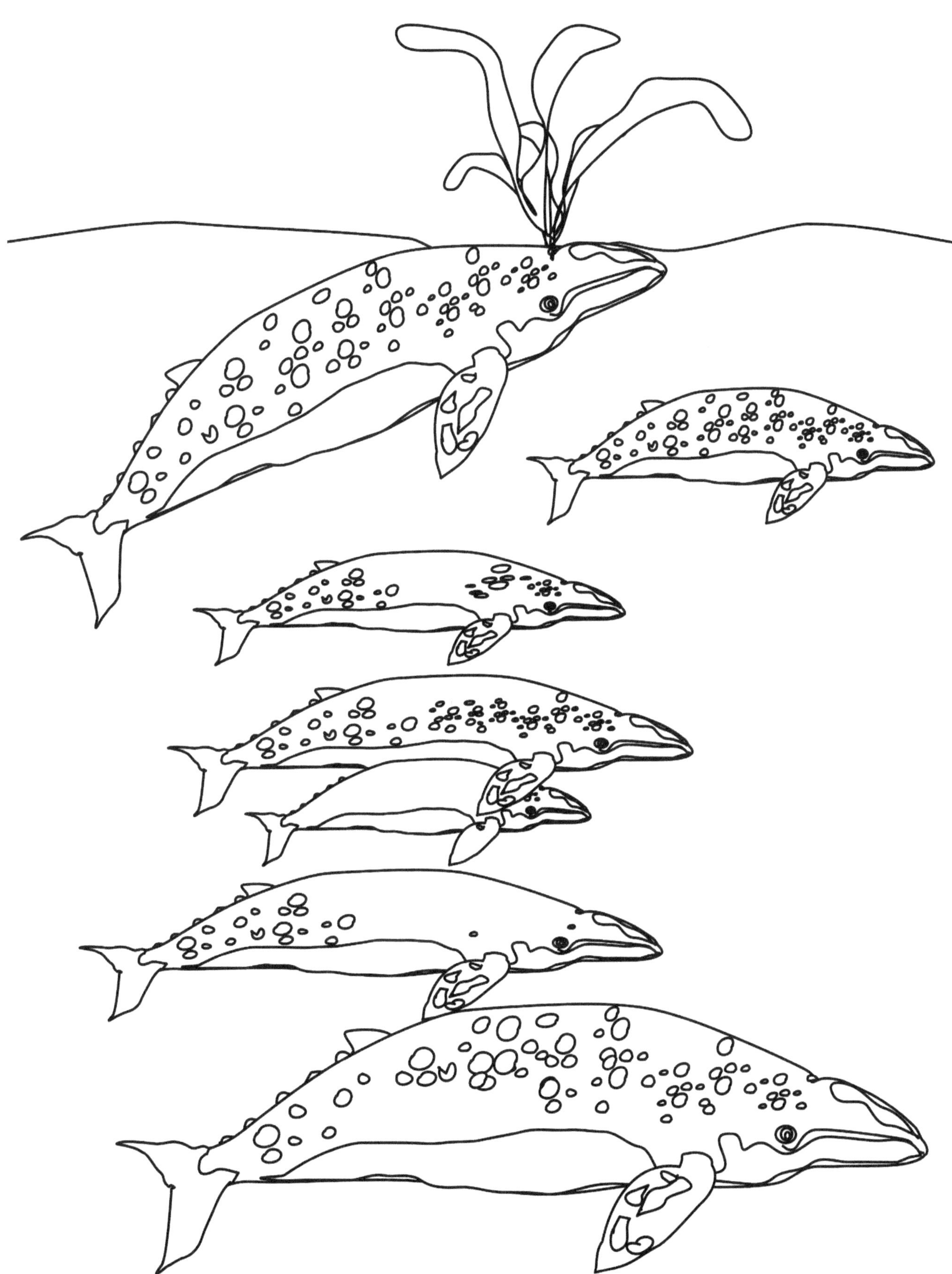

THIS PAGE LEFT INTENTIONALLY BLANK

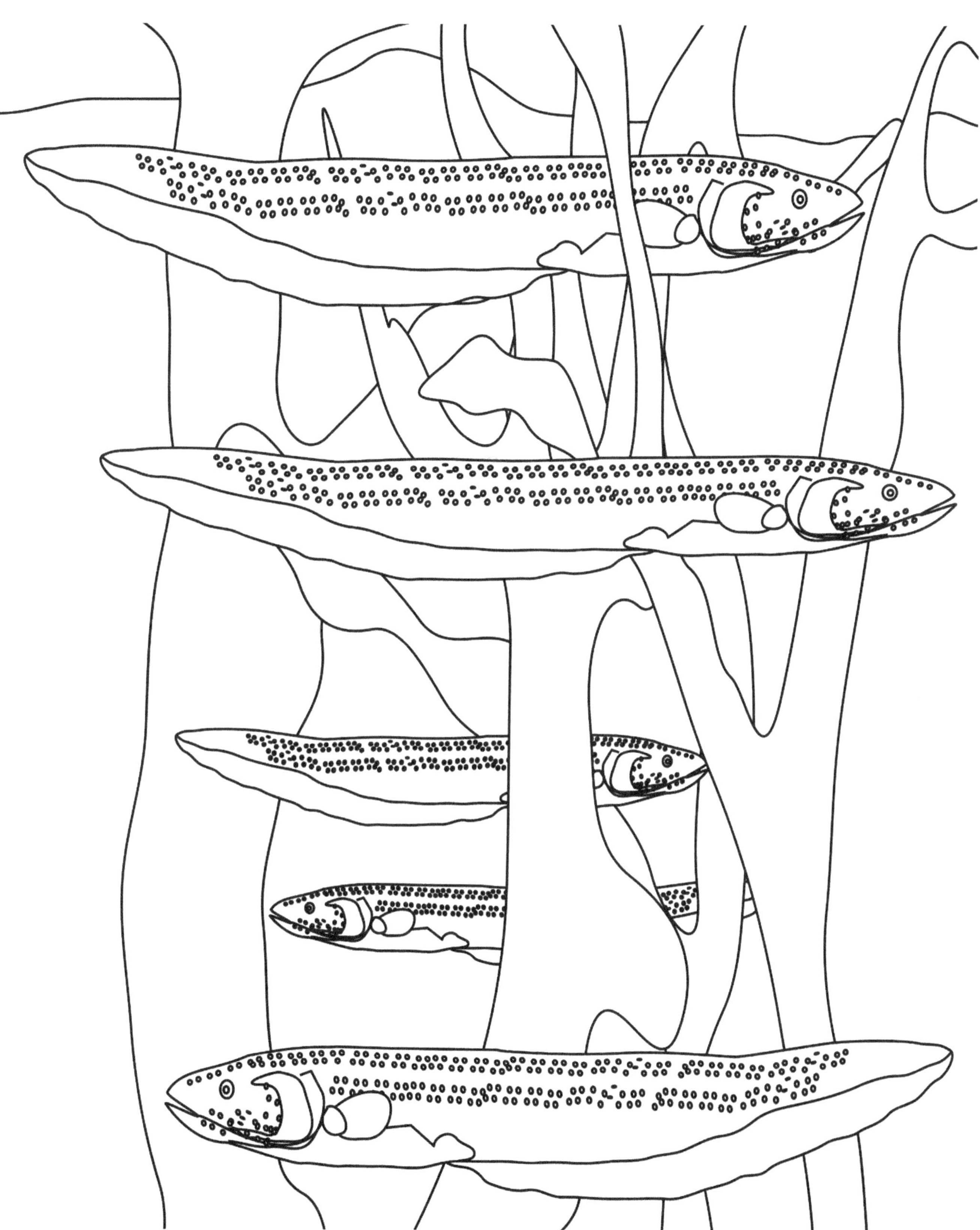

THIS PAGE LEFT INTENTIONALLY BLANK

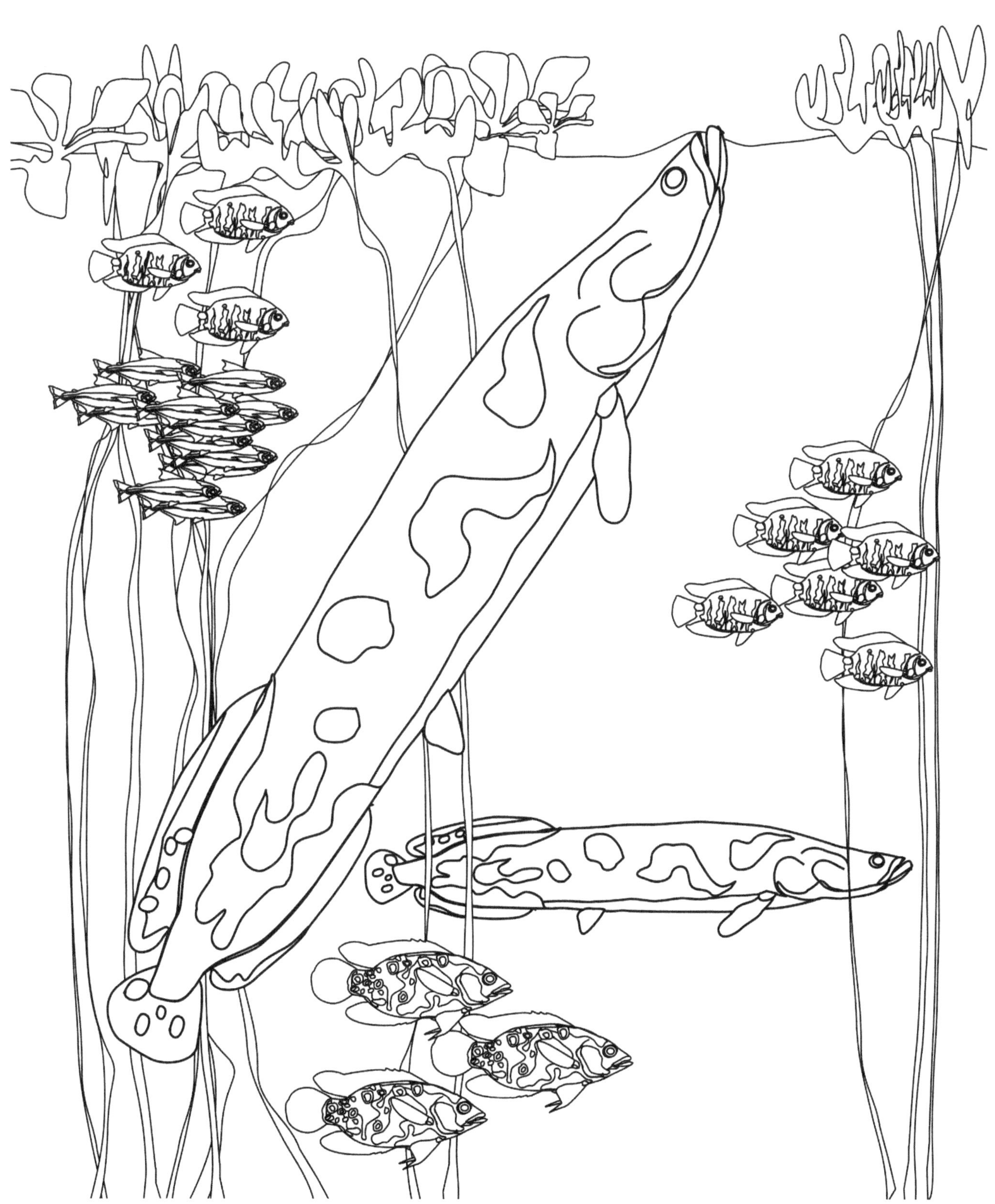

THIS PAGE LEFT INTENTIONALLY BLANK

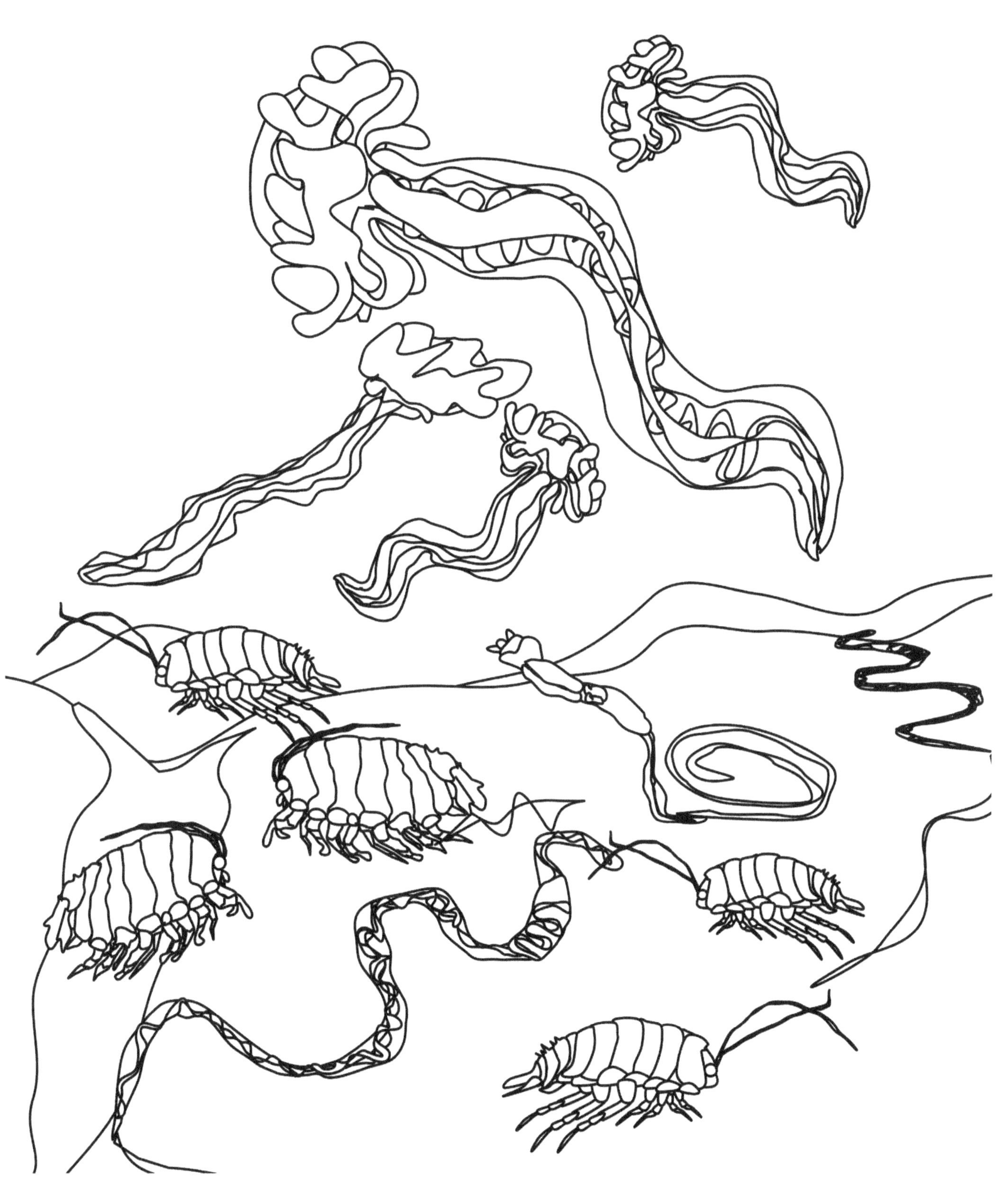

THIS PAGE LEFT INTENTIONALLY BLANK

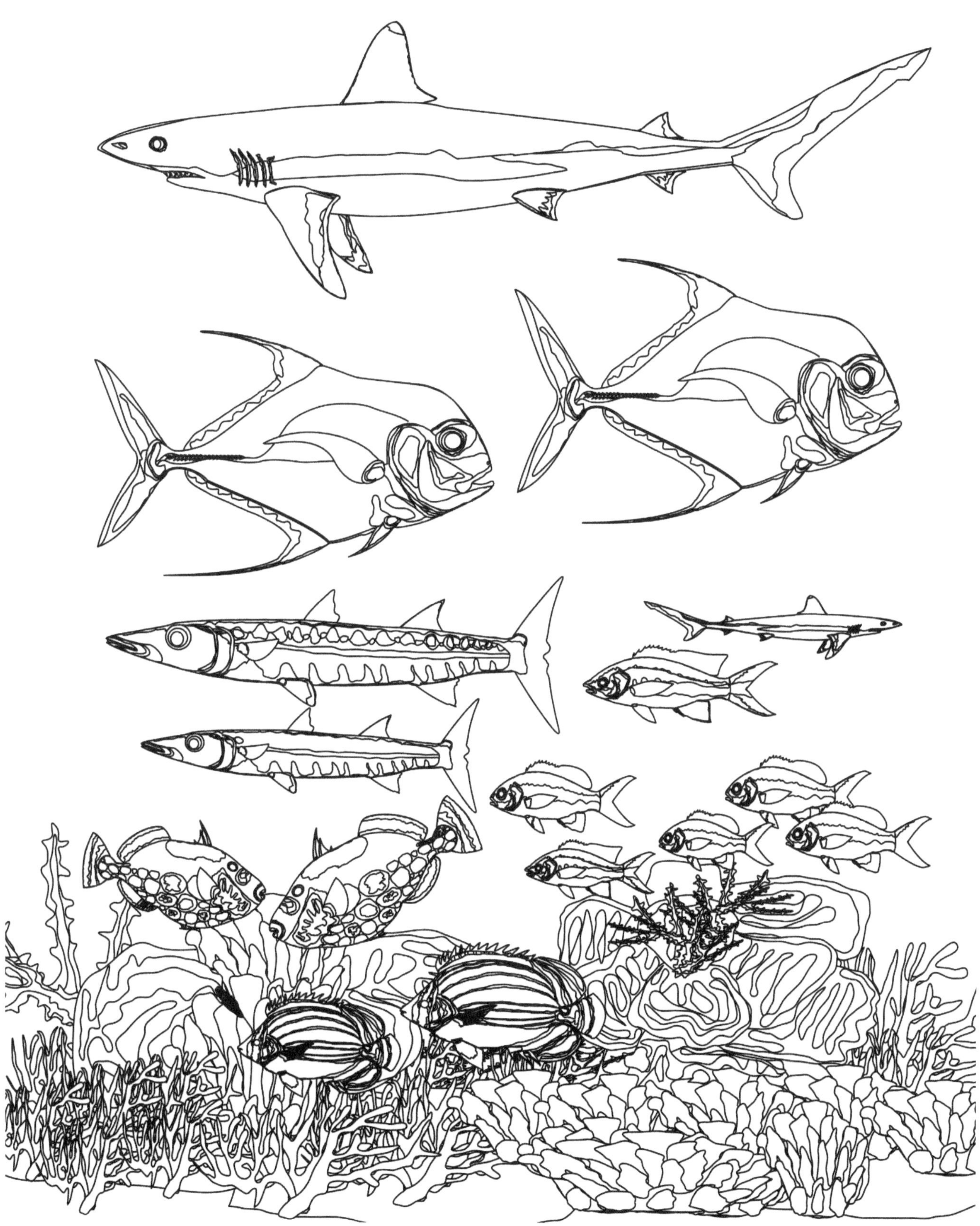

THIS PAGE LEFT INTENTIONALLY BLANK

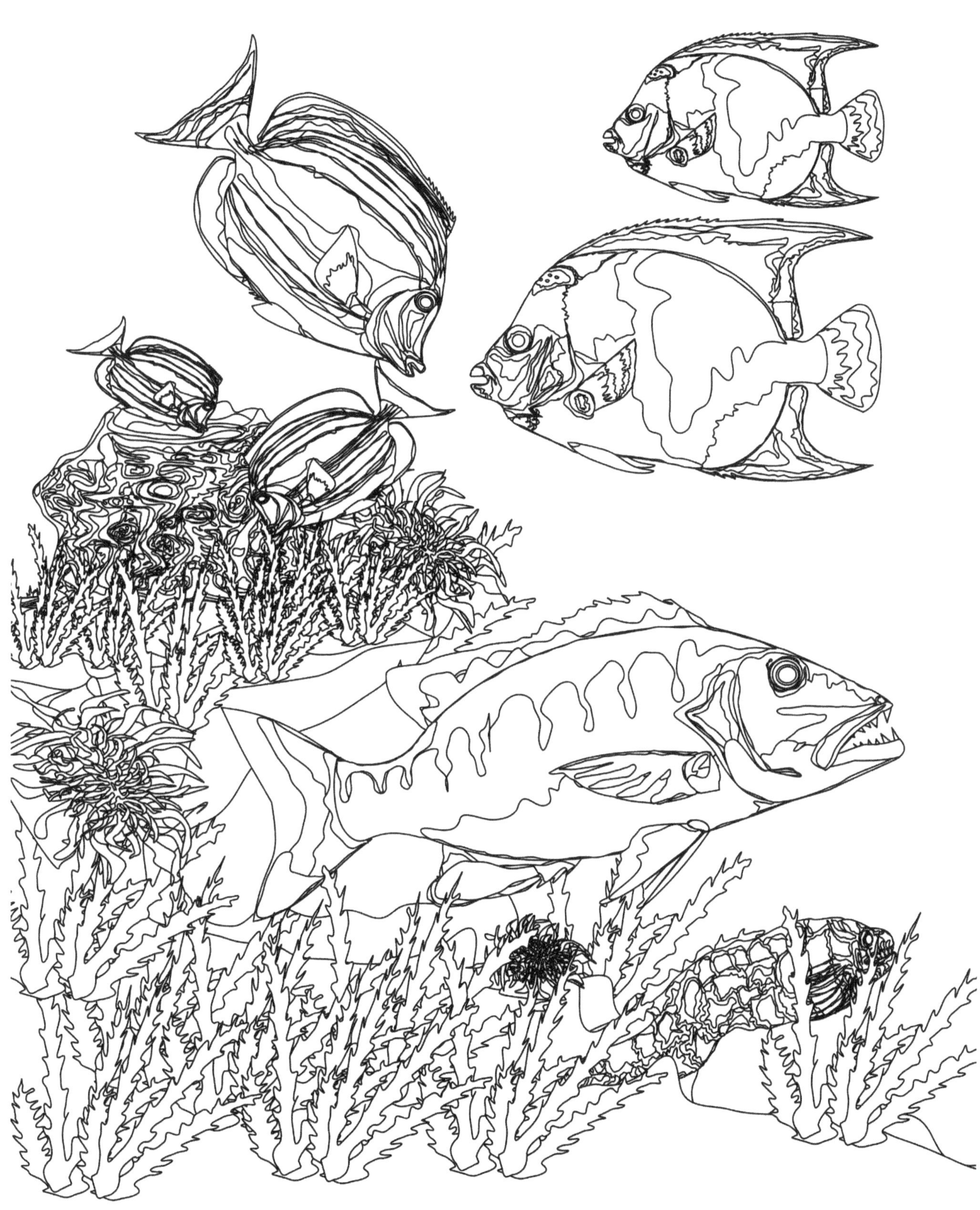

THIS PAGE LEFT INTENTIONALLY BLANK

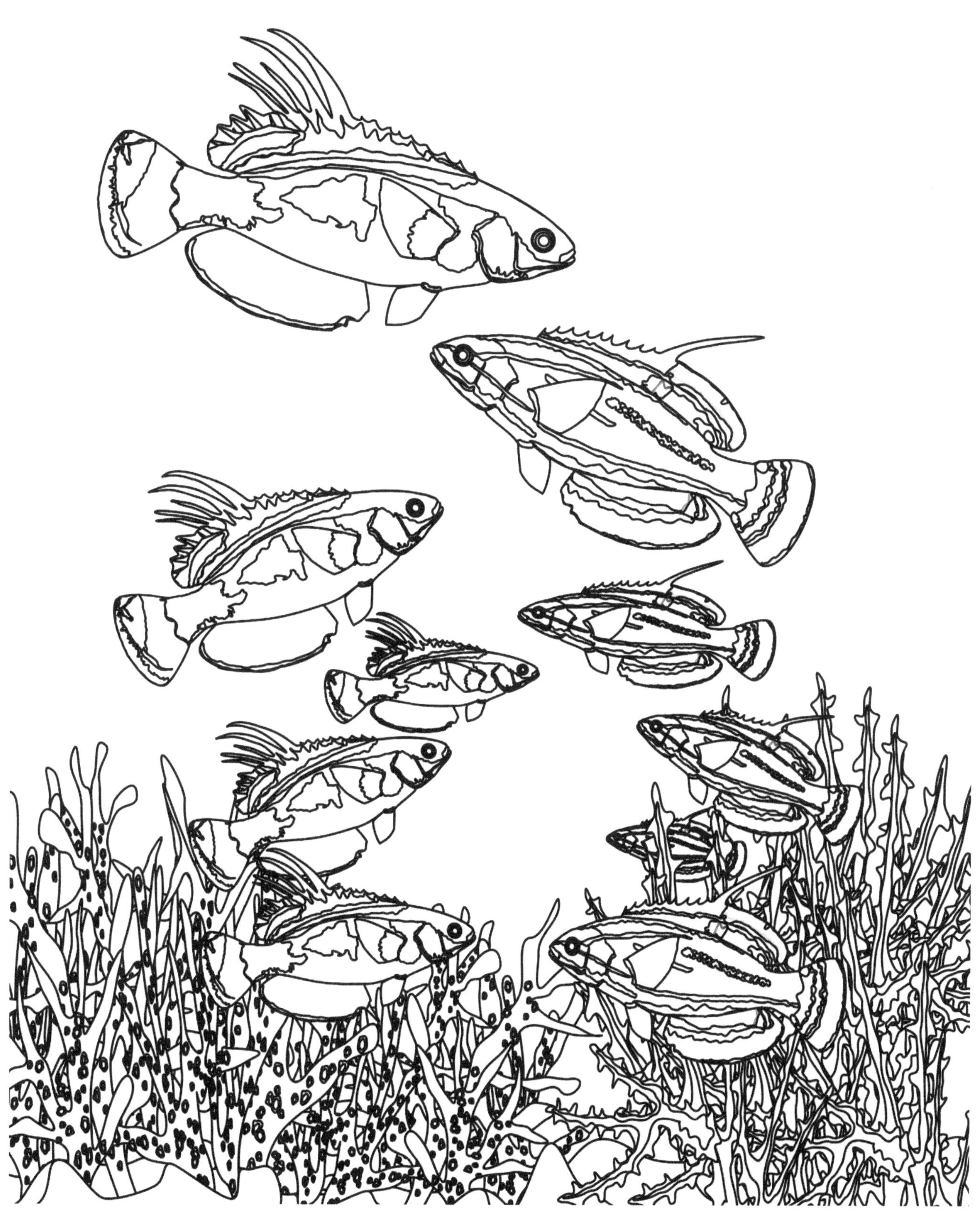

THIS PAGE LEFT INTENTIONALLY BLANK

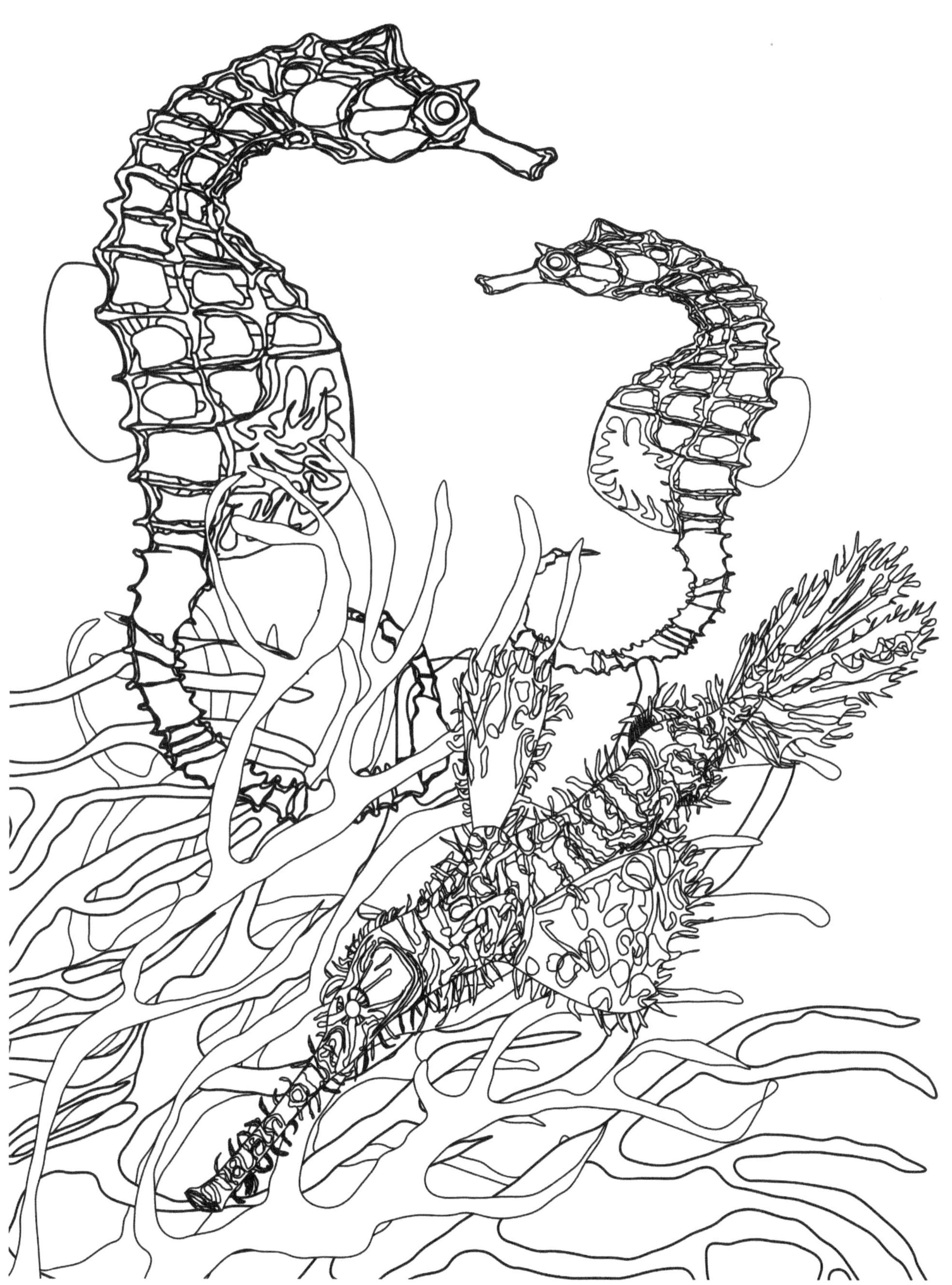

THIS PAGE LEFT INTENTIONALLY BLANK

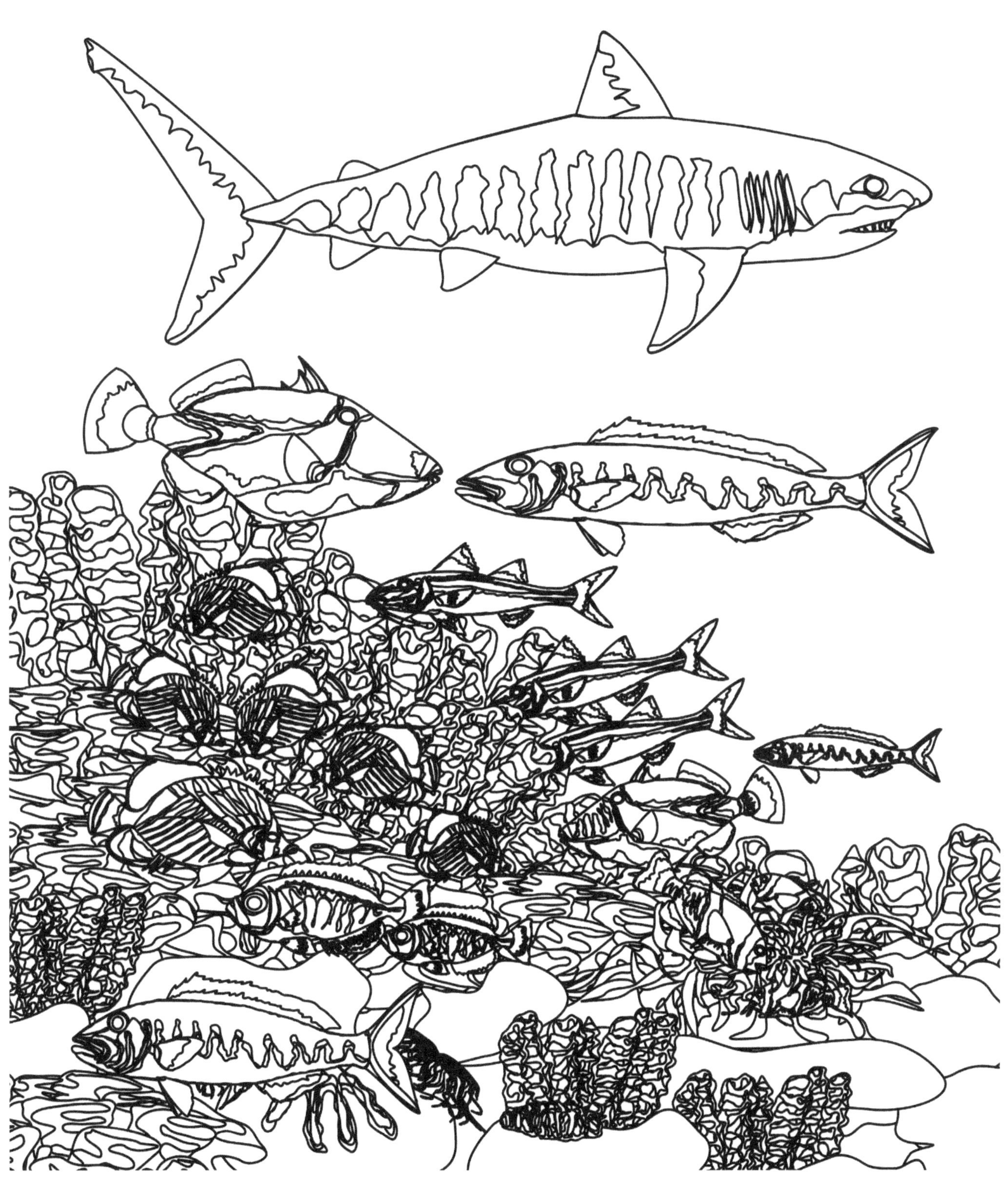

THIS PAGE LEFT INTENTIONALLY BLANK

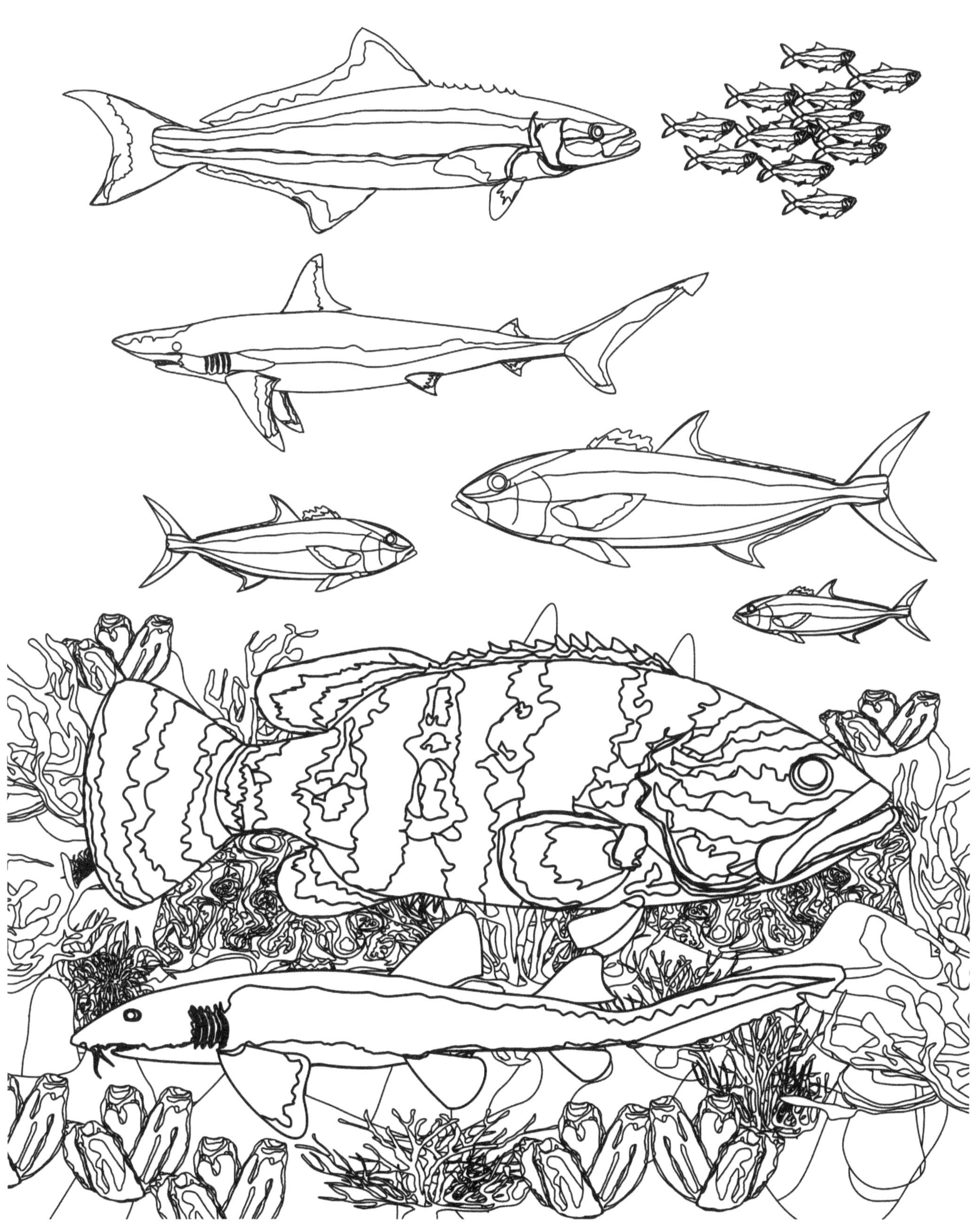

THIS PAGE LEFT INTENTIONALLY BLANK

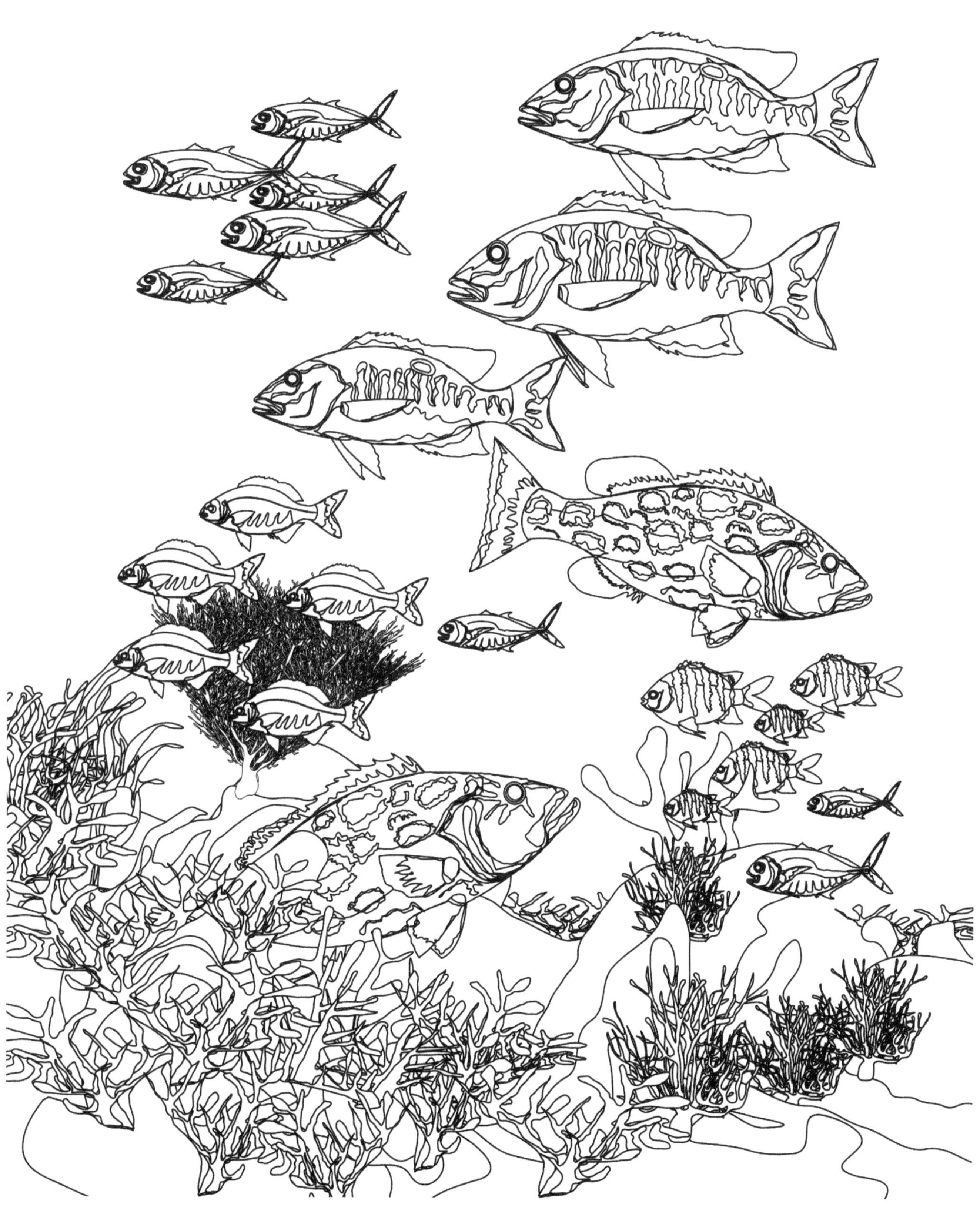

THIS PAGE LEFT INTENTIONALLY BLANK

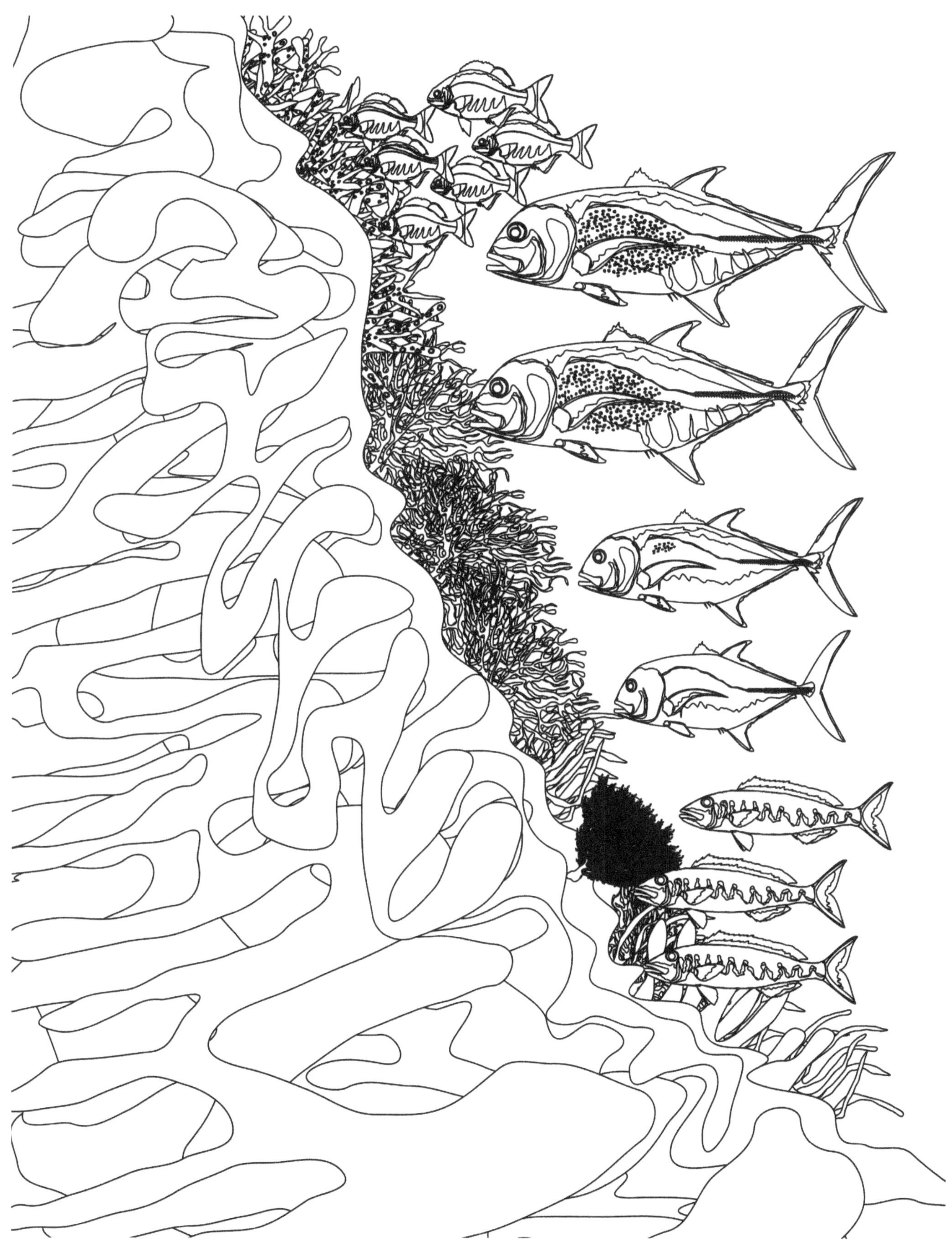

THIS PAGE LEFT INTENTIONALLY BLANK

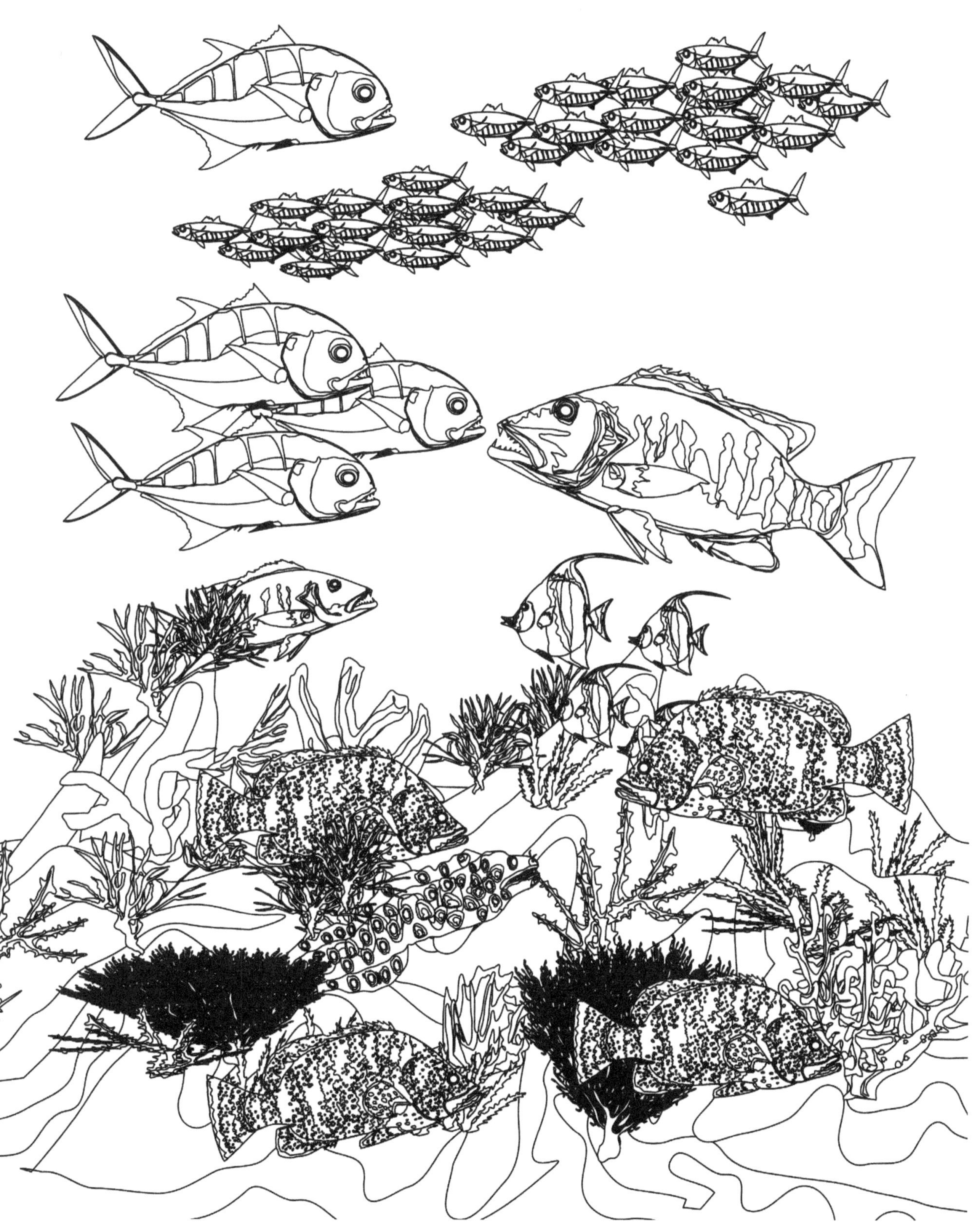

THIS PAGE LEFT INTENTIONALLY BLANK

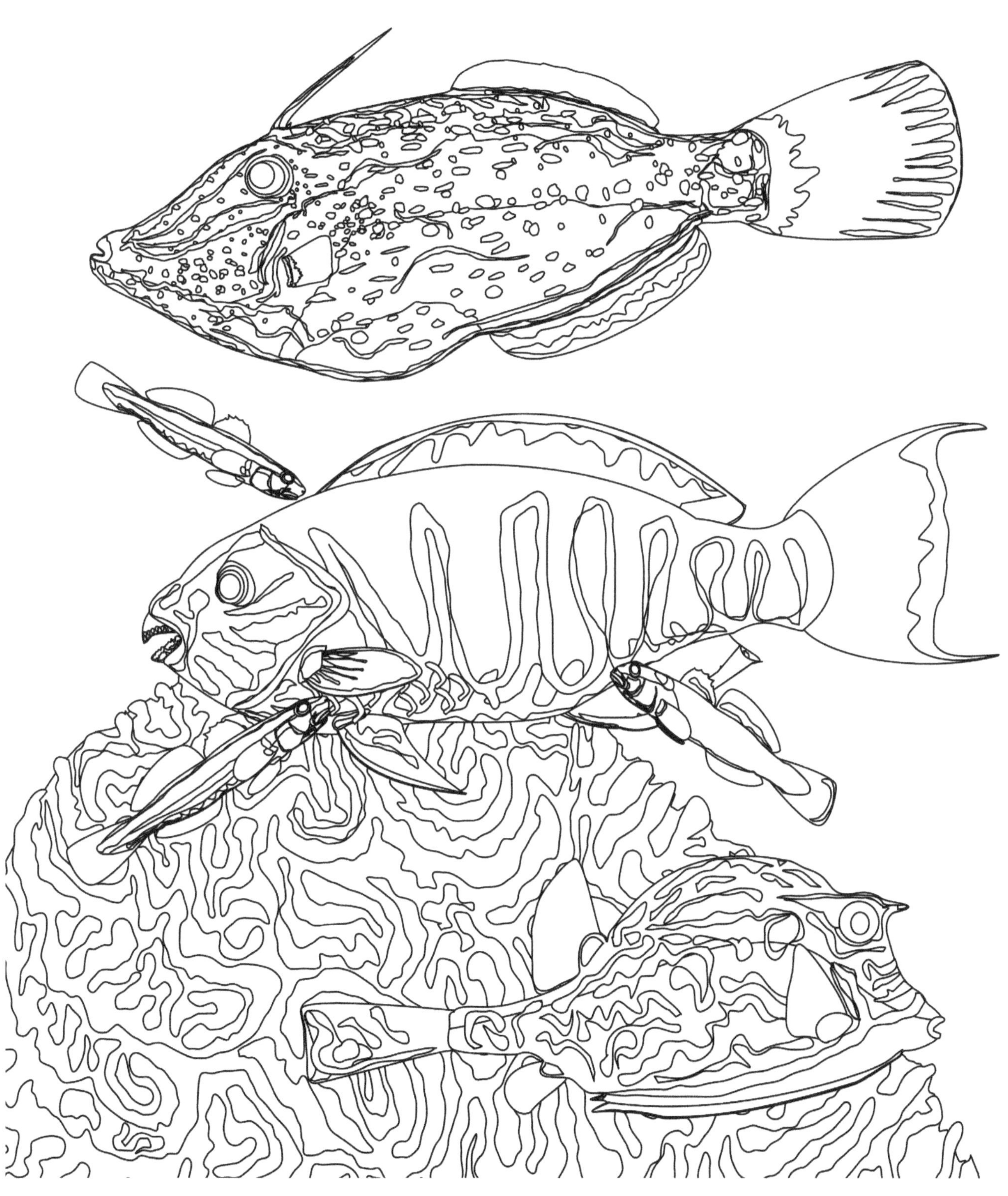

THIS PAGE LEFT INTENTIONALLY BLANK

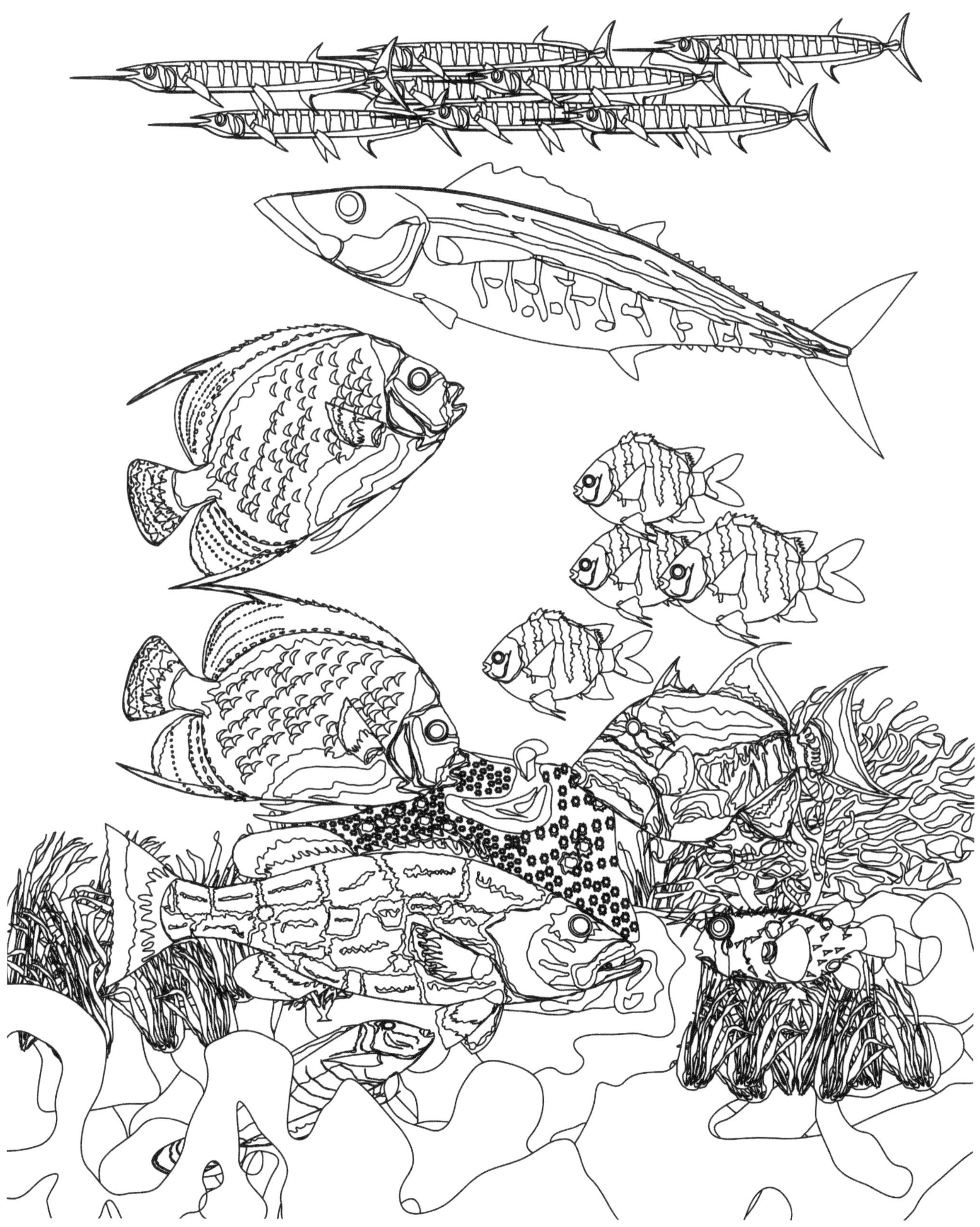

THIS PAGE LEFT INTENTIONALLY BLANK

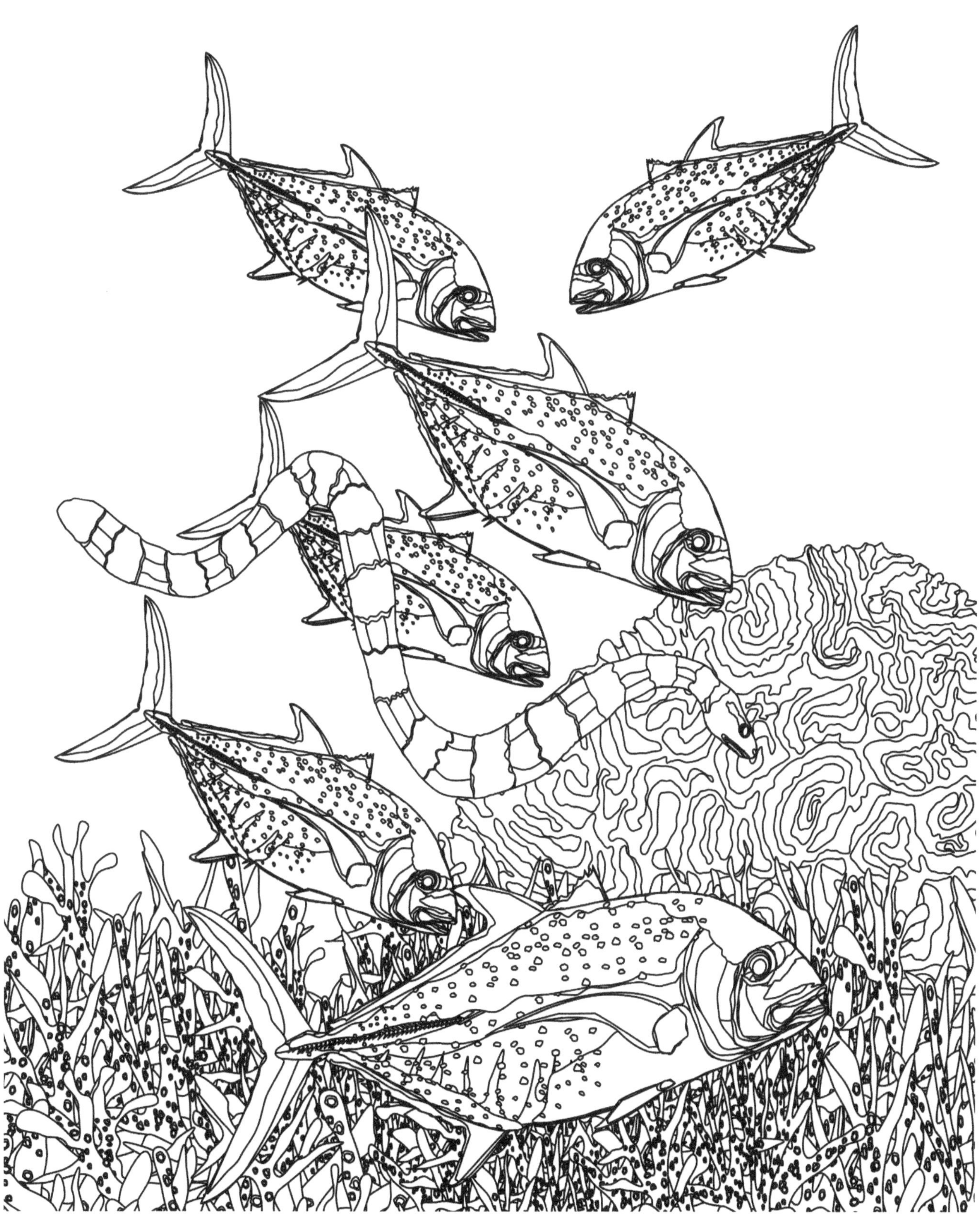

THIS PAGE LEFT INTENTIONALLY BLANK

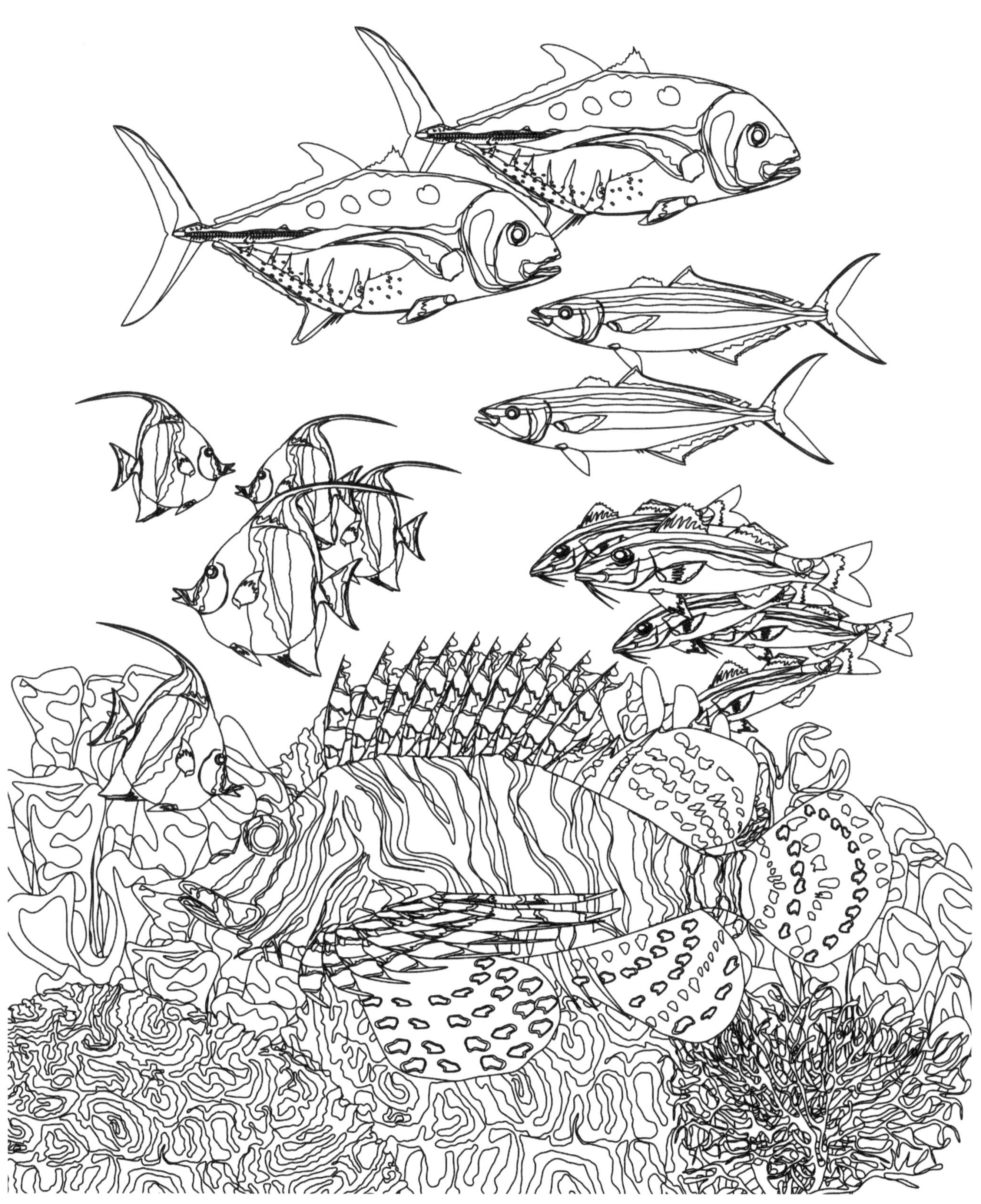

THIS PAGE LEFT INTENTIONALLY BLANK

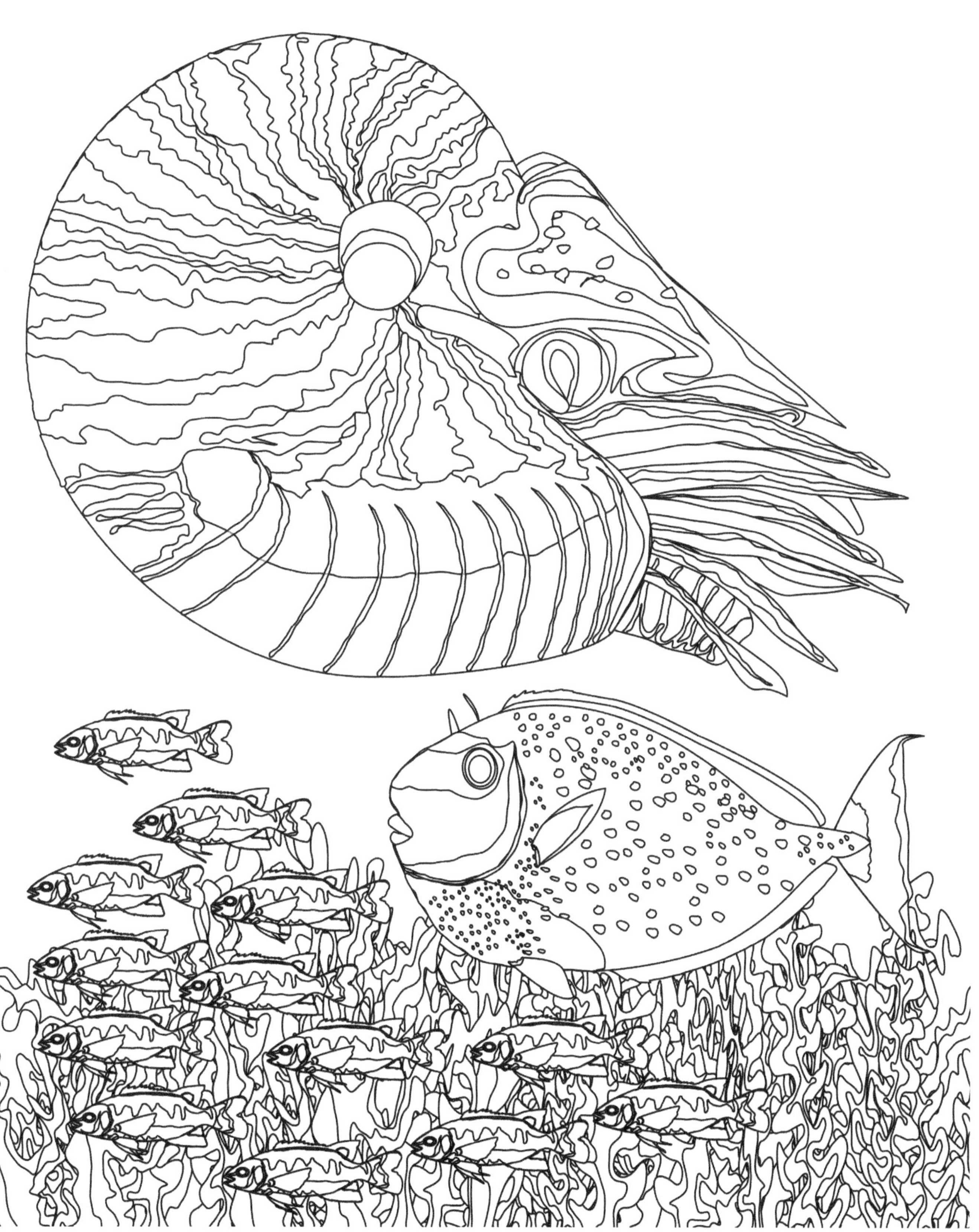

THIS PAGE LEFT INTENTIONALLY BLANK

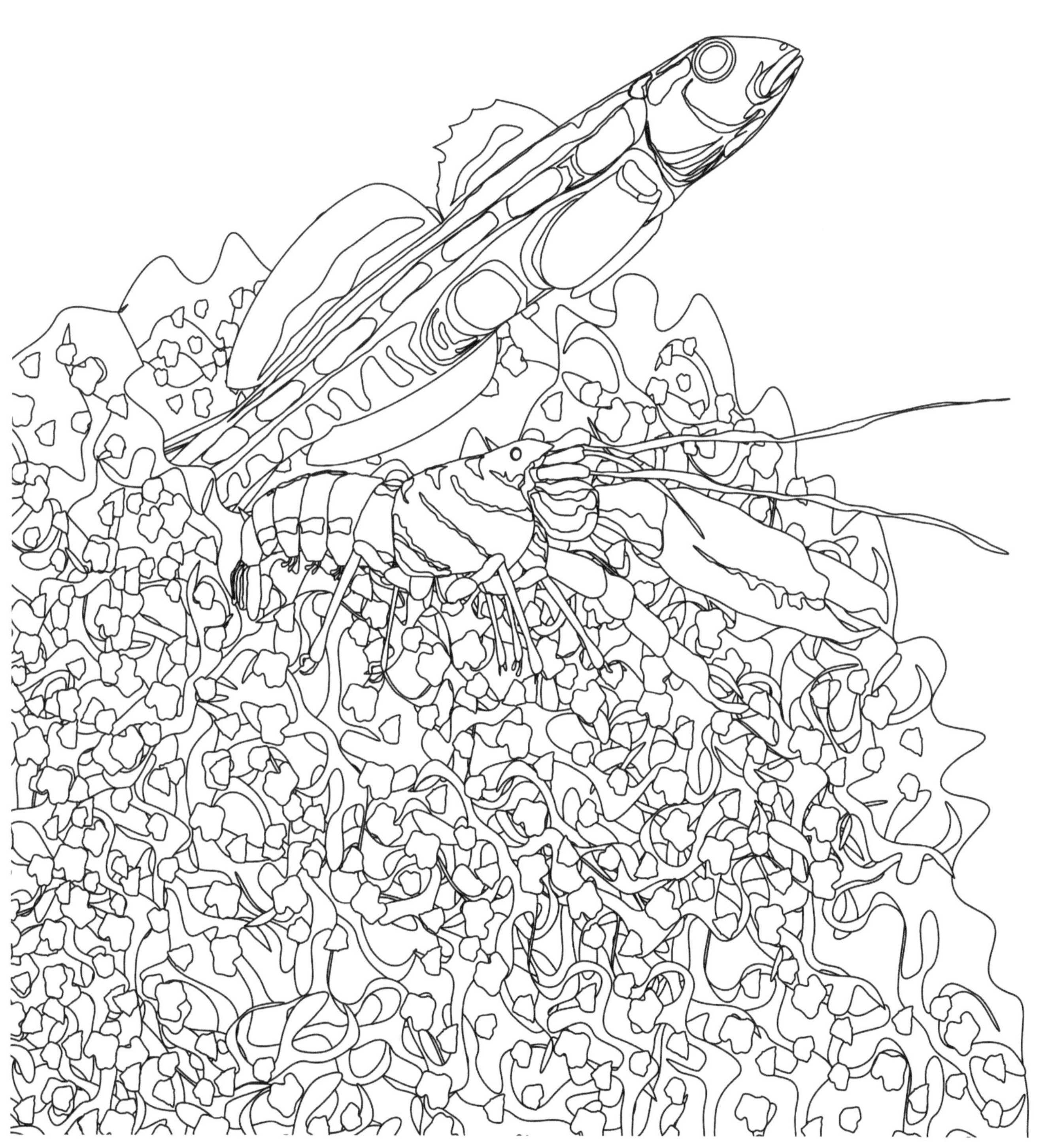

THIS PAGE LEFT INTENTIONALLY BLANK

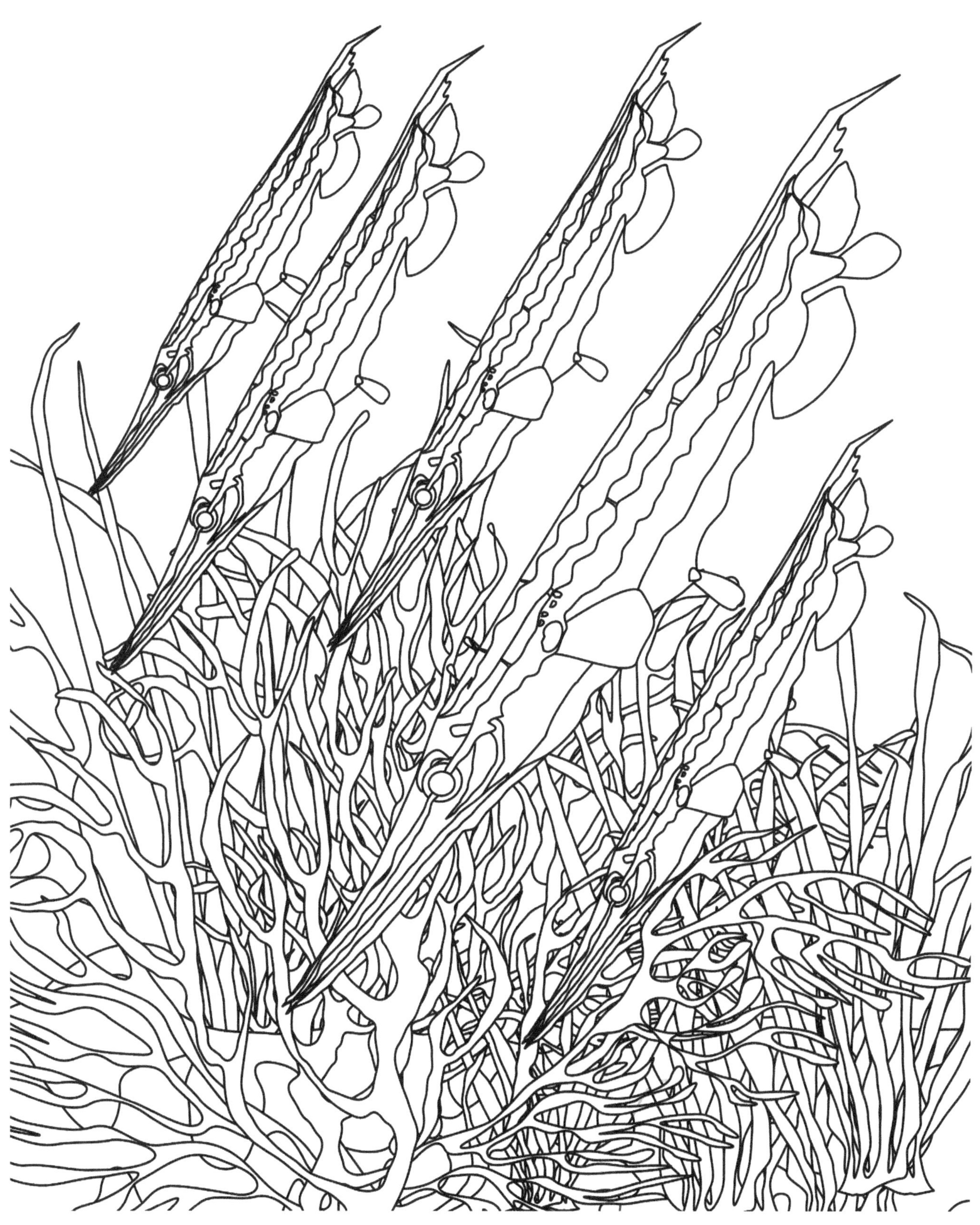

THIS PAGE LEFT INTENTIONALLY BLANK

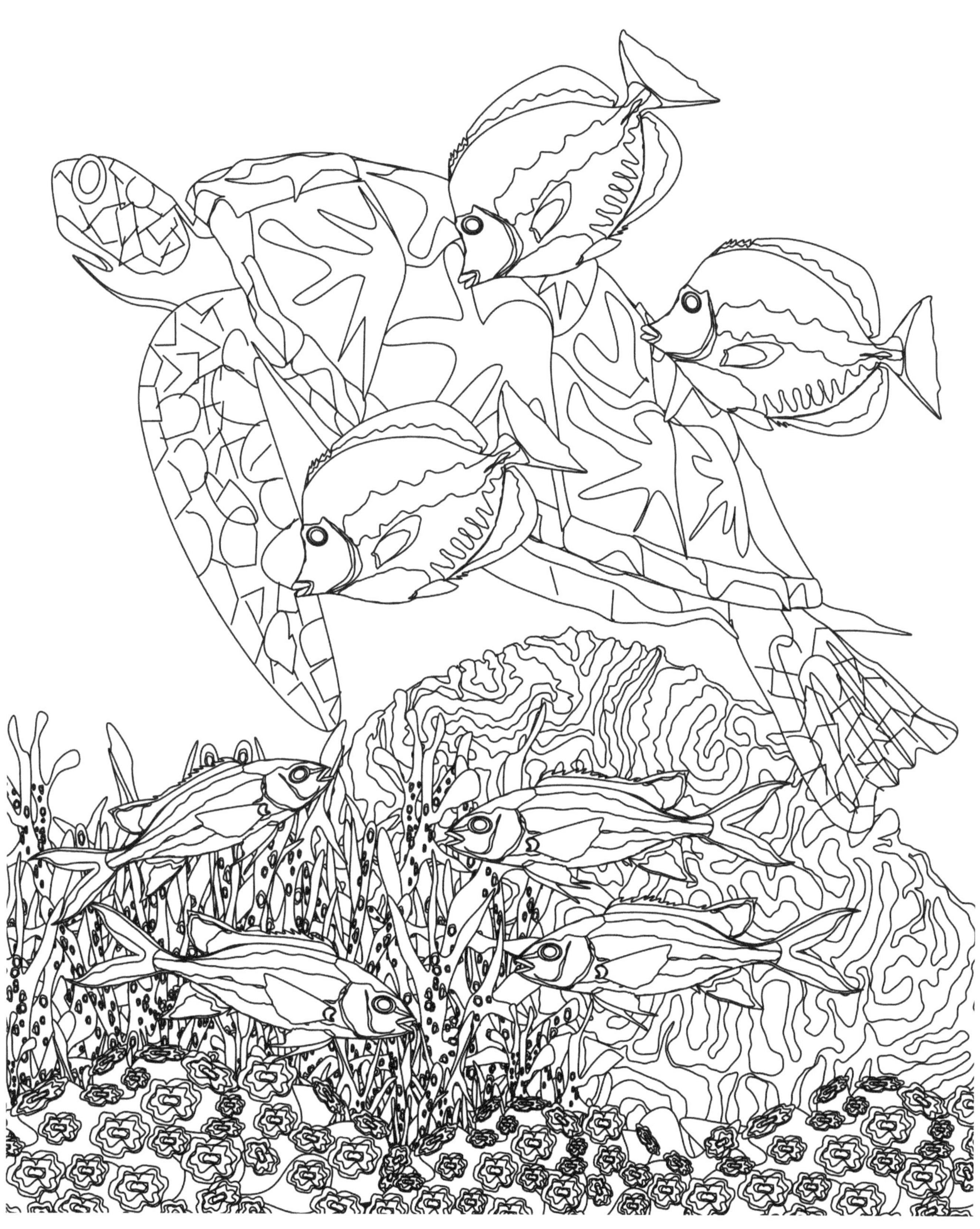

THIS PAGE LEFT INTENTIONALLY BLANK

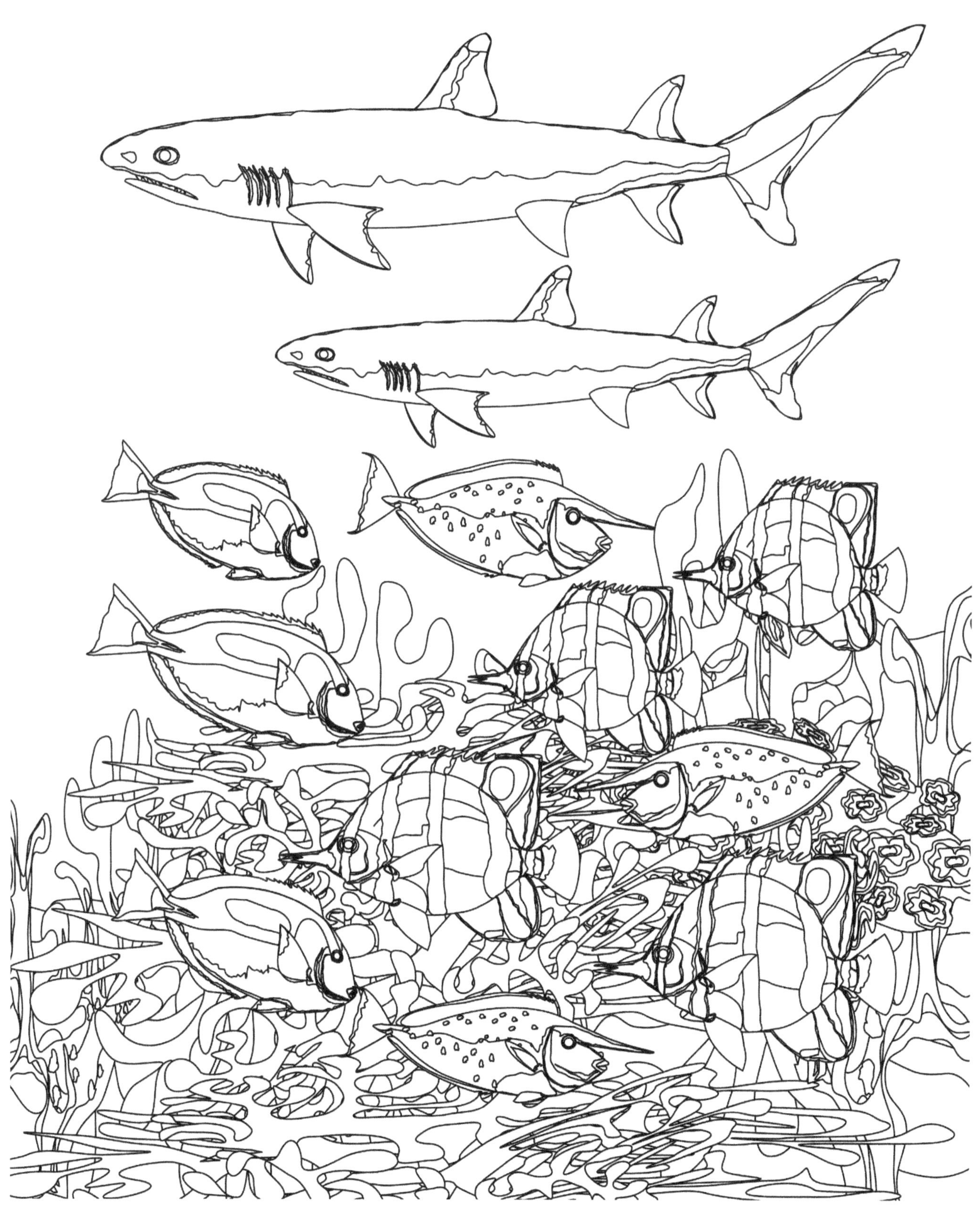

THIS PAGE LEFT INTENTIONALLY BLANK

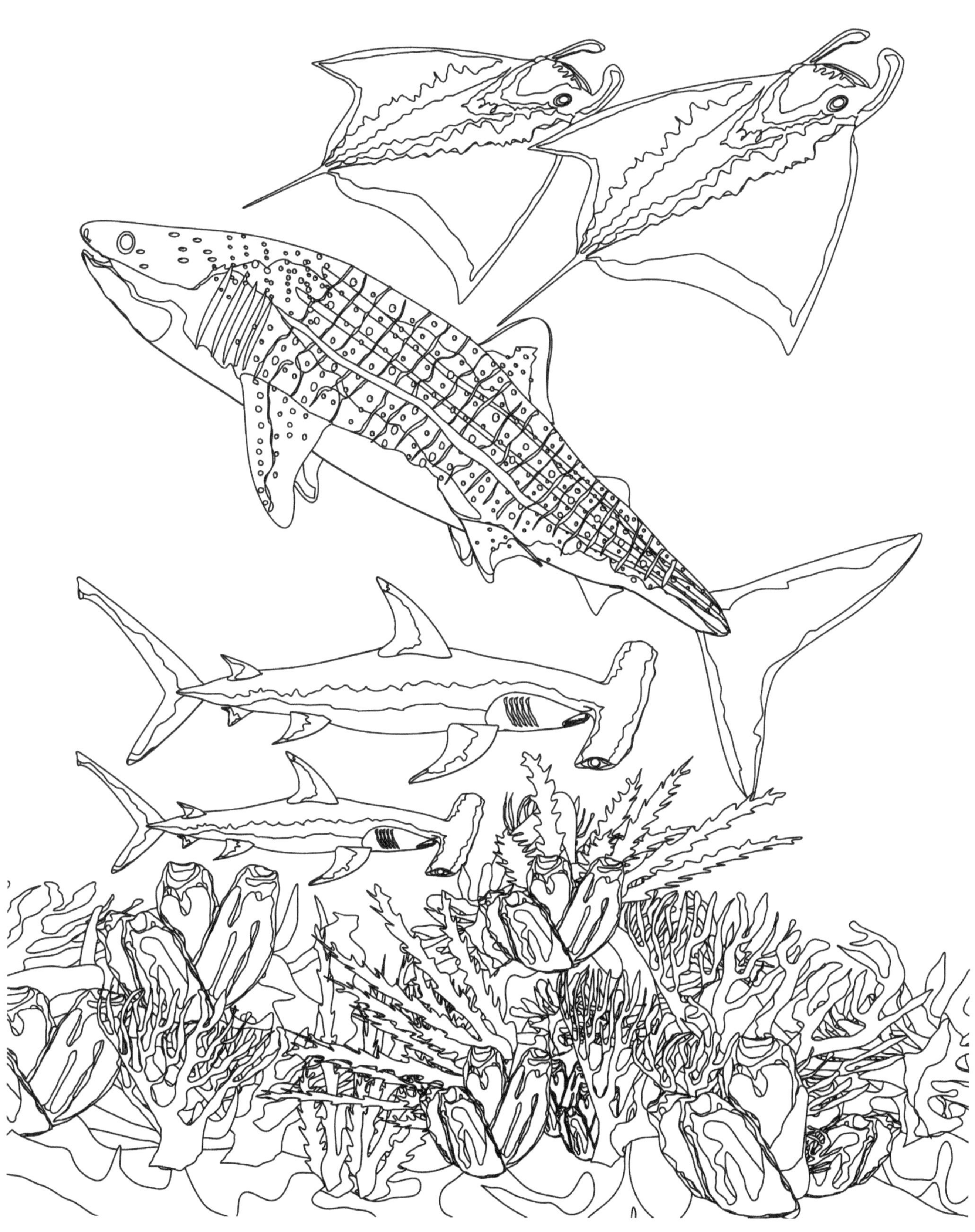

THIS PAGE LEFT INTENTIONALLY BLANK

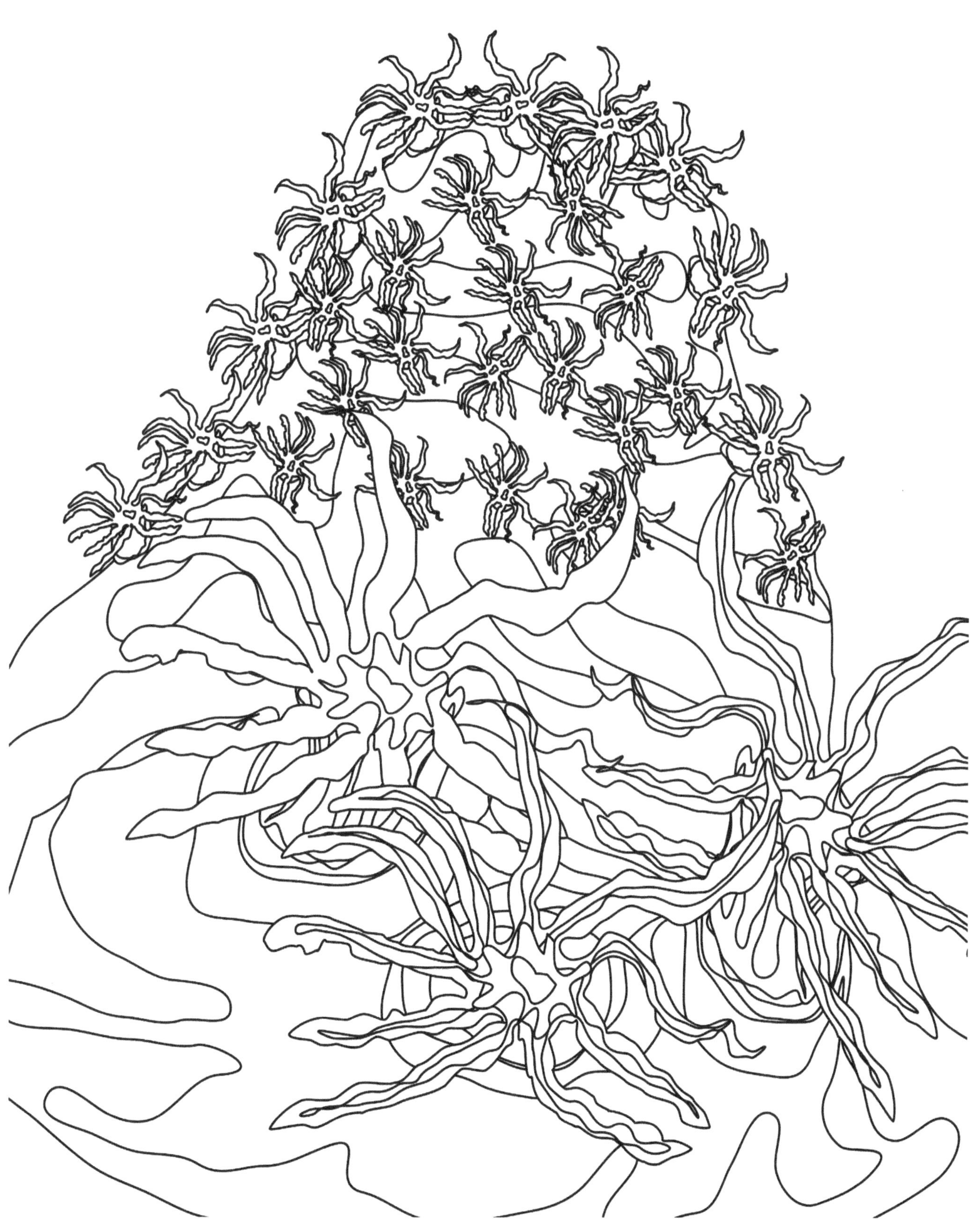

THIS PAGE LEFT INTENTIONALLY BLANK

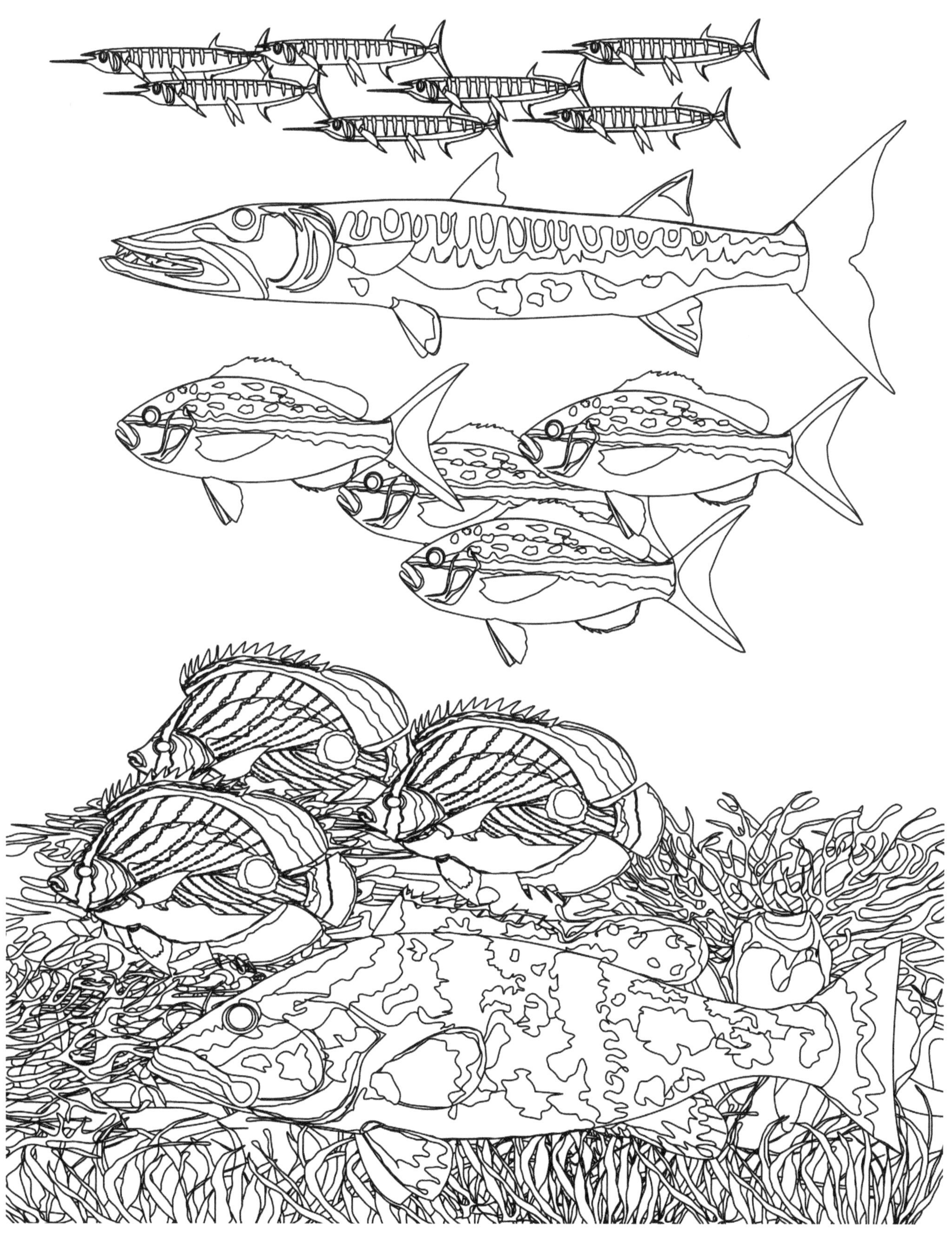

THIS PAGE LEFT INTENTIONALLY BLANK

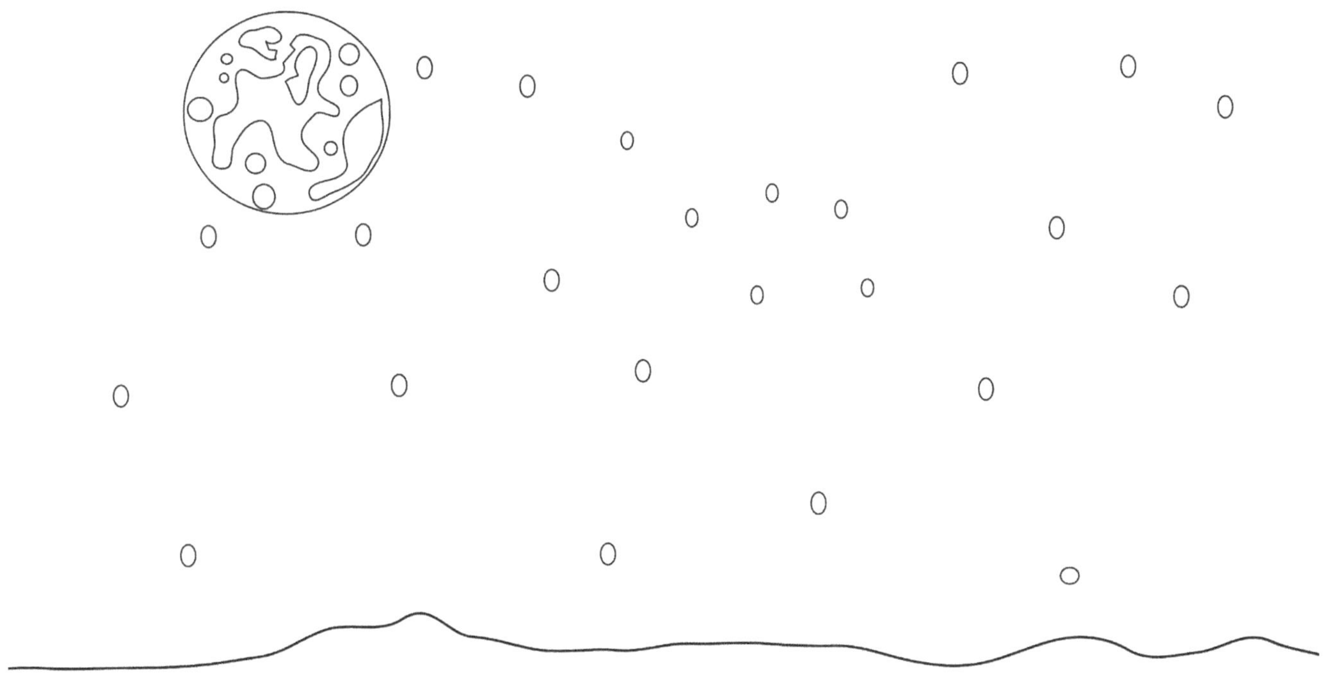
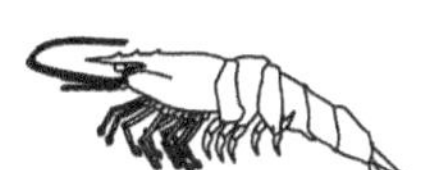
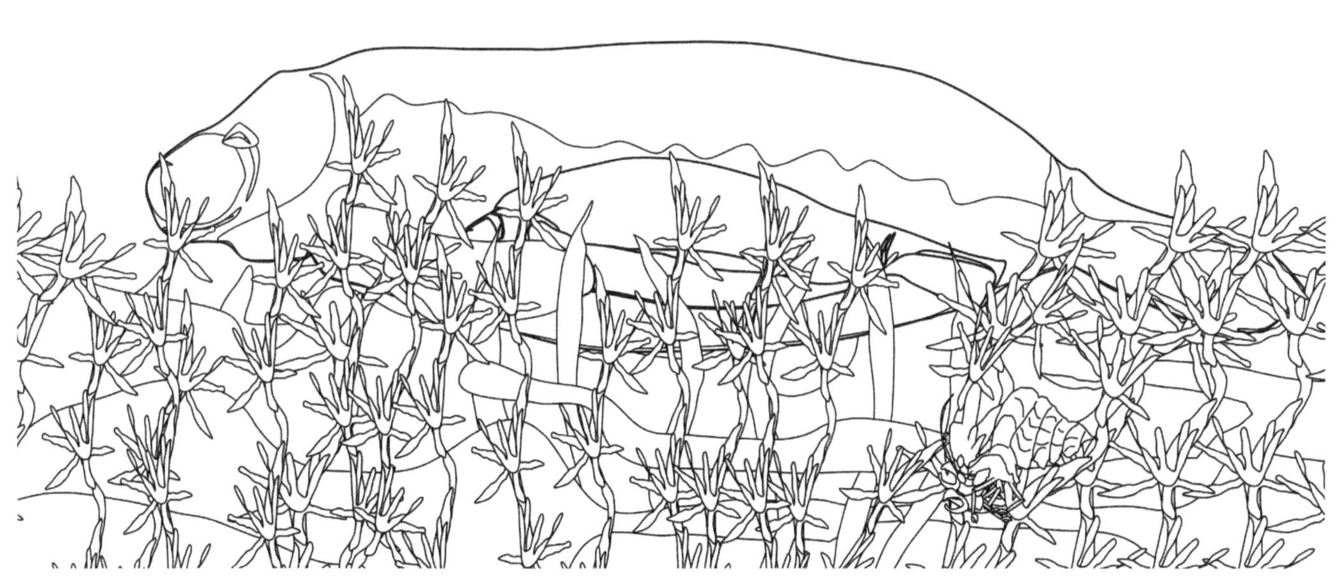

THIS PAGE LEFT INTENTIONALLY BLANK

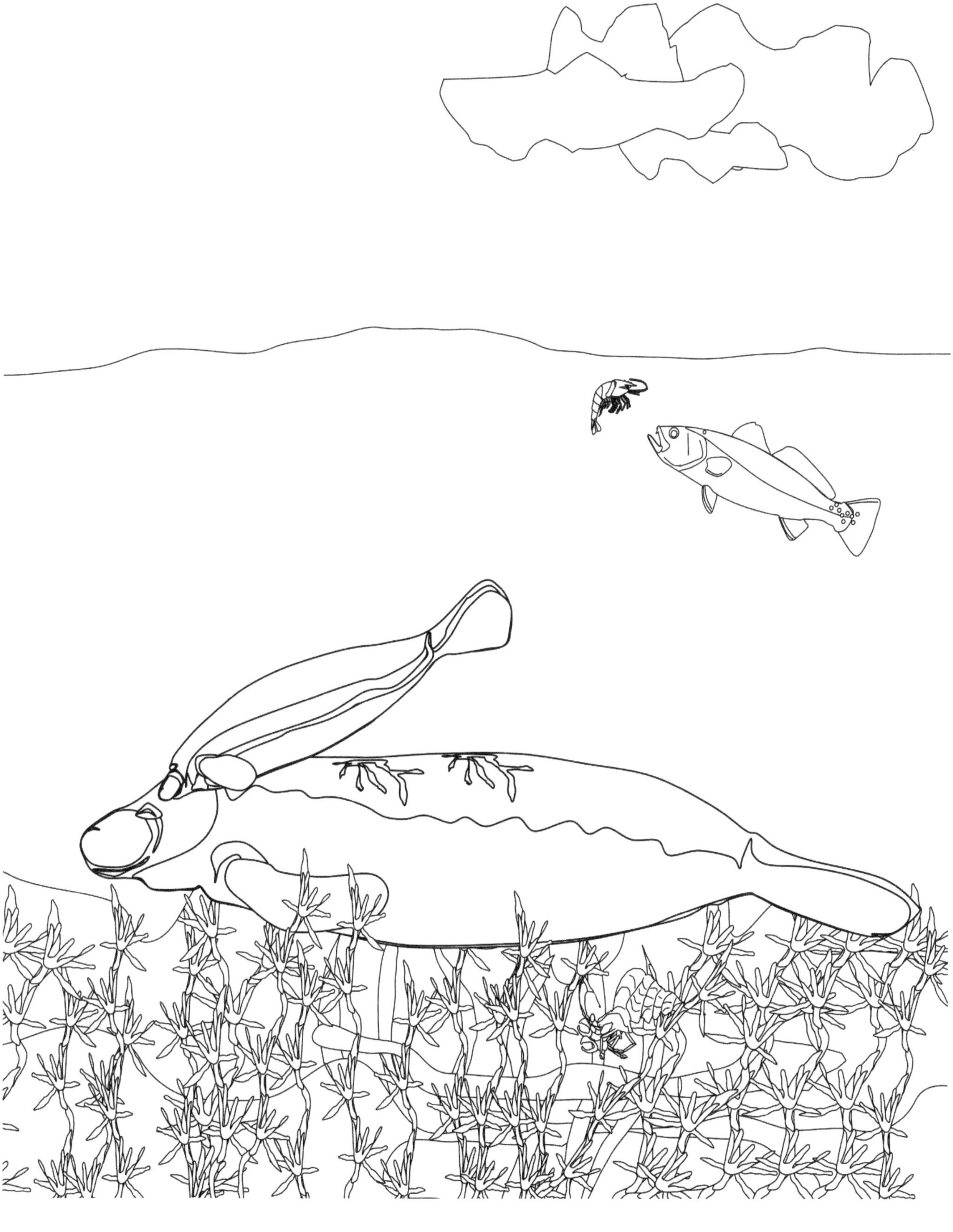

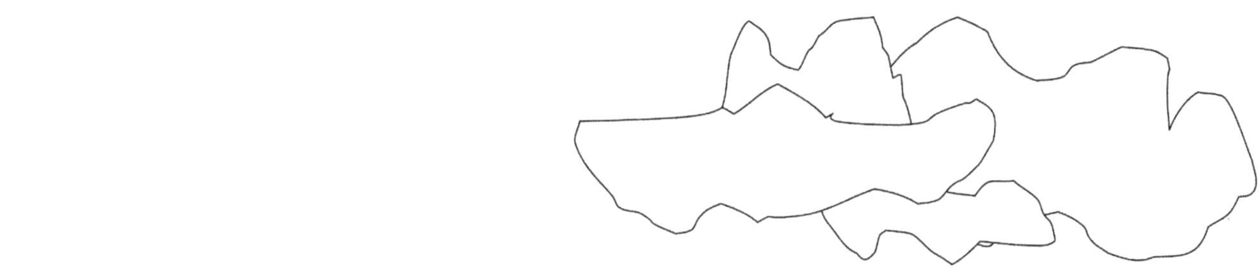

THIS PAGE LEFT INTENTIONALLY BLANK

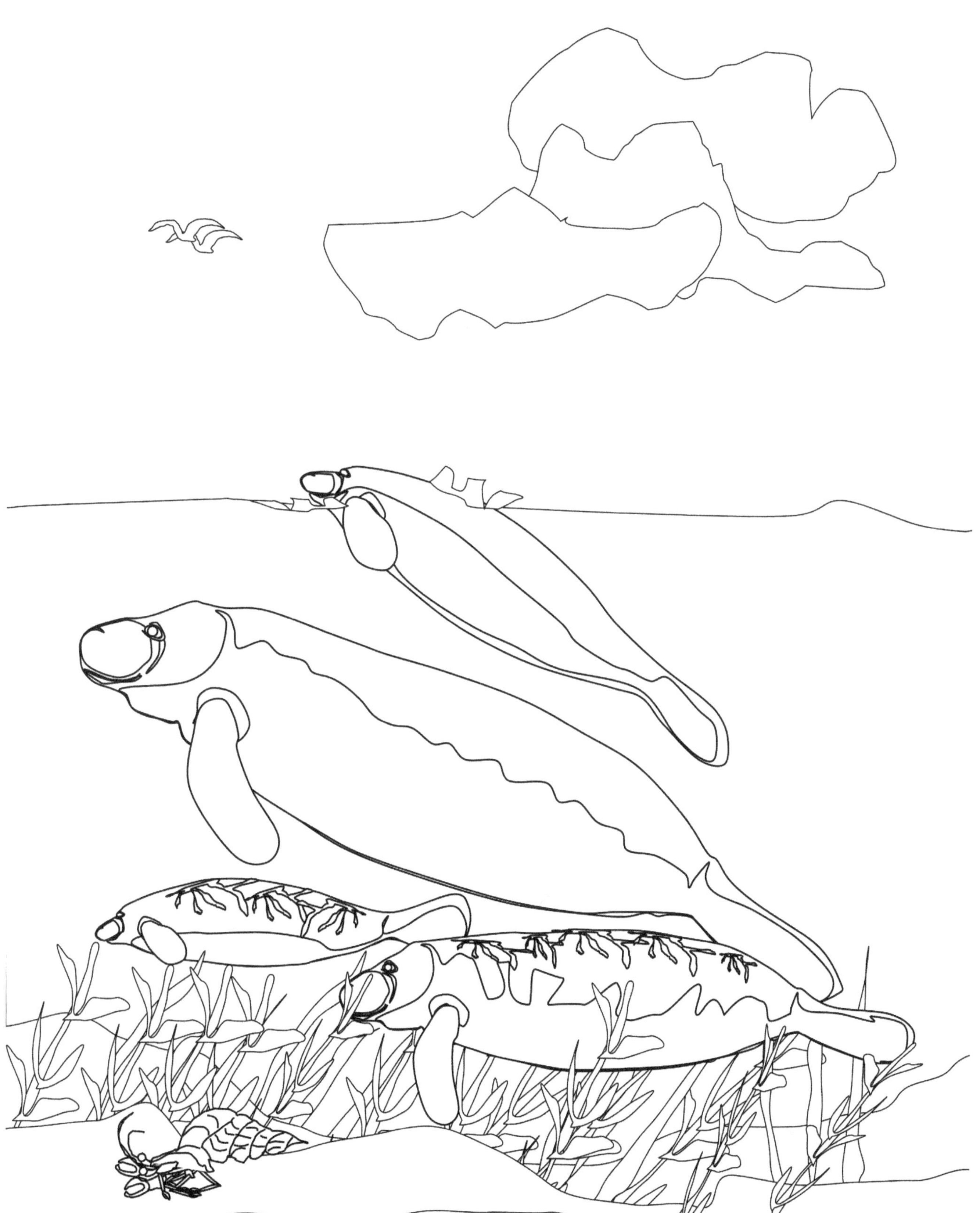

THIS PAGE LEFT INTENTIONALLY BLANK

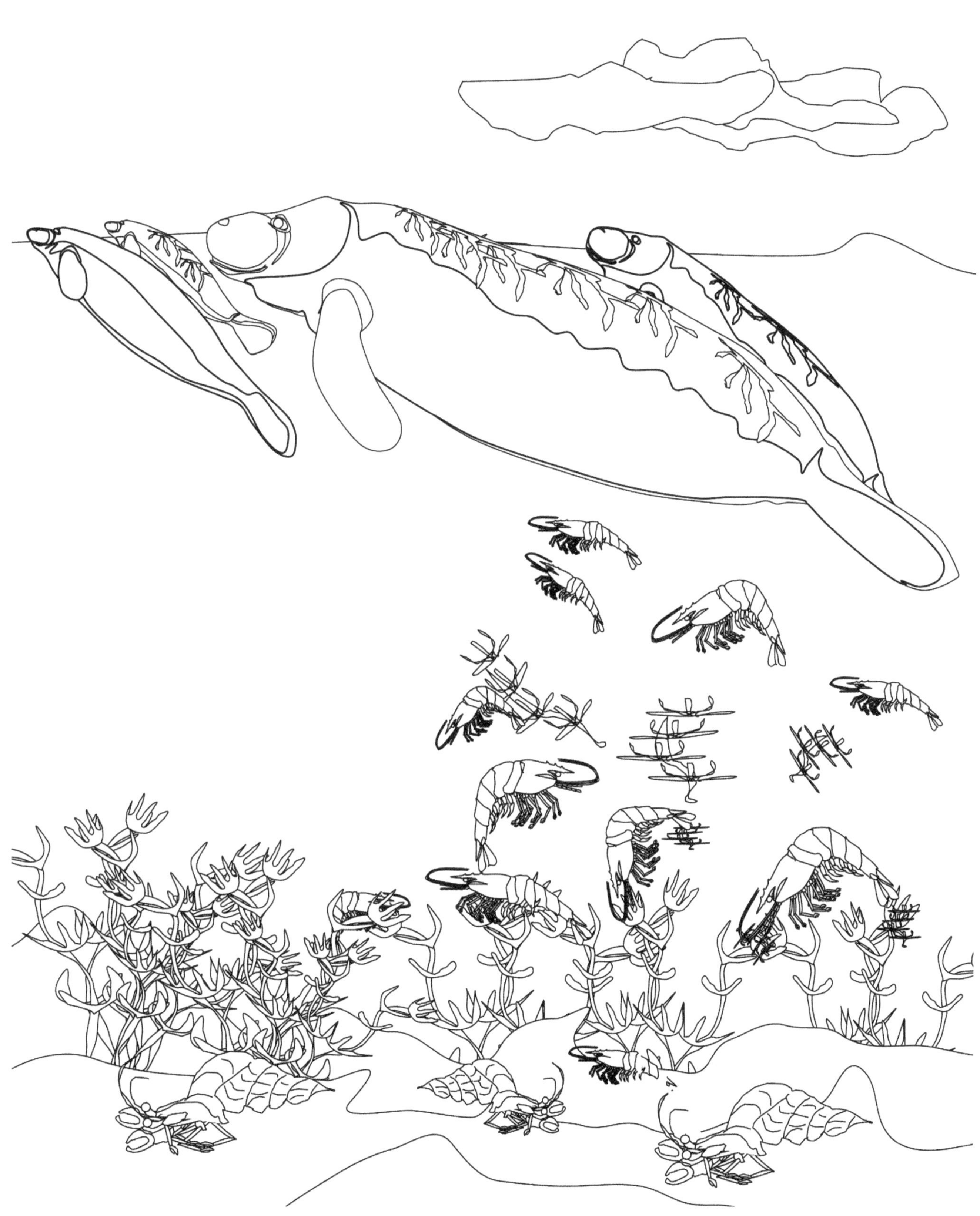

THIS PAGE LEFT INTENTIONALLY BLANK

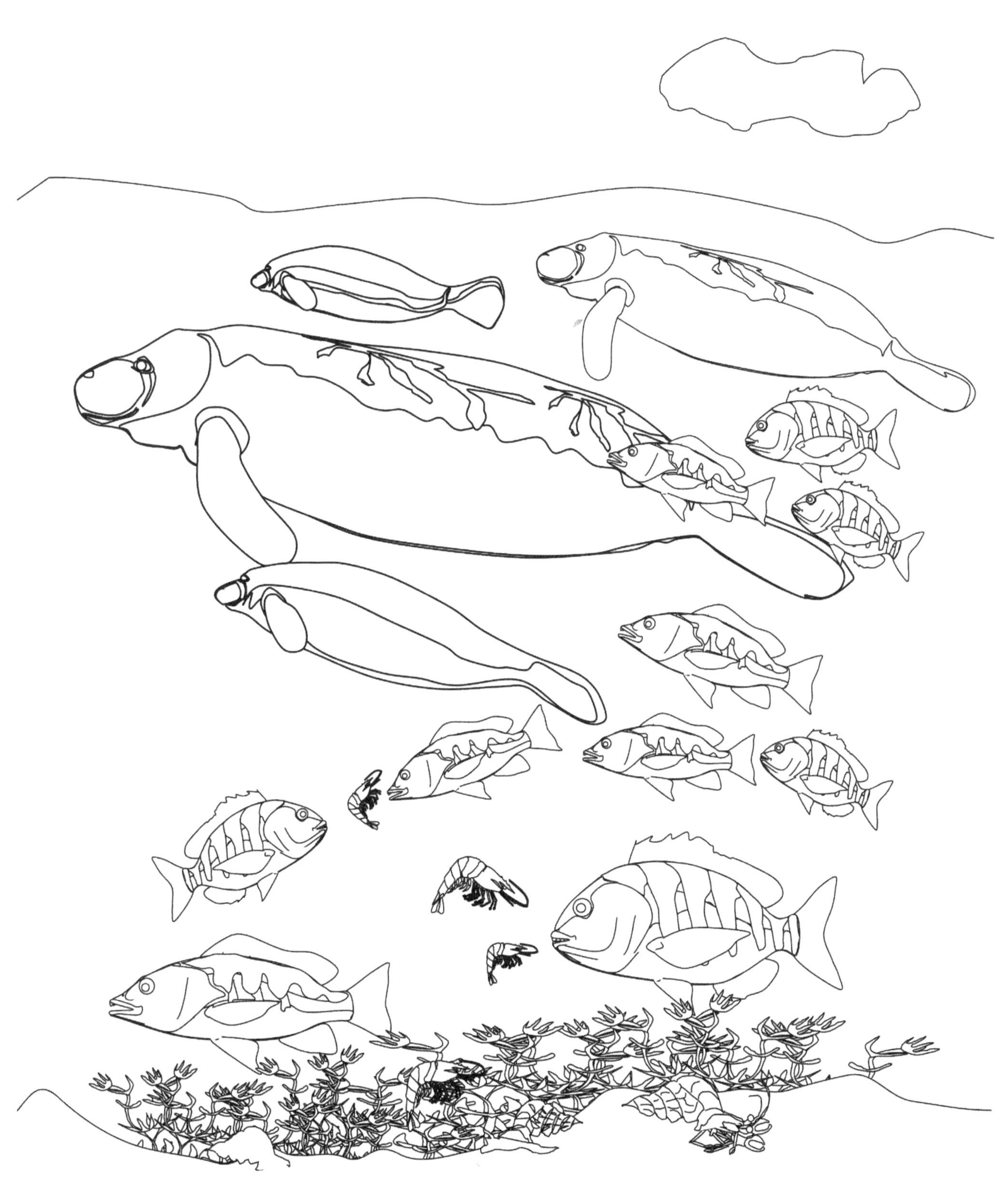

THIS PAGE LEFT INTENTIONALLY BLANK

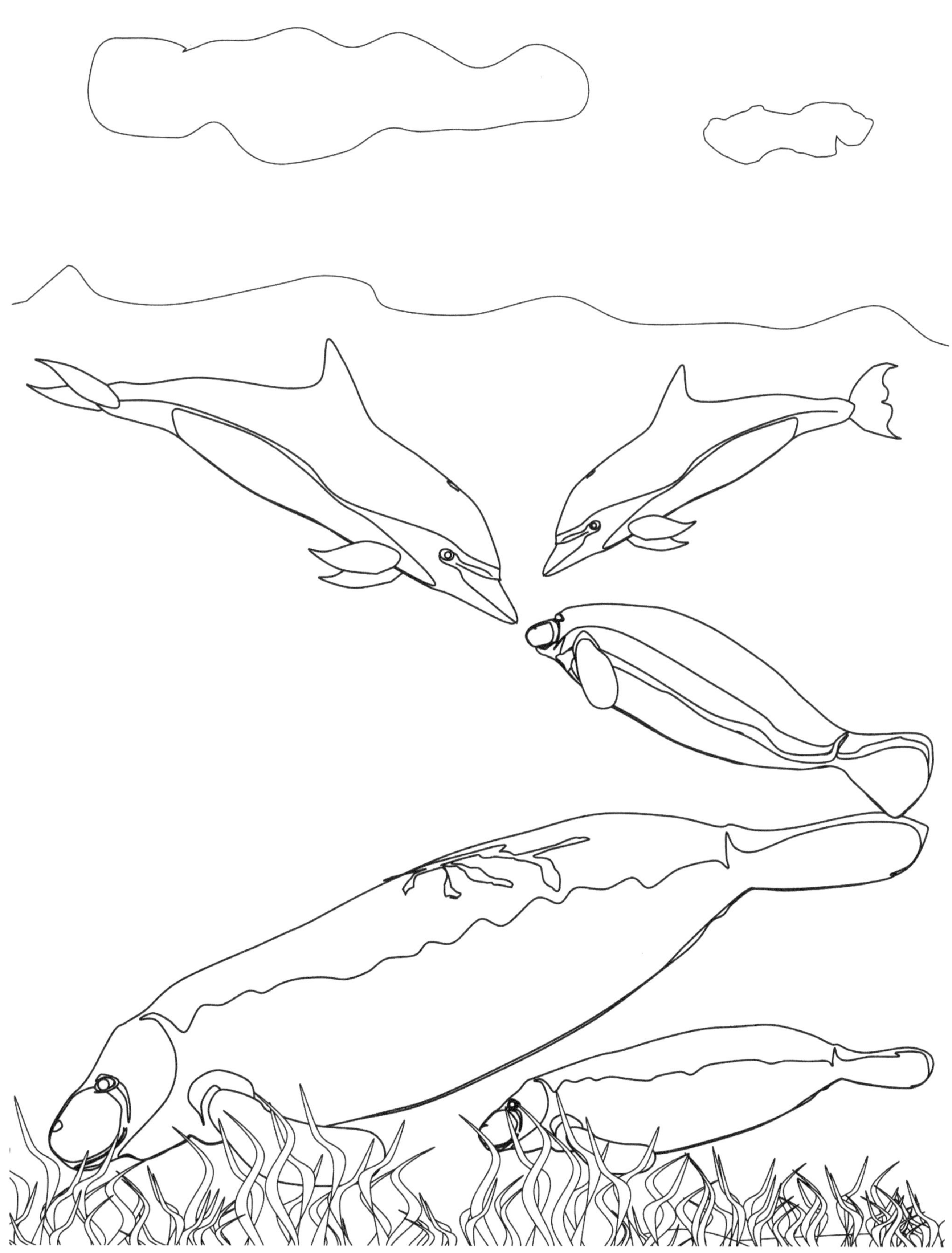

THIS PAGE LEFT INTENTIONALLY BLANK

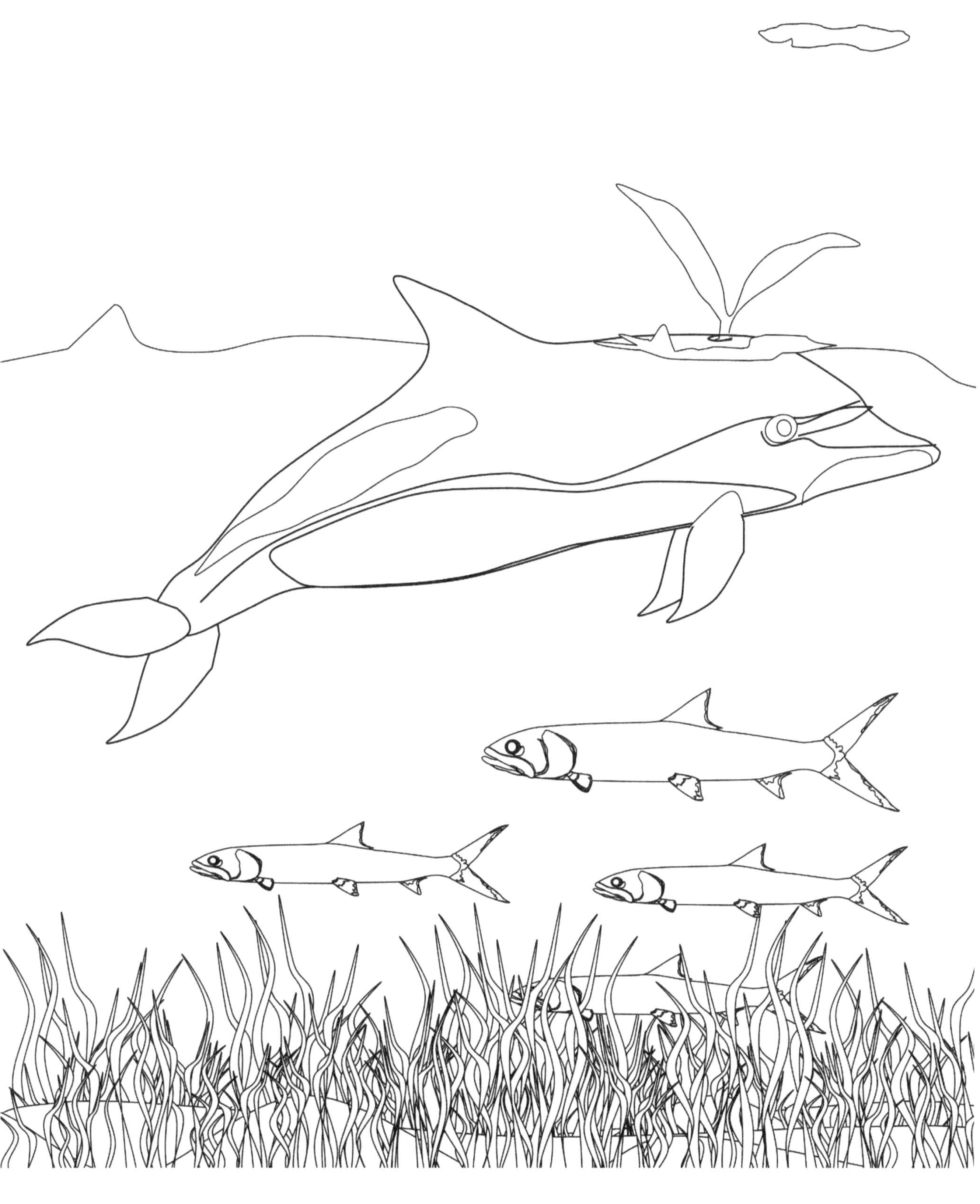

THIS PAGE LEFT INTENTIONALLY BLANK

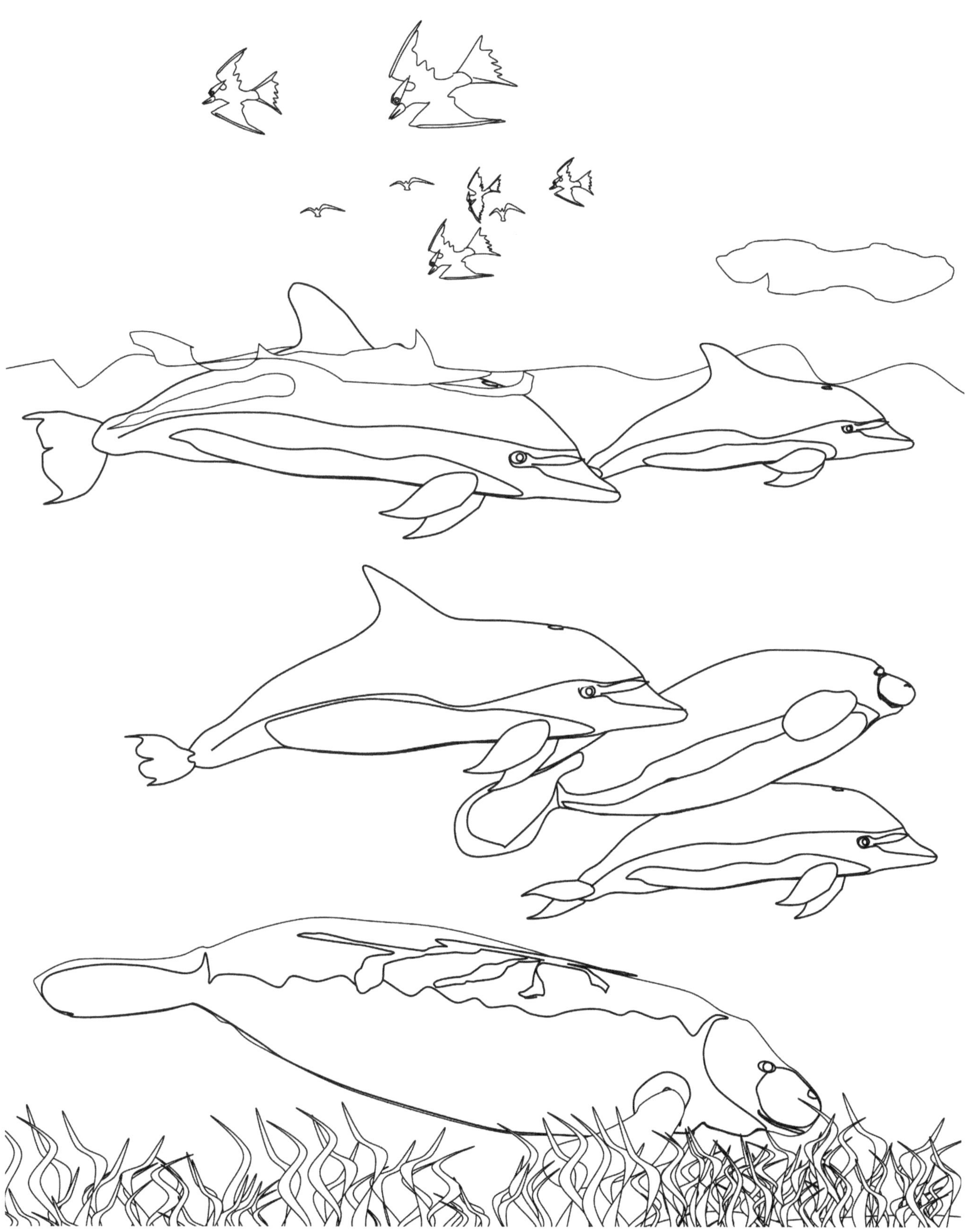

THIS PAGE LEFT INTENTIONALLY BLANK

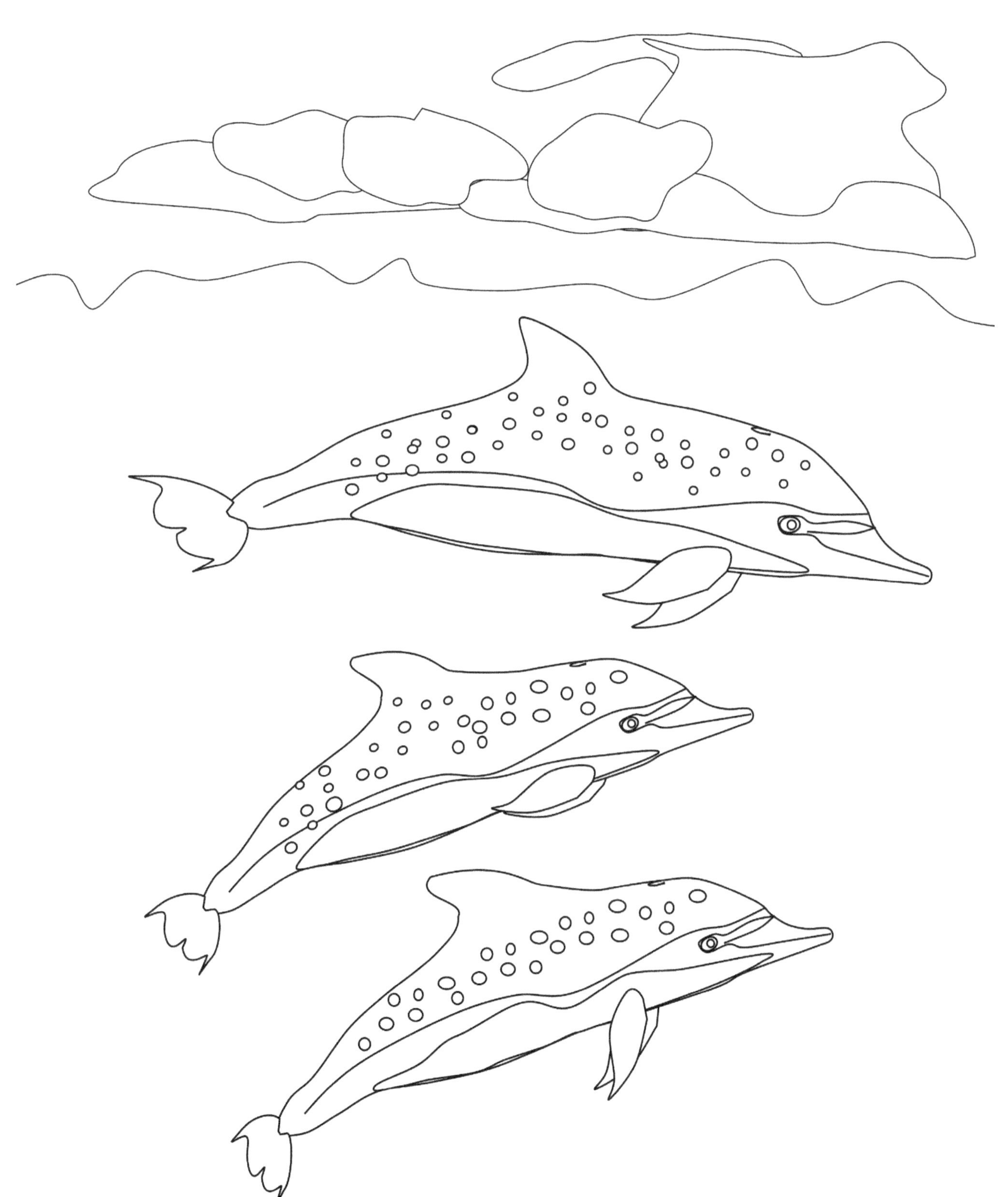

THIS PAGE LEFT INTENTIONALLY BLANK

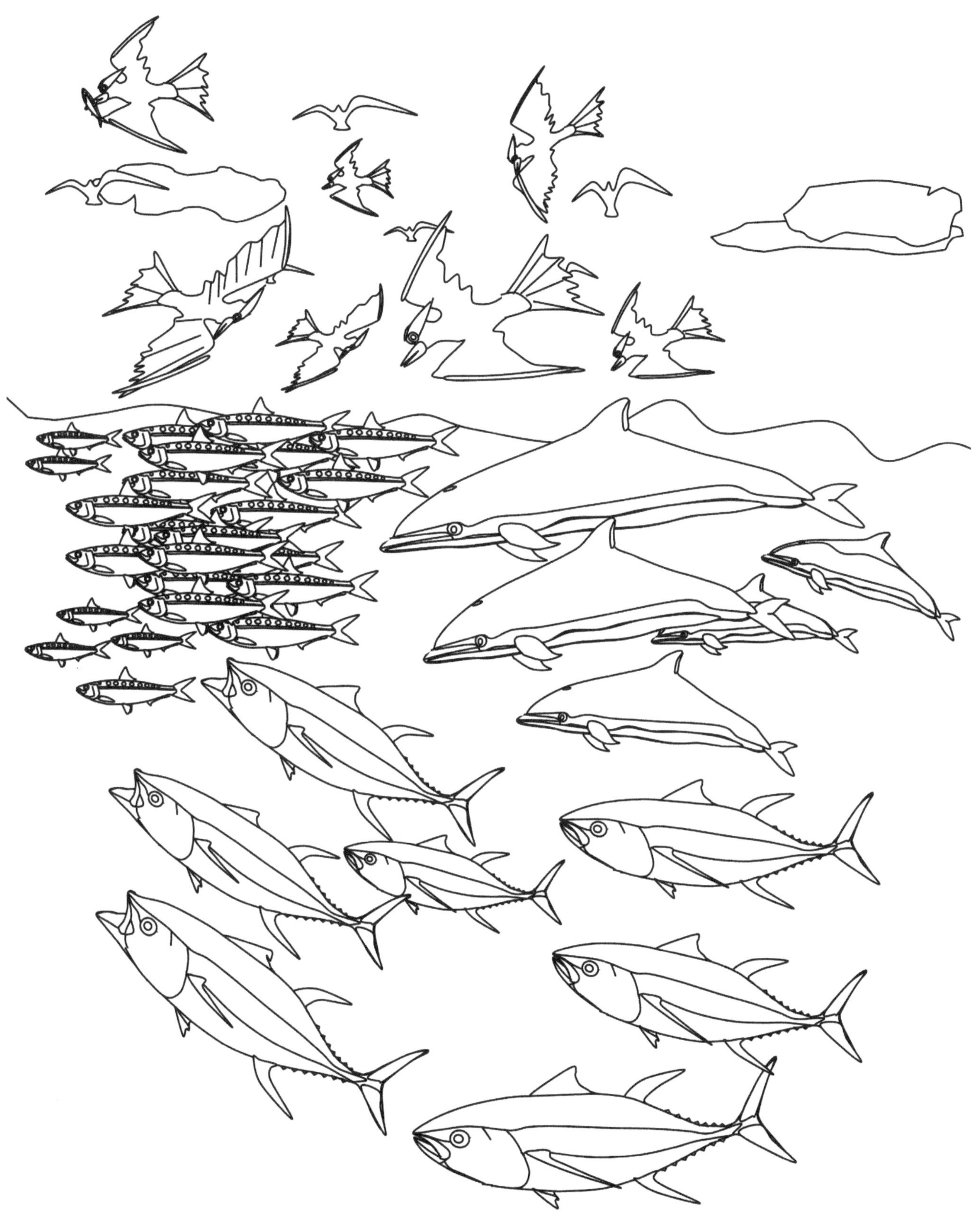

THIS PAGE LEFT INTENTIONALLY BLANK

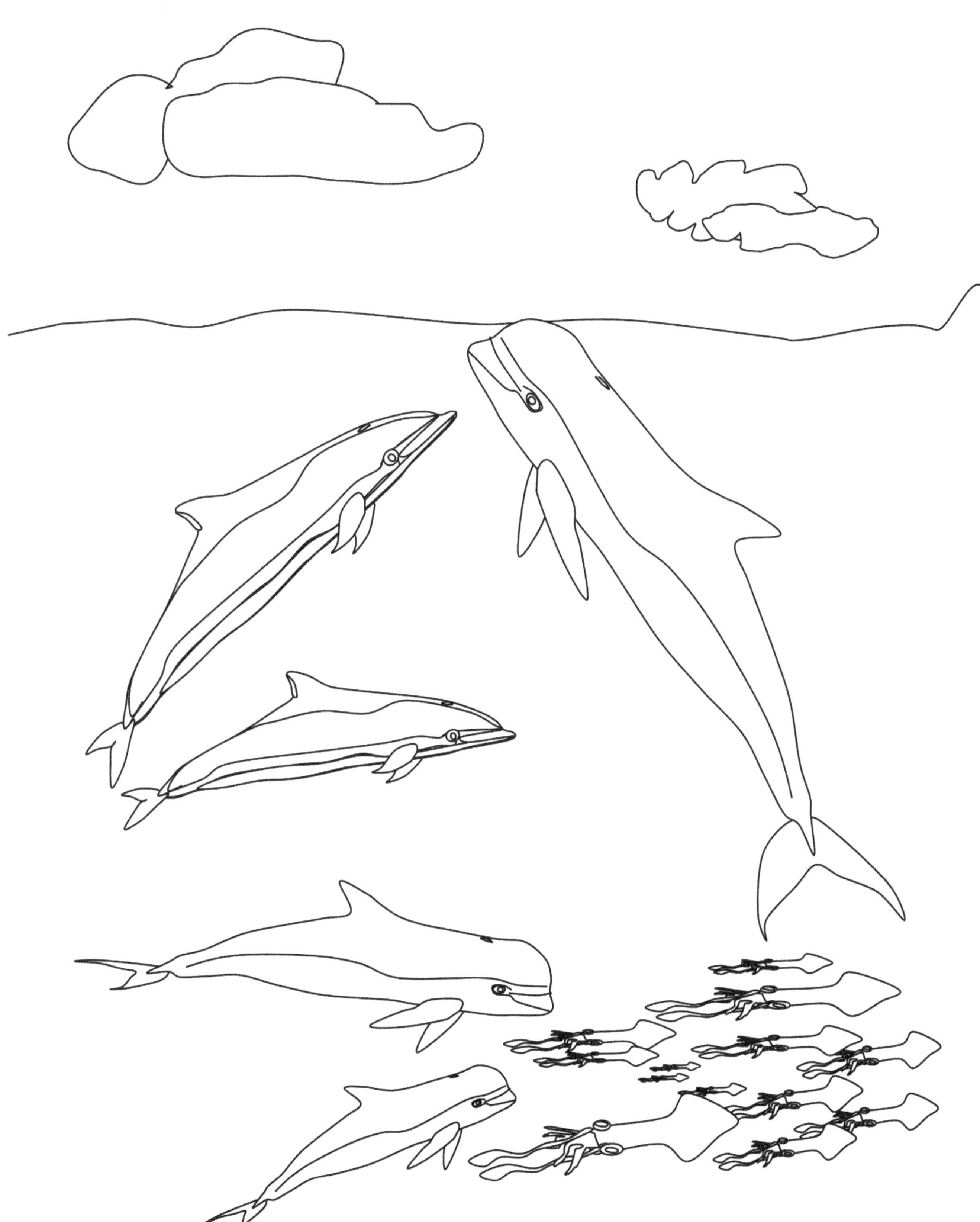

THIS PAGE LEFT INTENTIONALLY BLANK

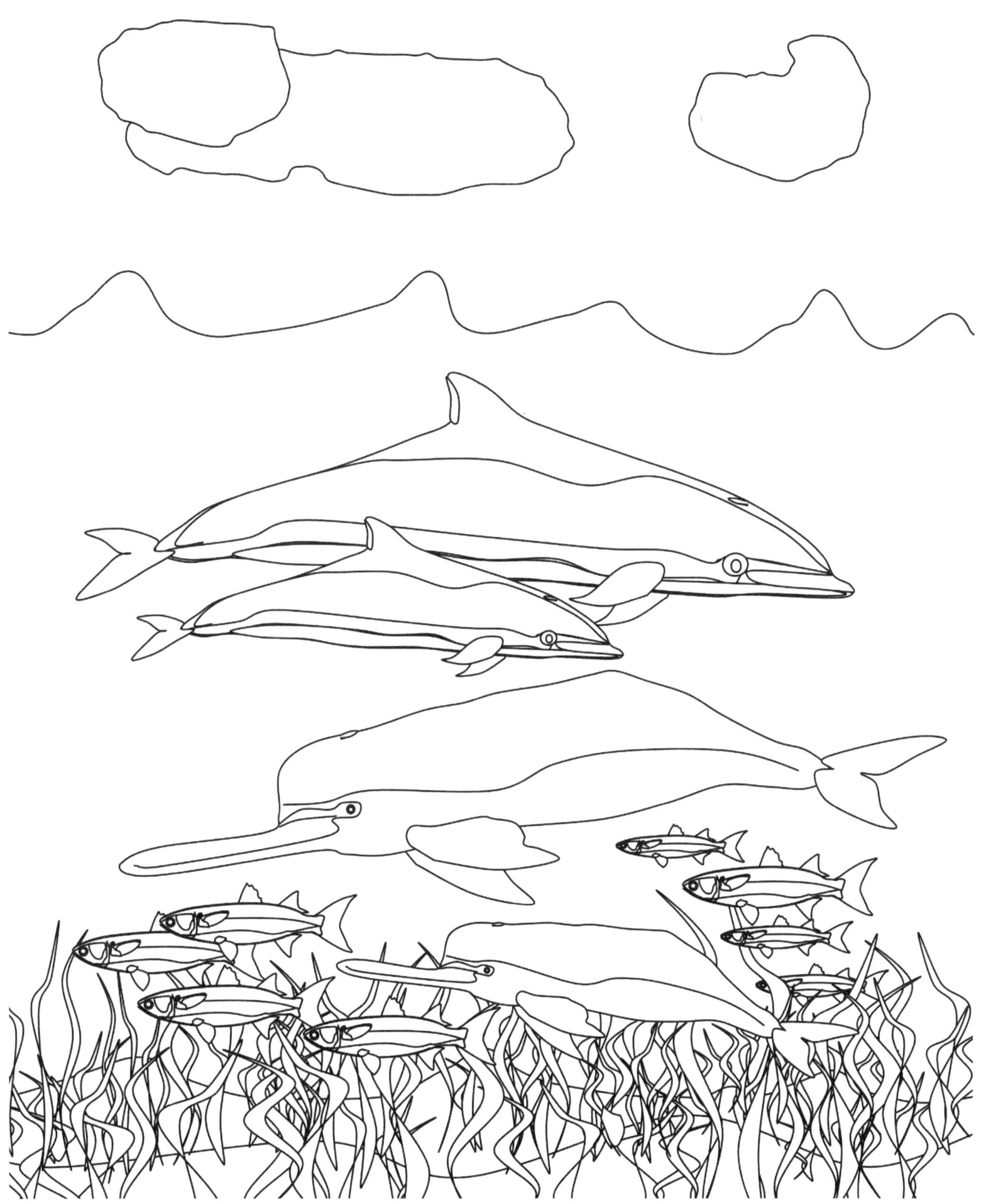

THIS PAGE LEFT INTENTIONALLY BLANK

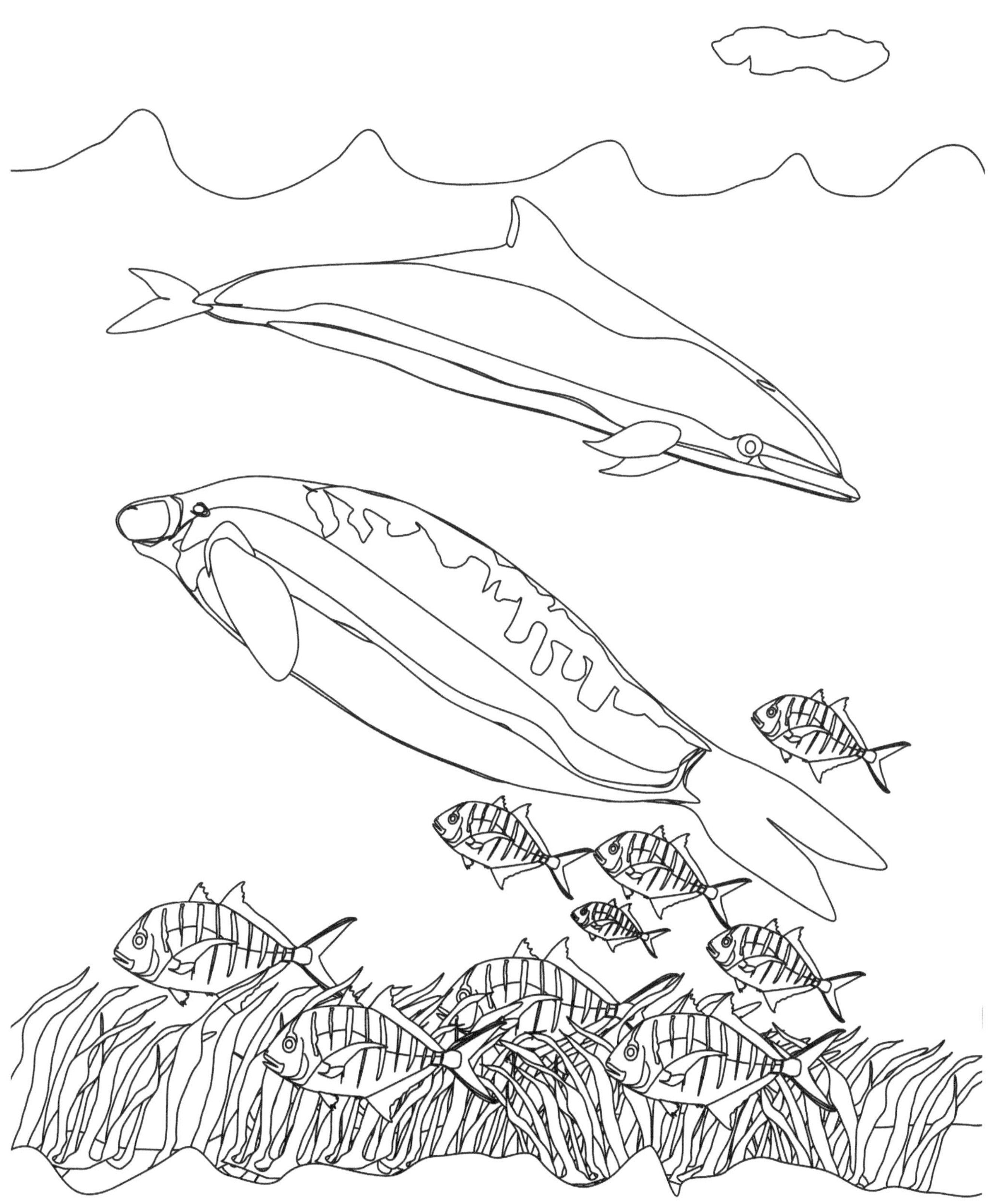

THIS PAGE LEFT INTENTIONALLY BLANK

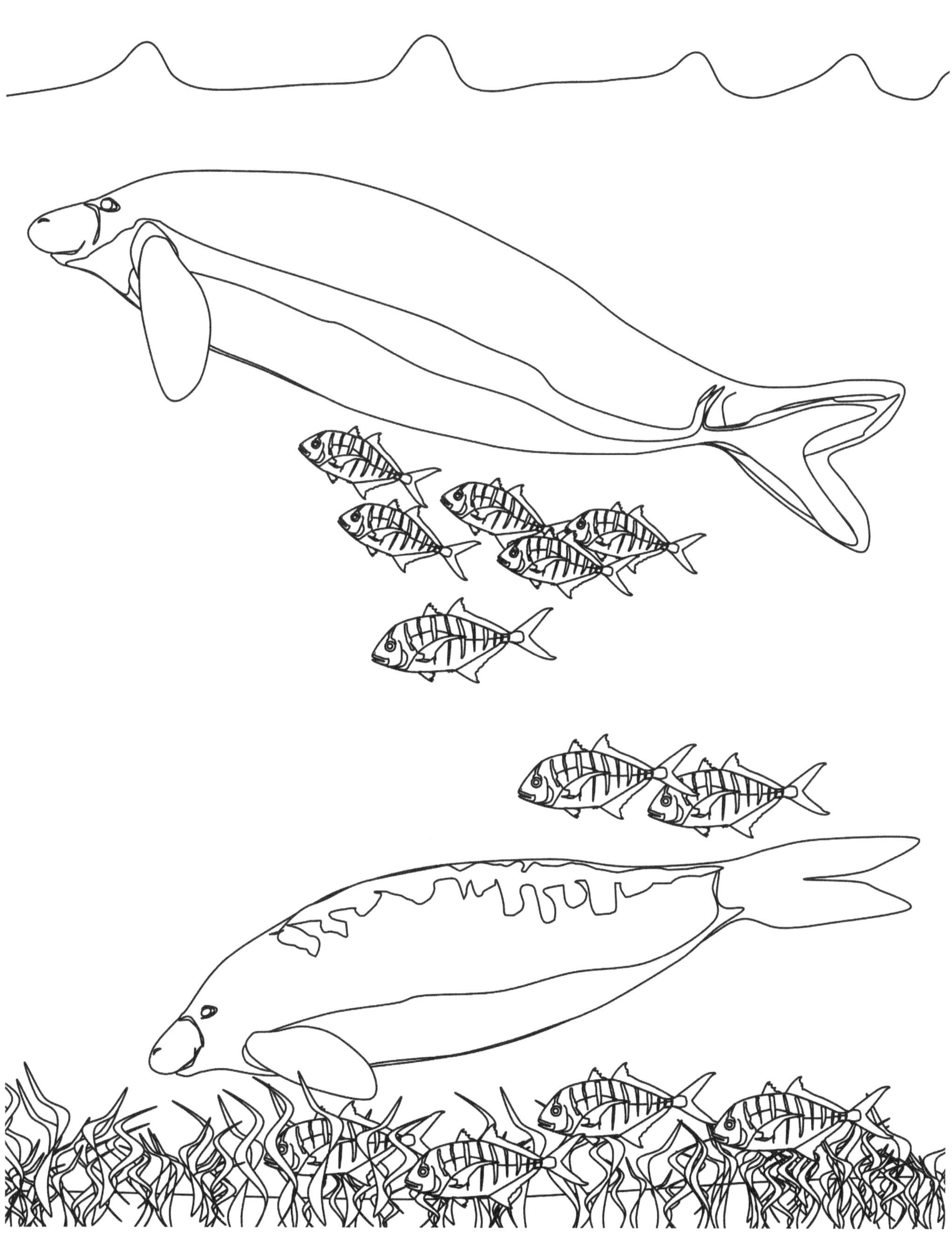

THIS PAGE LEFT INTENTIONALLY BLANK

Page #	Where?	What?
3	Tropical Northern Atlantic Ocean (as off the Florida Keys)	A Sargasso weed mat, with triggerfish, blue runners, mahi-mahi (dolphin fish), Little Tunny, and a Wahoo.
5	Open Tropical Ocean (any)	Skipjack Tuna school to avoid a pair of Black Marlin, while a Mako shark lurks below.
7	Arctic Ocean	A family of Narwahls, male (with tusk), female, and calf, below ice.
9	Southern Ocean near Antarctica	A pair of Minke whales swim between schools of krill, Antarctic Silverfish, and squid.
11	Ocean ice pack near Antarctica	Emperor Penguins chase krill, which are feeding under the ice edge. In the krill under the ice is an icefish. Below the penguins swims a Weddell seal.
13	Ocean near Antarctica	A pair of blue whales, and a trio of Minke whales feed on clouds of krill. Below swims a pair of Orcas.
15	Deep Southern Ocean near Antarctica	Three Collossal Squid track four Antarctic Toothfish.
17	Deep Southern Ocean near Antarctica (extreme ice edge)	Icefish, velvet cod, grenadier, and an octopus occupy an area of soft cold water corals, gorgonians, and sponges.
19	Ocean near Antarctica	Emperor Penguins chase krill, icefish, and silverfish near the surface.
21	Southern Ocean near Antarctica	An arrangement of Antarctic associated fish, including toohfish, silverfish, eel cod, velvet cod, grenadier, and icefish.
23	Southern Ocean near Antarctica	Weddell seals chase krill, squid, and a grenadier.
25	Winter ice near Antarctica	A Weddell seals keeps an ice hole ocean by chewing the ice, under the winter sky and Southern lights.
27	rocky coast (or island) near Antarctica	Southern Elephant seals, with a beachmaster male, and a group of females and pups.

Page #	Where?	What?
29	Ocean ice pack near Antarctica	Emperor Penguins escape to the water to feed, avoiding a pair of Leopard Seals. One of the leopard seals is chasing a Weddell seal.
31	Ocean ice pack near Antarctica	A female Leopard seal raised a rare pair of pups on the ice, while Leopard and Weddell seals swin below.
33	Ocean ice pack near Antarctica	Emperor Penguins stand on the ice, while others swim in the waters below.
35	Rocky beach near Antarctica	Rockhopper Penguins on a beach with males, females, and chicks.
37	Ocean ice pack near Antarctica	A groups of Emperor penguinsstand on the ice, while Perels and Skuas fly above, and a Skua stares down a penguin. An elephant seal swims below.
39	Land near Antarctica	A Skua and chick on ground, while krill feed under nearby ice.
41	Deep Ocean	Siphonophore Angler Jellyfish and Ctenophore Comb Jellies light the darkness.
43	A coastal river in Northern California	Coho (Silver) salmon climb rapids to get to their spawning grounds.
45	Upper Amazon River	Bicuda, Suckermouth Catfish, Tetras, and Headstanders swim in the rapids.
47	Deep Pacific Ocean	Swordfish chase Humboldt squid and a school of Escolar
49	Sacramento River Delta in California	White Sturgeon swim among mussel and clam beds, while Striped Bass and Steelhead swim above.
51	Amazon River	A biara chases sawtooth anchovies, above pacu, armored catfish, tetras, and highbacked headstanders.
53	Deep Ocean	Sperm Whales chase giant squid, one whale rams and bites into an inking giant squid.
55	San Fransisco Bay	Schools of Pacific anchovies and four leopard sharks swim above bat rays, and stingrays.

Page #	Where?	What?
57	Amazon River	Pellona chase sawtooth anchovies above pacu, pencilfish, tetras, prochilodus, tiger shovelnosed catfish, sawtooth catfish, and armored catfish.
59	Deep Ocean	Oarfish chase lanternfish.
61	San Fransisco Bay	Sevengill sharks hunt leopard sharks and rays.
63	Amazon River	Pacu and and elongate hatchetfish feed on figs as they fall from a tree, below them are silver dollar fish, watermellon fish, and discus fish.
65	Pacific Ocean off of California	Flag rockfish, vermillion rockfish, boccacio, and cabazon swim above a rockpile.
67	Pacific ocean, near a beach, southern California (Belmont Shores for example)	Mullet, mackerel, halibut, and guitarfish swim around the sands.
69	Amazon River (backwater)	Redbelly piranha, freshwater angelfish, and oscars hide under lillypads. A damselfly sits on a pad.
71	Deep Ocean	Dumbo squid, vampire octopus, and glass octopus swim the dark depths.
73	Amazon River	Giant river turtles cover a sandbar, while two spotted sorubim and a motoro stingray sit below.
75	Sea of Cortez beach off of Baha California Sur	Roosterfish chase and pin anchovies against the surf.
77	Deep ocean near the continental shelf	Ratfish swim near the bottom.
79	Farallon Islands, Pacific Ocean, California	A colony of Northern Elephant Seals sits above white shark filled waters, where a sea lion tries to avoid death.
81	Amazon River	Black caiman lounge on a mud bank near tall grasses.
83	Deep Ocean	A two female Anglerfish, a parasitic male, and a free swimming male. Lantern fish swim among them, and one lanternfish is being lured into doom.

Page #	Where?	What?
85	Southern California Pacific Ocean	Orcas chase a white shark.
87	Amazon River	An anaconda is about to grab a caiman while redtail catfish swim below.
89	Deep Ocean	An arrangement of Viperfish and Dragonfish
91	Kelp Bed off southern California Channel Islands	A kelp forest with Garabaldi, calico (kelp) bass, rockfish, white seabass, and giant seabass.
93	Amazon river (flooded forest)	A matamata turtle, Surinam toads, oscars, and tetras among leaf debris.
95	Deep Ocean	Amphipods, euphasids, and a deep sea shrimp.
97	Pacific Ocean Kelp Forest off of Southern California	Kelp Greenlings hide and swim near the kelp.
99	Amazon river (flooded forest)	Boto river dolphins look for fish among the flooded trees, while an arrowana hunts hatchetfish and a school of tetras above, and tetras, a peacock bass, discus fish, and festivus try to hide below.
101	Deep sea (north Atlantic ocean)	Conger eels hunt smaller fishes (lanternfish roughly) while hagfish swim, and crabs crawl the bottom.
103	Pacific Ocean Kelp Forest, Southern California (as off of La Jolla)	California barracuda, calico bass, opaleye, and rockfish, schools of mackeral and green jacks (scad) swim nearby. Bonito attack anchovies in open water.
105	Amazon River	Tucuxi river dolphins chase pellona
107	Deep Ocean	A megamouth shark, three frill sharks, and two sixgill sharks swim in the deep.
109	Pacific Ocean Kelp Forest as off of Alaska	Sea otters examine sea urchins (which they eat, and which in turn eat kelp)
111	Amazon River	Amazon river Manatees feed and swim, followed by cichlids and pacu.
113	Deep Ocean	A deep sea 'black smoker' vent, surrounded by tube worms, with amphipods and euphasids, clams, and crabs.

Page #	Where?	What?
115	Pacific Ocean rocky kelp	Male California sheephead, rockfish (copper, flag), lingcod, pacific wolf eels, and sculpins, near rocks with kelp.
117	Amazon River	A pair of bull sharks swim above redtail catfish and a motoro stingray, with a school of anchovies above.
119	Deep Ocean	Giant Deep Sea Jellyfish and Crosotta jellyfish
121	Pacific Ocean off of Southern California or Baha California	A kelp paddy with scads, california yellowtail, and a Mahi-Mahi. Shearwaters and gulls fly above.
123	Amazon River, backwater.	Amazon freshwater puffer fish feed on snails.
125	Deep sea off of Eastern Africa	Coelacanth swim near a trench
127	Pacific Ocean off of California	Bluefin tuna feed on sardines, while a striped marlin swims below, and a mola (ocean sunfish) basks on the surface.
129	Amazon River	Amazon river otters on a sand bank, while another chases piranhas and tetras below.
131	Deep Ocean	Pelican eels feed on lantern fish.
133	Pacific Ocean off of California	California gray whales migrate.
135	Amazon River (backwater)	Electric eels (actually a type of knifefish) lurk among flooded timber.
137	Amazon River (backwater)	A pair of arapaima among water weeds, with cichlids (festivus, oscars) and tetras
139	Deep Ocean	Isopods, and acorn and deep sea sea worms.
141	Great Barrier Reef	A grey reef shark above African pompano, a pai of yellowtail barracuda, clown triggerfish, oval butterflyfish and anthias.
143	Carribean sea	Blue Tangs, queen angelfish, and a Cubera snapper above a chain moray eel.
145	South Pacifc	McCosker's flasher wrasse and spottlined flasher wrasse
147	South Pacifc	Big belly seahorses and a harlequin ghost pipefish.

Page #	Where?	What?
149	Hawaii Coral Reef	Tigershark above humu wedge reef triggerfish, green jobfish, yellowstripe goatfish, thradfin butterflyfish, moontail bullseye, and sebae anemonefish.
151	Gulf of Mexico near Florida	Cobia chase a school of herring, a blacktip shark is over a trio of amberjack, a Goliath grouper, and a nurse shark.
153	Florida Keys Atlantic Reef	Three mutton snapper near a school of blue runners, above Bermuda chubs near a sea fan, near a gag grouper, near sergeant majors, and a hidden gag grouper below.
155	Hawaii ocean drop off (northeast shore of Maui for example)	Blue sea chubs hide from giant trevally. Three green jobfish are below.
157	Central America Pacific Ocean Reef	Crevalle Jacks and scads, near a Cubera snapper above Moorish Idols and Leather Bass, and a Jeweled Moray eel.
159	Florida Keys Atlantic Reef (ex: Looe Key Reef)	A scrawled filefish waits her turn while a blue parrotfish is cleaned by gobies. A cowfish swims below the brain coral.
161	Hawk Channel, Florida Keys	A school of ballyhoo are above a Cero mackerel, which is above a patch reef. The patch reef has French angelfish, sergeant majors, a queen triggerfish, a black grouper, a burrfish (porcupine puffer) , and a hiding razorfish.
163	South Pacific near Indonesia	Trevally and a sea krait (a snake) probe the corals for fish.
165	Red Sea	A pair of trevally swim above a pair of rainbow runners, a school of Moorish Idols, a school of Rosy goatfish, and a lionfish.
167	South Pacific near Indonesia	A chambered nautillus above south sea damselfish and a bignose unicornfish.
169	Florida Keys	A goby and pistol (snapping) shrimp guard a sponge. That popcorn sound you hear when snorkelling over a coral reef is made by lots of those tiny shrimp.

Page #	Where?	What?
171	Indo-pacific	Shrimpfish hover over a gorgonian.
173	Hawaii Coral Reef	Yellow tangs clean a green sea turtle, with blue chromis is the foreground (looking very big).
175	Great Barrier Reef	A pair of Whitetip reef sharks above Pallette Surgeonfish (made famous in a certain 'Finding' movie) with Whitemargin unicornfish and copperband butterflyfish.
177	South Pacific	A pair of manta rays are above a whale shark which is above a pair of hammerhead sharks.
179	tropical ocean coral reef	A closeup of coral polyps on a reef.
181	Carribean sea	Ballyhoo are above a great barracuda, which swims above yellowtail snapper and above Foureye butterflyfish and a Nassau grouper.
183	Homosassa River, Gulf of Mexico, Florida	West Indian Manatees (cow and calf) rest on the bottom below a moonlit starry sky. A shrimp swims above.
185	Homosassa River, Gulf of Mexico, Florida	West Indian Manatees (cow and calf) awaken at sunrise. A shrimp is chased by a spotted seatrout.
187	Homosassa River, Gulf of Mexico, Florida	A herd of manatees awaken.
189	Homosassa River, Gulf of Mexico, Florida	The herd of manatees stir shrimp and debris from the bottom as they move.
191	Homosassa River, Gulf of Mexico, Florida	Gray snappers and sheepsheads follow manatees to eat shrimp they flush from the weeds. They look like a cloud following the manatees.
193	Gulf of Mexico near Florida	Bottlenose dolphins investigate manatees.
195	Gulf of Mexico near Florida	A bottlenose dolphin above ladyfish.
197	Gulf of Mexico near Florida	Bottlenose dolphins investigate manatees as they swim.
199	Gulf of Mexico near Florida	Spotted dolphins.
201	Atlantic ocean	Fraser's dolphins and yellowfin tuna ball up sardines, with shearwaters above.

Page #	Where?	What?
203	Atlantic ocean	Dolphins encounter pilot whales, which are chasing squid below.
205	Ganges River Delta	Ganges River Dolphins (susu) encounter other dolphins among mullet.
207	Indian Ocean off of Austrailia	Dugongs encounter a dolphin with yellow trevally.
209	Indian Ocean off of Austrailia	Dugongs with yellow trevally.

Author's Notes:

Adult Coloring Books are not really a recent trend. Grown-ups have been borrowing kid's coloring books for years, and doodling since the stone age. However, since my sister, and sisters in law like to color in the latest crop of meditational art, they suggested a conversion of my existing children's book illustrations into a grown-up coloring book. Strictly speaking, any age could enjoy this book, but younger kids would have trouble with the fine lines and details in the images. The conversion process was very arduous, and in the end I ended up either changing the scenes heavily, or recreating scenes to take advantage of the adult coloring book format. Each fish had to be disassembled, since a simple color to black and white change was a disaster! As a result the scenes here in are almost completely unique, though will bear a resemblance to images from the *Fishes and Whales* book series.

I hope you very much enjoy this book, and it is mind building for you, as it was for me.

Calm seas, and fishy waters,

Bryce

If you liked this book, you will enjoy reading the *Fishes and Whales*$_{TM}$ series to any nearby kid:

Paige's Book of Fishes and Whales
Grant's Book of Manatees and Dolphins
Anna's Antarctica
Lily's Deep Sea Creatures
Audrey's Amazon River
Aidyn's California Oceans
Benjamin's Coral Reefs

Comming Soon:

Charlotte's Arctic Oceans
Madison's African Rivers

A kid's coloring book (which you may also like):

A Fishy, Dolphiny, Squidy, Penguiny, Coloring Book

You may also enjoy this short biology book:

What Fish Eats What: A Few Simplified Fish Food Webs

Every fish, whale, dolphin, manatee, dugong, seal, and penguin is available on clothing, decor, fabric, wallpaper, wrap, etc. on my page at:

http://www.combat-fishing.com

www.ingramcontent.com/pod-product-compliance
Lightning Source LLC
Chambersburg PA
CBHW080654190526
45169CB00006B/2105

* 9 7 8 1 5 2 3 8 5 5 7 3 5 *